D1598942

ALEXANDER
THE
GREAT

ALEXANDER THE GREAT

R. D. MILNS

PEGASUS · NEW YORK

SBN 7091 0201 1

Library of Congress Catalog Card Number: 74–105219.
First published in Great Britain in 1968

CONTENTS

6 Contents

Illustrations

The illustrations were supplied by the following:
The Mansell Collection, 1, 5, 6, 9, 10, 11 and 12;
Radio Times Hulton Picture Library, 2, 3 and 4;
Camera Press-Pix, 7, 8, and 14.

MAPS AND DIAGRAMS

PREFACE

In 1948 Sir William Tarn published his great two-volume work on Alexander, which immediately became canonical among scholars dealing with this period of Ancient History. However, it may fairly be said that Tarn had fallen too deeply under the spell of his subject and that consequently a somewhat romantic and over-idealized Alexander issued from his pen. Since then much work has been done—a large part of it in English—to redress the balance, to "de-romanticize" the hero and to see him, not as a "knight in shining armour", but as an astute, ruthless and somewhat sinister political manoeuverer and manipulator of men. Perhaps at times the reaction has been too violent and the truth lies somewhere between the two extremes. I have tried in this book to present a straightforward and fair account of the life and career of Alexander, drawing primarily on the ancient sources and testing their versions in the light of modern researches. Much of the narrative must inevitably deal with military affairs; for Alexander was, after all, and still is *the* type of the great soldier and conqueror and many authorities would rank him as the most outstanding commander of antiquity and among the greatest the world has ever produced. But I have also tried to trace the influences on and development of his character both through boyhood and as King.

The exigencies of space have necessitated the most summary or incidental treatment of such topics as Greek politics or the Macedonian homeland during Alexander's absence in Asia. Again, the Introduction is intended merely to give what seems to me sufficient "background" necessary for an understanding of the motives behind the Persian War and the Greek attitude towards Macedonia. The theme is Alexander and not the history of the Mediterranean world between 356 and 323 B.C. and for this reason the narrative centres around the person of the King, his court and his army.

Within the text references to ancient sources are given only where these sources are mentioned or quoted directly; for the reader who wishes to read the original writers for himself Appendix II gives details of modern English translations, where these are available. Nor have I indicated in the text—again, except where direct reference is made—the views of modern scholars which I have adopted when dealing with controversial issues. I have merely incorporated in the narrative the view which appears to me the most cogent and which harmonizes best with the character of Alexander as it developed. There is a reason for this: my book is not aimed at the Classical scholar or the professional Ancient Historian, who have both the opportunity and the training to discover for themselves and to master the huge amount of material, both ancient and modern, dealing with Alexander; rather I am concerned with the non-academic who finds the study of history and its great men a source of entertainment, interest and perhaps instruction. However, I may be allowed here to record my great debt to the stimulating writings of Professor E. Badian and, for the chapter dealing with the Gaugamela campaign, the recent book of E. W. Marsden.

My sincere thanks are due above all to two people: to my friend and colleague Dr. A. S. Henry, for his painstaking criticism and advice at all stages of this book's composition; and to my wife, who has uncomplainingly typed and re-typed my manuscript.

R.D.M.

INTRODUCTION

Philip II, Greece and Persia

Any book on Alexander must inevitably start with his father, Philip II, son of Amyntas, whose achievements made possible the career of his son. In a reign of twenty-four years (359–336 B.C.) this genius raised Macedonia from a backward and divided Balkan state, hemmed in all round by enemies who threatened the country with dismemberment, into the greatest power in Europe.

Internally Philip succeeded in uniting the semi-independent dynastic families of the Macedonian hill-country in a common allegiance to the crown, in raising the standards of living and prosperity among the peasantry, in attracting foreign talent—especially Greeks—to his court at Pella, and, most important, in creating a powerful and efficient national army, which both afforded internal security to Macedonia and enabled Philip to pursue an aggressive policy of expansion against his neighbours. Thus in 358 Paeonia, to the north of Macedonia, was brought under Philip's control, while to the east of the kingdom Thrace was annexed in 342 after a series of campaigns extending over ten years, thus bringing the boundaries of Macedonia up to the Dardanelles.

The main theme of Philip's reign, however, is his expansion southwards into the Greek peninsula and his relations with the Greek city-states. This penetration was facilitated by the discord and rivalries that were endemic among the Greeks themselves and was achieved by a combination of diplomatic cunning, subversion and brute force. Thus the Chalcidian League was destroyed in 348 and its territories incorporated in Macedonia; but to the Thessalian League and many small states in the Peloponnese Philip appeared as a liberator and champion against the imperialism of their fellow-Greeks in Athens, Thebes and Sparta. Thessaly, indeed, was so impressed with Philip that in 352 it voluntarily associated itself in a loose political union with Macedonia. The success of Philip's penetration of Greece won him the deep suspicion and opposition of Athens, the largest and most imperialistic of the city-states; and under the leadership of the eloquent Demosthenes Athens, after 346, pursued a policy of uncompromising hostility towards the Macedonian. Further, much of Philip's influence in Greece was won at the expense of Thebes, second in power only to Athens; and Theban concern at the growing power of Macedonia drove her into alliance with the great democracy, hitherto her most bitter rival. The Theban–Athenian alliance was smashed by Philip's army in August 338 at Chaeronea in Boeotia and the whole of Greece was now Philip's, to use as he wished.

Realizing the impossibility of holding down a reluctant Greece by means of a permanent occupation, Philip, early in 337, devised a highly statesman-like method of indirect control. The Greek states were organized into a League (called by modern historians the League of Corinth after its place of assembly). This League was intended to regulate the internal affairs of Greece, to maintain the peace and to uphold the autonomy of each state. The Macedonian King was not represented on the League's council and hence had no voice in its deliberations or decisions. But he was Hegemon (commander) of the League's military forces and only he—or his deputy—could initiate military action by the League; and he could also call on the League for aid against any recalcitrant member. His control over the Greek states, who were all, with the exception of Sparta, members of the League was by this means assured.

Though the League was intended to give the Greeks much-needed stability and peace, it was definitely an instrument of Macedonian domination and as such was deeply resented by the larger states with a long tradition of imperialism. The smaller states, who had always been the victims of the imperialistic cities, were probably quite amenable to the arrangement, which at least guaranteed their independence.

In the summer of 337, Philip announced to the Council a plan he had had in mind for some time—an invasion of the Persian empire—and invited the League to join him in it. The Council could hardly refuse and Philip was "appointed" commander-in-chief of the League forces that would take part in the invasion. Early in 336 an advance-party under Parmenion and Attalus, two senior Macedonian officers, crossed into Asia to secure the bridgeheads needed for the coming invasion.

To give the participation of the League states at least the appearance of a Greek Crusade the motives for the invasion announced by Philip were the exaction of vengeance from the Persians for the wrongs done to Greece 150 years earlier by King Xerxes and the liberation of the Greek cities of Asia Minor, which formed part of the Persian empire. Philip may have been influenced in this by an idea which had been prevalent among certain Greek thinkers for many years, but which is most closely associated with Isocrates, the Athenian teacher of political philosophy: the Greek states were to sink their differences and join in a combined expedition against Persia, the traditional enemy. Such an expedition would take the form of a war of conquest to wrest from Persia her western provinces in Asia Minor; it would enable the Greeks to focus their military ambitions on an external foe, while at the same time it would help to solve the social and economic problems of the Greek mainland. For the interminable wars between, and the frequent faction fights within, the city-states in the fourth century B.C. were disastrous to the poorer classes in particular, but in general to the losing side. Many of these ruined and exiled men took up service as mercenary soldiers—the only livelihood left to them—and, by their readiness to sell their swords to the highest bidder, contributed to the disorders among the Greek states. The conquered territory in Asia could be utilized to settle these homeless men, who would thus form a bulwark against Persia.

Isocrates propounded these ideas from 380 in the form of open political pamphlets, in which he suggested prominent Greek states or personalities as the leaders of such a Crusade. From 346 his attention turned to Philip as the possible Hegemon and in the next eight years addressed three open letters to the King, urging him to unite the Greeks and invade Persia. But on the question of the extent to which Isocrates influenced Philip in his decision, the Athenian is perhaps not being unduly modest when he says his own writings merely fell in with a design that Philip had entertained for some time.

For Philip had reasons of his own for attacking Persia, and the desire to unite the Greeks was not foremost among them. The eastwards expansion of Macedonia had brought her into direct confrontation with Persia, resulting in a steady deterioration in relations between the two empires. As early as 343 Philip can be seen putting out tentative "feelers" in Asia Minor (see Chapter 1); and in 340 the Persian government had committed an open act of hostility when it sent help to the city of Perinthus which Philip was besieging. Philip may thus have decided to solve his frontier-problem by the annexation of Asia Minor. Nor should the simple motives of conquest and booty be overlooked: ancient thought believed that, if a power had the resources and opportunity, it must inevitably expand itself by means of conquest; and the prospect of filling the somewhat depleted Macedonian treasury with Asiatic plunder must have had considerable attractions. Isocrates was not representative of Greek opinion; the Greeks themselves had little enthusiasm for being united or crusading; Philip must have realized this, and the invitation to the League of Corinth was perhaps little more than a specious means of ensuring the League's good behaviour during his absence in Asia.

The empire of the Persians, now facing invasion by the Greek Crusaders and the Macedonian King, was a colossal edifice extending from the eastern seaboard of the Mediterranean to the Hindu Kush and from the Caspian to the Arabian Sea. At its head, with his court at Susa, was an absolute monarch of the hereditary dynasty of the Achaemenids: to the Greeks he was the only monarch truly worthy of the royal title and was always referred to by them as the Great King. He was helped in his administration by an aristocratic governing class of Iranian stock, mainly Medes and Persians. The empire was divided into about twenty provinces, usually referred to by their Persian name of satrapies; and each area was governed by a satrap, who was appointed by the King and held office at his royal master's pleasure. Within his province the satrap had virtually unlimited powers—judicial, financial and military—and was answerable only to the central government; and herein lay the greatest danger of the system, since the satraps on the fringes of the empire were prone to rebellion and attempts to establish themselves as independent rulers.

Persia in the fourth century had long since abandoned any hopes of a European empire. In her dealings with the western world her only concern was with retaining the eastern coastline of the Mediterranean as an outlet to the sea. But retention of this seaboard entailed the incorporation in the empire of the numerous Greek states of Asia Minor; and these unfortunate cities became pawns in the sphere of international power-politics, since the imperialist Greek states of the mainland used the slogan of "freeing their fellow-Greeks" as an excuse to extend their own power. How sincere was the slogan can be seen from the way in which both Athens and Sparta in the previous 150 years

had "liberated" the Greeks, incorporated them in their own empire—
and then deliberately abandoned them again to Persia in order to win
Persian aid in their wars. The evidence seems to show that the Greeks
of Asia Minor were happier, both materially and politically, under the
mild Persian rule than during their periods of "freedom"; and not
unnaturally they were by now somewhat cynical about liberators from
the mainland.

Most of our accounts of Greco-Persian relations are written by
Greeks, above all Athenians, and the general impressions gained from
these are that all Greeks hated Persians and that the only foreign people
with whom the Great King was concerned were the Greeks. But, to
deal with the latter point, it is probable that the Persian government
viewed the mainland Greeks in much the same light as later the
Romans viewed the transrhenine German tribes—a potential danger
to a particular frontier-area; and, like the Romans with the Germans,
the Great King adopted the policy of neutralizing the Greeks by
fomenting internal discords among them (his vast wealth secured this
end) or by supporting any pro-Persian power against its rivals. To the
notion of all Greeks and all Persians being natural enemies a corrective
can be obtained by considering both the long-standing friendships
which existed between some mainland states and Persia and the large
number of Greeks to be found in employment with the Persian government: thus, apart from the Greek doctors, diplomats and engineers at
the Great King's court, there were at least 25,000 Greeks serving in the
imperial forces as mercenaries. The Persians, in fact, had taken to using
Greek mercenaries as their main infantry soldiers in conjunction with
their own excellent cavalry; and these Greeks, whose leaders often
attained high office in the King's service, displayed a remarkable loyalty
to their Persian paymaster.

The Persian realm was rich*, far-flung and seemingly eternal. But
the fourth century had given many indications that all was not well
with the empire. Revolts had been frequent in the outer-lying areas
and the government's attempts to crush them had usually been
singularly feeble: thus for most of the century Egypt was lost to Persia;
both Cyprus and Caria were virtually independent; between 368 and
359 the satraps of Asia Minor had participated in a great rebellion
against the King; and in the 340s most of Phoenicia had risen against
its Persian rulers. The unity of the empire was restored by the strong

* In the middle of the fifth century its annual income from tribute was
15,000 talents.

King Artaxerxes Ochus (reigned 358–338): his Greek general, Mentor of Rhodes, reconquered Phoenicia, enslaving the people of Sidon, and cleared up all pockets of rebellion in Asia Minor; Ochus himself, with 10,000 Greeks among his army, reconquered Egypt in 343. But the recovered areas were far from reconciled to Persian rule and Egypt again rose in revolt in 337. To make matters worse, Ochus himself was murdered in 338 through a palace conspiracy. His successor, who sent aid to the beleaguered Perinthus, reigned only two years, when he too was assassinated. In June, 336, a member of a collateral branch of the Achaemenid family, Darius Codomannus, ascended the throne of Persia, with the title of Darius III. His reign was not destined to come to a happy end; but neither was that of the Macedonian King who had been preparing to take advantage of the troubles of Persia.

1

The Early Years to 336 B.C.

On the sixth day of the Macedonian month Loüs, 356 B.C. (26th July*) a son was born to King Philip and his wife Olympias. The boy was given the name of Alexander—"the protector of men". On the same day, says popular legend, the temple of Artemis at Ephesus was burnt to the ground: the goddess was absent at the time, bringing Alexander into the world. Twenty-two years later Alexander was to repay the goddess for her midwifery by rebuilding her temple.

The marriage between Philip and Olympias had taken place about a year before this. They had met at a celebration of the wild mystery religion that was performed in Samothrace. Olympias, who was then named Myrtale, was the orphaned daughter of a King of Epirus, the country bordering on Macedonia to the west, and the niece and ward of the reigning King, Arrybas. The two fell in love at the first meeting and requested the consent of Olympias' guardian to the marriage. Such an alliance had strong political possibilities for the Epirote King and Arrybas gladly gave his consent. He was to live to regret it; for fifteen years later he was driven from his throne by Philip and replaced by a brother of Olympias.

Among the Greeks—and one may include the royal houses of Macedonia and Epirus in this category—a powerful instrument of political propaganda was the ability to trace one's descent to a hero or god, a process to which the rich mythology of the Greek people readily lent itself. His parentage gave to Alexander a splendid galaxy of divine and heroic forebears both to flaunt and to model himself upon. Among the

* But cf. Hogarth, *Philip and Alexander of Macedon*, p. 284 ff., who dates the birth to October, 356.

A.T.G.—B

mythical ancestors of the Macedonian royal house—the Argead dynasty—were numbered Perseus, the slayer of the Gorgon, Heracles, whose twelve labours and assumption to the ranks of the immortals provided an ever popular source of material to poets and moralists, and Macedo, son of Zeus and founder of the Macedonian people. The Epirote royal family could trace its descent back to the greatest of Greek heroes, Achilles, and—paradoxically and indirectly—to the greatest of the Trojan warriors, Hector. For the founder of the race, Molossus, was the son of Neoptolemus, who was the brother of Achilles, and Andromache, the widow of Hector, who had been taken among the captive women at the fall of Troy. This illustrious ancestry was to influence Alexander deeply and to act as a stimulus to much of what he thought and did.

The love-match between Philip and his wife, which Plutarch describes,[1] was not destined to be of lengthy duration. Philip was an excellent general and a shrewd politician, but in his private life was much addicted to drink and to sexual licence. Whatever may have been the Macedonian law of marriage, Philip was not a believer in monogamy, though it must be stated that most of his marriages were of a political nature, formed for the purpose of cementing some desired alliance. One Greek writer wittily remarks that Philip was not at all like the Great King of Persia, who went on campaign surrounded by his wives—Philip used to acquire his wives on campaign.[2] Already (perhaps in 359 B.C.) he had taken to wife a Macedonian noblewoman, Phila, by whom he had begotten a son, Caranus; the fate of Phila is unknown. In 358 he had taken two more wives: an Illyrian princess, Audata, who presented him with a daughter, and a Thessalian woman, Philinna, who produced a son. The daughter, Cynna, was later married by Philip to Amyntas, son of Perdiccas, by whose deposition Philip himself had come to power. That Amyntas was allowed to live and, even more, allowed to marry his deposer's daughter was a rare act of generosity and humanity on Philip's part; Alexander was to be less clement to his brother-in-law. Philinna's son, Arrhidaeus, was probably older than Alexander by one year. His feeble wits were later to save him from the same fate as Amyntas.

Olympias, then, when she married Philip in 357, was not his first wife, nor was she his last. For in the course of the next twenty years the King took to himself another three wives (Nicesipolis, from Thessaly, in 353; Meda, a princess from one of the Danubian tribes, in 339; and Cleopatra, a Macedonian, in 337). He is also said to have sired innumerable children by other women; Olympias herself presented him with another child the year after Alexander's birth—this time a daughter who was named Cleopatra. Though Olympias' illustrious descent and forceful personality secured her predominance in this harem at least down to 337—it is likely that she was the legal wife, while the technical status of the others was that of concubine—she was a woman of great pride and a passionate disposition, and it seems probable that she viewed Philip's marriages and amours with a considerable resentment and wounded vanity. Philip, for his part, found his wife's domineering and violent nature irksome. Besides, there was something frightening and mysterious in her unrestrained participation in the wild and orgiastic mystery religions. When the rift between the pair began cannot be said; but the hatred which was unleashed by her repudiation in 337 indicates a bitterness and odium on Olympias' part towards her husband that was not newly formed.

Thus the young Alexander was brought up in an atmosphere of mutual dislike between his parents. Of his father he could have seen but little during the first ten years of his life, for Philip was usually away on campaign during the years 356–346. Hence his formative years were passed under the control of his mother, who did all in her power to fill the boy's head with an awareness of his descent. His ancestors were more than mortal and he must strive to emulate them. It was Olympias who secured the appointment of Alexander's first tutors: a relative of her own, Leonidas, and the aged Lysimachus. Leonidas, who had general charge of the boy's education, was a stern and unsympathetic man. Lysimachus, an Acarnanian, had few pretentions to intellectual talent, but—no doubt encouraged by Olympias—called himself Phoenix, Alexander Achilles and Philip Peleus. This won him great popularity with the prince; for Phoenix had been the tutor of Achilles and Peleus his father.

Olympias intended her son to have a great future, and she and the tutors directed all their efforts to making him realize that he was somebody set apart from the common run of mankind. He was destined one day to be the greatest of Kings and to surpass all other men in his achievements. Some indication of the influence she exerted over her son's outlook during his childhood—an influence from which Alexander never completely broke free—can be seen from Plutarch's story that when his swiftness of foot led someone to ask him whether he would be willing to compete in the footrace at the Olympic games,

Alexander replied that he would—if he were to have Kings as his fellow-contestants.[3]

Not only did Olympias encourage Alexander to believe in an outstanding destiny; but she also seems to have tried to turn the boy against his father, perhaps by belittling his achievements and pouring scorn on his moral laxity. Certainly in the later years of Philip's life there was a deep dislike—even hatred—between father and son, and Alexander himself was eager, when King, to disclaim the parentage of Philip. Olympias, on the other hand, he always held in the deepest respect and admiration and some of her most horrible atrocities were passed over with little more than a mild rebuke. The reluctance—called by some restraint—that Alexander showed with regard to sexual matters may well stem from the deep hold that Olympias exerted during the first twelve years of his life and from the dislike of his father she instilled in him. One hesitates to indulge in the technical jargon of modern psychology, but there are many indications in Alexander's life of the notorious Oedipus complex.

It was partly because of the disruptive influence of Olympias that, in 343 B.C. when Alexander was thirteen years, Philip decided to take a hand in his son's education, and issued an invitation to one of the leading scholars of Greece to come to Macedonia as tutor of the Crown Prince. This was no other than the great Aristotle, resident on the island of Mitylene. The philosopher was at this time aged forty-one, a bald man with small penetrating eyes, a lisp, and with a scrupulous regard for the niceties of dress. For a scholar, his life had hitherto been surprisingly mobile. Born at Stagira, on the Chalcidic peninsula, he had gone to Athens at the age of seventeen to study under Plato at the Academy. In 348–7 Plato died and Aristotle left Athens for the city of Assos, situated in the Troad in North-western Asia Minor. His departure, which may have been the result of his disapproval of the new head of the Academy, Plato's nephew, Speusippus, was like a minor migration of the school to Asia, for he was accompanied by several of Plato's best students, including Xenocrates, a future head of the Academy. In the year 348–7 Philip and his troops, operating in the Chalcidic peninsula, stormed Stagira, and razed it to the ground. Aristotle was thus "at one stroke ... deprived both of his ancestral and of his spiritual home."[4]

Assos at this time formed part of the domain of the eunuch tyrant Hermeias. A slave of the previous tyrant of Assos, he had made himself ruler, on his master's death, of the city and the neighbouring town of Artarneus, gaining recognition by the Persian government as a vassal-prince. He became friendly with two ex-students of Plato and under their influence became a keen disciple of the master's teachings, allegedly even going so far as to moderate the form of his tyranny.

Aristotle and Hermeias quickly made a deep and lasting impression on one another; Aristotle actually married the adopted daughter of the eunuch, Pythias, by whom he had a daughter, also named Pythias. At Assos, Aristotle was joined by his nephew Callisthenes of Olynthus, a promising historian who was destined to become central in the story of the philosopher's relations with Alexander. Here too perhaps the learned circle was joined by the botanist Theophrastus, from the island of Lesbos. It has been said that "nothing less than a colony of the Academy was taking shape at Assos at this time, and there was laid the foundation of the school of Aristotle".[5] In 345, perhaps at Theophrastus' instigations, Aristotle moved to Mitylene on Lesbos, where he remained till Philip's invitation.

Why did Philip choose Aristotle as his son's teacher? For there were other figures as well qualified and more famous nearer home. The aged Isocrates for example, head of one of the most flourishing schools of "philosophy" at Athens, was a keen supporter of Philip and viewed him as the means of uniting the Greek people and ending their troubles. Isocrates would have been only too happy to have the chance of educating—and indoctrinating—Philip's heir. To Plutarch the answer was simple: Aristotle was "the most famous and learned of Philosophers". [6]But this is to view Aristotle's academic standing in the light of his future achievements. In 343 he can hardly be spoken of in these terms. However the family connection of the philosopher with the Macedonian court may have been influential, for Aristotle's father, Nicomachus, had been court physician to an earlier King of Macedonia, Amyntas. But perhaps the decisive factor was political considerations. As early as 343–2 Philip seems to have been thinking in terms of a future invasion of Persia. For such an expedition a bridgehead in Asia Minor was a necessity; the Troad was ideally situated for this and Hermeias an ideal potential ally, especially since Persia was engaging in a drive in the west to bring under firmer central control the independent and rebellious vassal-rulers and an· alliance with Macedonia could be an attractive proposition to Hermeias. "Everything indicates that it was the connection between Hermeias and Philip that really suggested . . . the association of the thinker and the Great King (Alexander)".[7]

Aristotle, for his part, would have been happy to renew his family connections with Pella, while the prospect of liberal royal patronage for the conducting of his researches was no small incentive to take up the appointment. No doubt, too, the philosopher hoped to be able to exert some influence on the beliefs and outlook of the heir to the throne of the most powerful state in the Greek world; the Academy had never been remiss with its advice to monarchs.

The story of Hermeias has an interesting outcome. A secret alliance does seem to have been formed between him and Philip, but this turned out to be of little value to the tyrant. For in 341 he was treacherously captured by the commander of the Persian King's mercenaries, Mentor of Rhodes, in the course of the operations mentioned above, sent to Susa and tortured with every refinement of the art to try to make him reveal the details of the "secret" treaty with Philip. In Athens, Demosthenes exulted that, "the Great King will hear of all Philip's activities—not through our accusations . . . but from the mouth of the very man who helped form the plot and was working for its fulfilment".[8] But Hermeias proved Demosthenes wrong and died under torture without talking; his last words were "Tell my friends that I have done nothing weak or unworthy of philosophy". His son-in-law, Aristotle, was deeply impressed by his death; he wrote a fine lyric poem in memory of "Hermeias' Virtue," and had erected at Delphi a statue of him. Callisthenes, too, wrote a moving "Encomium on Hermeias". Aristotle, as will be seen, did not have a high opinion of the Persians; the Hermeias episode can hardly have raised them in his esteem.

Philip is said to have paid Aristotle "a noble and appropriate tuition-fee,"[9] for he rebuilt and repopulated the city of Stagira and restored it to those of its citizens who were in exile or slavery. As a place of study, away from the noise and activity of the palace at Pella, there was assigned to master and pupil the precinct of the nymphs near Mieza (to the south-west of Pella, at the foot of the wooded heights of Bermion); in Plutarch's day a tourist attraction was still "the stone seats and shady walks of Aristotle". The place was a natural beauty-spot and legend situated nearby the celebrated gardens of King Midas, where the King was believed to have captured the drunken satyr, Silenus, and conversed with him on the meaning of life.

In these congenial surroundings the formal education was begun and continued for the next three years. One would be wrong to envisage master and pupil locked in monastic seclusion at Mieza; rather, the prince was surrounded by the youth of the Macedonian nobility as fellow-students and Aristotle was aided by other scholars, such as his nephew, Callisthenes (the tradition that makes Callisthenes a fellow-student of Alexander is incorrect). Among Alexander's young companions were the son of Antigonus and future historian, Marsyas of Pella; undoubtedly Hephaestion, Alexander's *alter ego*, and Ptolemy, the future King of Egypt, were there too; perhaps also Cassander, the son of Antipater, younger by one year than Alexander. Antipater, who had negotiated the notorious peace-treaty of 346 B.C. with Athens, was one of Philip's senior generals and a hard and ruthless politician; he also had claims to literary ability, having written his memoirs of the campaigns of King Perdiccas. With Aristotle he formed so close and lasting a friendship that it has been suggested that he filled in the philosopher's affections the place left vacant by the death of Hermeias. His son, on the other hand, was to become one of Alexander's bitterest enemies.

Aristotle was an Academic and pupil of Plato, and the education Alexander received from his hands seems to have been mainly on the lines of the typical Academic curriculum of the day: discussions of poetry, both "classical" and modern; rhetoric; geometry; astronomy; and eristics—the art of arguing a point from either side. It was an education that laid itself open to the charge, so often directed nowadays by unthinking and so-called specialists in education against the Classical disciplines, of excessive formality and of not "preparing the pupil for life". Indeed, the senile Isocrates, who had a long-standing feud with the Academy and felt snubbed that he himself, a fervent partisan of Philip, had not been offered the post as tutor, when writing a turgid epistle to Philip in 342, added a shorter letter to Alexander in which, in veiled and courtly language, he attacked the Academics and their philosophy and gave Alexander the advice to "drop" Aristotle. The warning, of course, went unheeded.

Outside the Academic fields of study, we are told by Plutarch[10] that the teacher inculcated in his pupil an interest in medicine; "for he was not only fond of the theory of medicine, but actually came to the aid of his friends when they were sick and prescribed for them certain treatments and regimens". The same writer[11] says that Alexander received from Aristotle the philosopher's ethical and political discourse and that he participated in the more secret and profound teachings called *acroamatic* ("fit only for oral teaching") and *epoptic* ("fit only for the initiated")—though how much a fifteen-year-old boy would understand is a debatable matter.

On a more practical level, Aristotle was a dedicated student of politics and human behaviour—we have treatises of his on "Ethics" and "Politics"—and one may legitimately ask to what extent he influenced his pupil in these matters. That Aristotle believed in the superiority of the Hellenic race over all others, especially the servile "barbarians" of Asia is well enough known; and it is highly likely that the incident of Hermeias had turned his contempt of the Persians into active dislike. But whether he looked to Alexander as the man who would unite the Greeks, and so help them attain that invincibility he is certain would result from such a unity, is nowhere recorded; and if he did, he was to be badly mistaken in his unifier. Again, on one occasion of unspecified date, he is recorded as having given Alexander the advice to conduct himself as Hegemon (leader) to the Greeks, but as *despotes* (master of slaves) to the "barbarians"; to look to the former as friends and kinsmen, but to treat the latter as animals and plants. But Alexander, when he had crossed into Asia and come into contact with the "barbarian animals", was to adopt a course exactly the opposite of what Aristotle recommended; to the nobility of Iran he showed, indeed, not only repect but even admiration.

Indeed, one may agree with the verdict of the modern writer, that in the three years of their acquaintance "Aristotle never succeeded in exercising definite political and philosophical influence upon Alexander", and "that it would seem . . . that the meeting of genius with genius (leaving minor details out of the question) remained without a deeper meaning and without effect. The great creations of either were conceived and grew and took effect without any mutual impressions worth mentioning".[12]

Of the "minor details" Alexander's interest in medicine has already been noticed. Aristotle seems also to have built well on the foundations laid by Olympias and Leonidas and to have given the future King a genuine love of Greek poetry, especially Homer—though here he was sowing on particularly fertile ground. For Alexander, it has been said, lived to a large extent out of the Iliad; to him the deeds of his mythical ancestor, Achilles, were as real as those of his father and were to be imitated and surpassed. Still in the field of literature, the influence of Aristotle is to be found in the interest that Alexander always displayed in eristics, and it was this art of arguing both sides of a case with equal readiness and facility that was later to recoil on the teacher through the person of his nephew, Callisthenes. Apart from this the former Academic made as little impression on the way of life of the future ruler of the world as his master had made on the Sicilian tyrant, Dionysius.

On a more personal level, the relations of teacher and pupil seem to have been excellent. "Aristotle he admired at the first", says Plutarch,[13] "and loved him, as he himself used to say, no less than he did his father; for to Philip he owed his life, but to Aristotle a good life. Later he held him somewhat in suspicion, not so as to do him any harm, but the fact that his kindly attentions did not have their usual ardour and affections were signs of an alienation". This alienation, however, probably did not come about until considerably later than the years of instruction at Mieza. The three years away from Pella, surrounded by his friends, must have been the most untroubled and perhaps the happiest time in Alexander's life.

Then, in 340 B.C., Philip decided that his son's formal education was now sufficiently complete and Alexander, now aged sixteen, was re-called to Pella by his father to gain practical experience in affairs of state. The school at Mieza broke up and Aristotle retired to his newly rebuilt native-city of Stagira, where both he and the botanist Theophrastus owned estates; there they remained for the next six years.

On his recall, which coincided with an increased tension in the Gallipoli peninsula and the disaffection of the important Macedonian allies of Perinthus and Byzantium, necessitating the absence from the capital of Philip yet again, Alexander was left at Pella as Regent of Macedonia in charge of the Royal Seal. To help him in this task Antipater was left as adviser and here began the association that was to be of great importance to the prince during the difficult days of the later part of Philip's life. As Regent—and almost certainly with Philip's permission—Alexander undertook his first independent command when he subdued the rebellious tribe of the Maedi, a Thracian tribe on the upper reaches of the River Strymon, and settled in their territory a military colony of mixed population; the name of this colony was Alexandropolis—"the city of Alexander"—perhaps a deliberate imitation of Philippopolis, which his father had founded two years previously. It has been suggested that this was the occasion when Aristotle composed for Alexander his (lost) treatise "On Colonies", as a manual for the prince's guidance; a later date and different motives are more likely.

Two years later, at the age of eighteen, Alexander was placed by his father in command of the left wing of the Macedonian army, when the final test of strength took place at Chaeronea, between Philip and the combined Thebans and Athenians. Opposite him, on the allied right, were stationed the elite Theban corps, the Sacred Band. Needless to say, Alexander was given some of the most seasoned generals as his advisers. Philip himself held the traditional post of the King, on the right of the army and facing the Athenians. In the battle it was the Prince's fierce and determined assault that shattered the Sacred Band and ensured victory for his father. Plutarch relates[14] that in his day, nearly 450 years later, there was an ancient oak-tree still called "Alexander's Oak" near the river Cephisus near which Alexander is supposed to have pitched his tent before the battle. After the battle, perhaps as a reward for his valour, Alexander was delegated, along with Antipater, to restore to the Athenians the bones of their dead, who had fallen in the fight, and to begin negotiations for peace. It must have been an impressive moment for the prince as he rode solemnly into the noblest and most magnificent city in the Greek world; Antipater had had previous experience of the city and its excitable people. We may believe, too, that Alexander was in close attendance on the King during the months following Chaeronea, when Philip was busy with the organization of the defeated Greeks into a League under his hegemony, whose meeting-place was to be at the Isthmus of Corinth. The League was given a double function by the Macedonian: to guard and uphold the Common Peace which he established for the Greeks; and to join him in a war of conquest against the Persian empire.

The reputation of the young prince had been steadily rising during the years 340–337 B.C.; Plutarch, indeed, goes so far as to tell how the Macedonians began to call Alexander their King and Philip their general—to Philip's great delight, we are asked to believe.[15] But it was precisely during these years that the domestic troubles, with which Philip, like every Macedonian King, was afflicted, began to erupt into open dissensions and faction-quarrels at the court—perhaps due to the very fact that Alexander was now becoming a power to be reckoned with. It was around the question of succession to the throne that the trouble centred itself.

Alexander, it will be remembered, was not the only son of Philip II with a claim to the throne; and there were other possible pretenders outside the immediate circle of Philip's family—Amyntas, the son of Perdiccas, whom Philip had deposed, was still very much alive, and from the princely house of Lyncestis the three sons of Aëropus—Arrhabaeus, Heromenes and Alexander—could all advance sound genealogical claims to the regal position. Alexander, himself, from

Philip's family, obviously had the best claims to succeed his father at this time; for his half-brother, Philip Arridaeus, was said to be feeble-minded. But Alexander was not universally popular, especially among a large and influential section of the Macedonian nobility, which had the powerful families of Parmenion and Attalus at its head. One reason for this unpopularity may have lain in the fact that Alexander was not of pure Macedonian birth, the nobility wanting a full-blooded Macedonian on the throne. But this by itself need not have been an insoluble problem; the prince's descent on his mother's side was illustrious enough to made up for his Epirote blood. The main reason is in all probability the hatred with which the arrogant overbearing Olympias was regarded by the nobility—and Alexander was clearly very much attached to his mother and deeply influenced by her; so much so, that his attitude towards Philip was strongly coloured by Olympias' detestation of her husband. To the nobility, then, the prospect of Alexander as King, with the dowager Olympias ruling through him, was unbearable. Besides, Alexander himself had given clear indications that he had a different view of kingship from his father. Philip was open and affable—a *primus inter pares*, addressed by his fellow-peers by his name and not by any royal title. Alexander, on the other hand, had shown a haughtiness and sense of his royal position more fitting to a Persian monarch than a Macedonian King. Such a man would be far less concerned with their status and privileges than his father.

That Philip, though his relations with Alexander were, at the best, difficult, was statesman enough to realize that at the time Alexander was the only possible successor, is obvious from the care he took over his son's education and the important posts with which he entrusted him after it. But Philip seems to have been under strong pressure from 340 onwards from the nobility opposed to Alexander's succession to take a new Macedonian wife, by whom he could produce a more accept-able heir; and in 337 he formally divorced Olympias—"a jealous and evil-tempered woman", as Plutarch calls her[16]—and took as his lawful wife Cleopatra, the daughter of Antiochus and niece of Attalus. The latter was, by this time, connected by marriage with Parmenion, whose daughter he had married; and it is possible to discern the nucleus of a powerful faction here. Attalus was a bitter enemy of Alexander.

The marriage of his father with Cleopatra dangerously weakened Alexander's position. Henceforth he would be Crown Prince only until such time as the hoped-for son of the new marriage came of age;

then he could be discarded. On one friend he could rely—Antipater—
who must have seen his own influence at court waning before the
faction of Parmenion and Attalus.

The bitterness between Alexander and his father and the hatred
between Alexander and Attalus are well illustrated by the incident that
took place at the wedding. During the banquet that followed the
ceremony the drink naturally flowed freely, and most of the guests
were near to drunkenness. Flushed with triumph, Attalus, now the
father-in-law of the monarch, proposed a toast: "to a *legitimate* heir
to the throne". The remark may have been a reference to Alexander's
Epirote blood; more likely it was directed at the rumour that Philip
was not the father of Alexander, and that Olympias had shown as
little regard for matrimonial fidelity as her erstwhile husband. The
remark had meant to wound and to taunt Alexander. But Attalus could
not have reckoned with the young man's fierce and uncontrollable
temper. Blazing with fury, Alexander hurled his goblet into Attalus'
face, shouting "Do you dare call me a bastard?" Philip, himself drunk
and roused to fury by his son's action, lurched to his feet, drew his
sword and made for Alexander—only to trip and fall flat on his face.
"Look", mocked Alexander, "this fellow was preparing to cross from
Europe to Asia, and he goes head over heels crossing from one table
to another".[17]

Leaving the banquet, Alexander took his mother and escorted her
back to her brother, the King of Epirus. He himself then departed north
and he took up residence among the wild tribes of Illyria, where he
proceeded to stir up sedition among the tribesmen against his father—
an activity whose fruit he himself was to reap later.

The open split in the royal family was bad for Philip's prestige both
at home and with the Greeks. Besides, the activities of Alexander in
the north and Olympias in Epirus, where she was goading her brother
to take vengeance on Philip, were full of potential danger. Accordingly,
a reconciliation was arranged with Alexander, the more dangerous of
the two, through the agency of the aged Greek adventurer, Demaratus
of Corinth. Whatever terms brought Alexander back to Pella—perhaps
a verbal promise from Philip that Alexander would still be the successor—the reconciliation was an uneasy one. Neither father nor son
trusted each other, as the following incident shows. Pixodarus, the
satrap of Caria, had received word of the intended invasion of Persia
by the Macedonians. Wishing to secure his own position in the event
of the invasion succeeding, he entered into negotiations with Philip

to arrange a marriage between his daughter and Philip Arrhidaeus. Philip was not reluctant; the more "fifth columns" in Asia, the better for his enterprise. Alexander, however, learned of the proposal and immediately jumped to the conclusion that Philip was again trying to oust him from his succession. By means of his own agent, the tragic actor, Thessalus, he secretly informed Pixodarus that a marriage to himself, Alexander, was a much better proposition than the imbecile Arrhidaeus; and Pixodarus, who could not have followed the power struggle at Pella closely, agreed. The plot was discovered and reported to Parmenion; his eldest son, Philotas, informed the King and another violent quarrel ensued, the results of which were that Pixodarus obtained neither Alexander nor Arrhidaeus as his son-in-law. Thessalus was sent to Macedonia in chains, and several of Alexander's friends, including Harpalus, Ptolemy, Nearchus, Erigyius and his brother, were sent into exile. Philip seems to have decided, now that he had Alexander back at court, to isolate him still further.

The problem of Olympias and her brother was more easily solved. The following year, 336, Philip offered Alexander of Epirus the hand of Cleopatra (the daughter of Olympias and sister of Alexander) in marriage. It was a skilful move; the Epirote preferred a peaceful settlement by marriage to the highly dubious issue of war. The wedding-date was fixed for the early summer, to be held at Aegae, the old Macedonian capital. Philip was successfully circumventing all the machinations of his son and Olympias. After the wedding would follow the departure to Asia, with the neutralized Alexander following the army. Something drastic had to be done, and quickly. A suitable opportunity offered itself at the wedding-festival.

Philip spared no expense on the celebration, which included musical and athletic contests. Guests were invited, not only from Macedonia and Epirus, but from all Greece. The marriage was to be a grand propaganda spectacle to the Greek world of the splendour and munificence of their new master—and of the superhuman nature of his achievements, which made him worthy of comparison with the Olympian gods. Divine honours had already been granted spontaneously to Philip by certain cities in Asia Minor. He too was deluded by his success, and in the sacred procession with which the games opened there was carried alongside the statues of the twelve Olympians a thirteenth statue—that of Philip himself, "the King thus showing himself enthroned among the twelve Gods".[18]

The procession took place in the theatre, which was crowded with people. After the gods, Philip entered the arena, dressed in a white cloak and unattended by his bodyguards, who stayed some distance from him at his express orders; "for he was trying to show all that, protected as he was by the universal goodwill of the Greeks, he had no need of a guard of spearmen".[19] He was on foot, escorted on one side by his son, Alexander, and on the other by his new son-in-law, the Epirote King. As he moved forward into the applause of the waiting multitude, a man suddenly rushed forward from the shadows and plunged a sword through his side, killing him on the spot. Then, amid the shocked silence, the murderer ran for the gates where horses were waiting tethered. Three men—Leonnatus, Perdiccas and Attalus (son of Andromenes)—led the pursuit which ensued. The man had a good lead and would have made his escape, had he not stumbled and fallen. His three pursuers were upon him and despatched him with their javelins as he lay in the dust. The whole scene could have taken little more than a minute to play.

The man was named Pausanias, a young Macedonian noble. The reason for his murder of Philip is said to have been as follows: eight years previously he had suffered an unforgivable insult at the hands of Attalus, who had made him drunk at a dinner-party and then handed him over to his muleteers, by whom Pausanias was sexually assaulted and then beaten up. Pausanias took his grievance to Philip, but the King, afraid of offending the powerful faction of Attalus, refused to take any action. For eight years Pausanias nursed his resentment until the time of the wedding of Alexander's sister to Alexander of Epirus; then he had decided to exact his revenge.

This is one version of the story. Alexander's official propaganda, after his accession, turned Pausanias into just one of a wide-spread conspiracy, whose members were paid agents of Persia, which saw in Philip's murder a means of stopping—or at least postponing—the projected Persian expedition. Ancient writers, however, were not all blinded by this screen of propaganda and modern writers are inclined to agree with them. Plutarch says that "most of the blame devolved upon Olympias, on the ground that she had added her exhortations to the young man's anger and incited him to the deed; but a certain amount of accusation attached itself to Alexander also".[20] Justin says that "it was also believed that Pausanias had been instigated by Olympias, the mother of Alexander, and that Alexander himself was not without knowledge of his father's murder".[21]

In fact, it does appear highly likely—though, of course, it can never be proved conclusively—that Olympias and Alexander were the forces that impelled Pausanias to the deed. Pausanias had his long-standing grievance; but it is doubtful whether, after eight years, he would have dared to do such a deed alone and without the promise of powerful support. Olympias and Alexander were both smarting under more recent insults from Philip and neither was the sort to allow an insult to go unavenged. Moreover, the question of motive—*cui bono?*—must inevitably point to Alexander. His position at court was being continually weakened; he was now at best a stop-gap successor. The time was ripe for making sure that the succession did go to his own person. For both Parmenion and Attalus, the senior members of the anti-Alexander and Olympias faction, were both away in Asia, having been sent that same spring as commanders of the advance-party of the expeditionary force, whose task was to secure a bridgehead at the Dardanelles. Of the other great nobles, Antipater was still at court—friendly towards Alexander, disgruntled at his own influence diminishing before that of Parmenion and Attalus, and filled with dislike for Philip's pretentions to divinity. Antipater, as will be seen, was to play the decisive role in Alexander's accession.

It is highly likely, therefore, that the following reconstruction is correct: Olympias and Alexander decided to use the situation of the wedding of Cleopatra to rid themselves of Philip and secure Alexander's succession; Pausanias was persuaded to act as the assassin and Antipater was also, perhaps, included in the plan. If Pausanias was induced by promises of immunity and large rewards when the deed was accomplished, he sadly overrated the honesty of his employers. For Pausanias knew too much and while he lived, would always be a source of danger to Alexander. The scheme must have been extended to include Alexander's three close friends, who were perhaps also his personal bodyguards. Perdiccas, Leonnatus and Attalus were posted close by the place where Pausanias was to attack the King. Then, when the murder had been perpetrated and Pausanias was about to make his escape, the trap was to be closed on him. He was to be killed whilst attempting to avoid arrest and so be silenced forever. There can be little doubt that Alexander became King by becoming a parricide.

NOTES

1 Plutarch, *Alexander 2*
2 Satyrus, at Athenaeus, *Deipnosophistae*, XIII, 557 B–D
3 Plutarch, *Alexander 4*

4   W. Jaeger, *Aristotle*, p.105
5   Ibid., p.115
6   Plutarch, *Alexander 7*
7   Jaeger, *Aristotle*, p.120
8   Demosthenes, *Philippic* III.xx
9   Plutarch, *Alexander 7*
10 Plutarch, *Alexander 8*
11 Ibid.
12 V. Ehrenberg, *Alexander and the Greeks*, p.98
13 Plutarch, *Alexander 8*
14 Plutarch, *Alexander 9*
15 Ibid.
16 Ibid.
17 Ibid.
18 Diodorus XVI 92.5
19 Diodorus XVI 93.1
20 Plutarch, *Alexander 10* (Loeb translation)
21 Justin IX 7.1

2

Securing the Throne

Amidst the confusion that followed the death of Philip, Alexander was taken to the army by Antipater and acclaimed—as constitutional procedure demanded—as King by the soldiers. There then ensued a series of murders motivated partly by revenge, partly by the need of the young King to rid himself of all possible rivals to the throne. Amyntas, son of the former King, Perdiccas, and King himself until his deposition by Philip, had been allowed by that monarch to live on with honour; he had even married one of Philip's daughters, Cynna (or Cynanne). Alexander had this harmless man executed. Three possible pretenders were the sons of Aeropus of the Lyncestian royal family; they were arrested and accused of complicity in the deed of Pausanias. Two—Heromenes and Arrhabaeus—were killed; the third, Alexander (known as "the Lyncestian" to distinguish him from the new King), was spared. For he had been the first to salute Alexander as King, and, more important, he was Antipater's son-in-law.

Olympias returned to Macedonia, filled with hatred and burning for vengeance. To her savagery Alexander gladly sacrificed Cleopatra, Philip's recent bride, and her baby daughter. Olympias had the baby murdered in her mother's arms and then drove the unfortunate Cleopatra to suicide by hanging. The brother of Cleopatra, Amyntas, son of Antiochus, was compelled by the enmity of Alexander and Olympias to fly into exile. He went to Persia, where he took up service as a mercenary-captain. Nor did the queen-mother try to hide her exultation at the murder of her former husband. Justin narrates that as well as showing honours to the corpse of Pausanias she dedicated to Apollo, under her maiden name of Myrtale, the sword with which Philip had been killed. "She seems to have been afraid that it might not be proven that the crime was committed by her".[1]

From the Macedonian point of view, there was now only one source of danger left for Alexander. This was Parmenion and Attalus in Asia at the head of the advance-force of the expedition. But here lay the greatest peril. For both men were popular with the troops and a revolt in the army might have serious repercussions with the bulk of the army in Macedonia. Attalus, of course, was implacable. To his feud with Alexander had been added the murder of his niece, and he realized that he himself could expect no mercy from the new King. Immediately after Philip's death he entered into treasonable negotiations with Athens to undertake joint action against Alexander. The key figure was Parmenion, whose adherence to either side could be decisive. An agent was sent by Alexander to try to win Parmenion. The old general decided that there was greater profit to be had from supporting Alexander than from opposing him in rebellion. He therefore connived at, if he did not actively participate in, the assassination of Attalus by Alexander's agent. "Thereafter the Macedonian forces in Asia were free from any incitement to revolution".[2] Parmenion secured the King's throne, but his price was heavy. When the expedition set out for Asia, all the top positions were filled by relatives and friends of Parmenion; and one of Alexander's hardest fights in the early years of his reign was to break the power of this faction.

But domestic enemies were not Alexander's only difficulty on his accession. The news of Philip's death spread rapidly in all directions. To the north—both eastwards and westwards—the barbarian tribes beyond the frontier were preparing to throw off their allegiance to the Macedonian crown and resume their raids and depredations. To the south, the Greek peninsula was in a state of ferment. The League of Corinth had dissolved itself, considering that its obligations to the Macedonian crown had ended with the death of Philip. Athens had openly rejoiced at the murder, voting a crown to Pausanias, and had (see above) entered into negotiations with Attalus. Thebes had voted to expel its Macedonian garrison. Aetolia and Ambracia were in revolt; and even in the Peloponnese and Thessaly, traditional homes of Macedonian influence, movements were afoot to end the foreign hegemony. The situation looked grim and his counsellors, foreseeing a return in Macedonia's position to that of 359, advised Alexander to let the Greek states go by the board and to negotiate a peaceful settlement with the tribesmen to the north.

Alexander however, decided on a bolder course of action—quite properly, since any signs of weakness in such a youthful King would quickly bring all Macedonia's enemies down on him. The southern threat seemed the more dangerous, and so, gathering his forces, he swept down through Thessaly, where the Thessalian Federation, surprised at the rapidity of his movement, hurriedly voted him as Archon (or chief magistrate) of Thessaly in succession to his father. At Thermopylae a meeting of the Amphictyonic Council was summoned. This body was basically a religious organization, formed from several leading Greek states who represented a primitive tribal structure for the worship of the god Apollo at Delphi. It had, however, become a political body with much prestige among the Greeks. A resolution was passed by the Council giving Alexander the leadership of the Greeks. Since the Council was not competent to confer such a distinction, the resolution amounted to nothing more than a formal recognition by this prestigious body of Alexander's claims.

Passing on from Thermopylae, he entered Boeotia, approached Thebes and encamped near the city. The Thebans were thrown into confusion at his approach and hastily dropped their plans for securing their independence. The Athenians, across the border in Attica, sent envoys to Alexander asking his pardon for being so slow to recognize him; and, taking no chances, they evacuated Attica to within the city-walls.

The next step taken by the King was to convene a full meeting of the Greek League at Corinth. He had already secured piecemeal formal recognition by the most important sections in Greece—the Thessalians, the Amphictyonic Council, Thebes and Athens; he now intended to have the same thing done by the Greek states in common. The Hellenic League followed the lead of its most powerful members and voted Alexander as its Hegemon in place of Philip and as *strategus autocrator* (General Plenipotentiary) of the alliance formed for the invasion of Persia. Alexander could now return northwards. The Greeks had been startled and cowed by the speed of his descent; but it was soon to become evident that not all of them were reconciled to the fact of the hegemony of Macedonia in general and Alexander in particular.

The winter of 336–5 was spent in setting domestic affairs in order and in training the army. In the spring of 335, Alexander felt himself ready to take the army out on campaign against the barbarian tribes with which Macedonia was surrounded and which had shown their readiness to revolt at the time of his succession. The ensuing campaign—

rightly described as one of the most brilliant of Alexander's smaller campaigns—was undertaken for three reasons: firstly, to suppress any rebellious tendencies among the tribesmen; secondly,—and here we see the King's sound grasp of strategic needs—to advance the northern frontier of the kingdom to the River Danube; and thirdly, to give the army a thorough "work-out" under his command before the invasion of Asia. The forces which were employed were, with the exception of the Agrianian javelin-men, all Macedonians, and probably amounted to 15,000 in number.

The sphere of operations was to be the vast tract of land extending from the Adriatic eastwards, and south of the Danube, as far as the Black Sea. The main opponents were the Triballi, who lived to the north-east of Macedonia roughly between the River Danube and the Balkan Mountains, and the Illyrian tribes who were situated all along the western flank of Macedonia, extending as far southwards as Epirus.

The army began its march from Amphipolis, at the mouth of the River Strymon, and moved in a north-easterly direction, passing close by Philippi, with its famous gold-mines. Crossing the River Nestus (modern Mesta), it then struck northwards through the territory of the "autonomous Thracians", so called to distinguish them from their kinsmen who were subject to Macedonia, as far as the Balkan Mountains (the Haemus range, as the ancients knew them).

The route chosen for the crossing of the mountains seems to have been the Shipka pass, but when the army arrived there it found the pass, which rises to the top in a steep, though level, slope, held and blocked by a strong force of "autonomous" Thracians. These had drawn up a line of wagons at the top of the slope as though to serve as a stockade. But Alexander was quick to realize their real purpose, which was that they should be sent rolling down the slope, if Alexander tried to force the pass, so as to smash into the advancing troops at high speed and sweep them away. The Thracians could then charge down upon the confused ranks of the enemy and cut them to pieces. Alexander is said to have countered this danger by instructing the phalanx, which was in two columns, to part its ranks wherever possible; but where this could not be done, to lock their shields together over their heads (presumably kneeling down) and let the wagons' impetus carry them without harm over the heads of the phalanx. The manoeuvre sounds, at worst, highly improbable, at best highly dangerous; but it is said to have been so successful that not one man perished beneath the carts. Then the phalanx, supported by the archers, charged up the slope and easily routed the Thracians and secured the pass. 1,500 of the enemy were killed, though their nimbleness and absence of heavy armour meant that no prisoners were taken apart from the women and children of the Thracians, who now became part of the booty.

The army crossed the mountains through the pass and entered the territory of the Triballi, advancing as far as the River Lyginus (either: Osma, Vid 'or Iskre). The Triballian King, Syrmus, on the approach of the Macedonians had sent the women and children of his tribe to an island in the River Danube named Peuce, to which he himself also withdrew. His army, however, by means of clever manoeuvring, managed to slip in behind the advancing Macedonian army and occupy the mountain passes in their rear, forcing Alexander to turn to deal with them. To send the phalanx into the wooded glen where the Triballians were encamped would have been suicide. Alexander therefore attempted to lure the enemy out into the open. The light-armed missile troops were sent to the glen, with orders to shoot at the enemy and retire before their counter-attack, luring them out of the woods. The ruse was successful; the Triballians, both annoyed by the missiles showered on them and thinking they had the light-armed at their mercy, pursued them into the open. There the trap was sprung: caught on the front by the phalanx and on the flanks by the cavalry, the Triballians were routed and 3,000 of their number were killed. Alexander's rear was once again secure.

Three days later the army reached the Danube, opposite the island of Peuce, and was here joined by a squadron of warships which had sailed up the Black Sea from Byzantium and had then been rowed upstream of the Danube. Alexander had obviously anticipated before setting out that some naval assistance would be necessary. Embarking troops aboard the warships he made an attempt to force a landing on Peuce. However, the banks of the island were steep and precipitous, the current of the river was swift and the men on board ship insufficient in number to force a landing. Hence the operation had to be called off.

A further complication was added by the presence on the northern bank of the river of the large and hostile force of the Getae, who inhabited roughly what is now Moldavia and Bessarabia. Alexander decided to attempt the crossing of the Danube. Two motives impelled him: he wanted to show Syrmus and the Triballians on Peuce the strength of the Macedonian army in action; and, says Arrian, he was seized with a *pothos* to cross the Danube.[3] This Greek word whose meaning is "fierce, ardent desire", is used on several occasions by

Arrian in connection with Alexander's exploits—here for the first time —and usually denotes in the King an almost irrational desire to perform some act that nobody had ever done before. In view of the large forces of Getae assembled on the opposite bank, the crossing had to be made at night, when the Getae had retired inland to their camp. 1,500 cavalry and 4,000 infantry were transported across the river in one night on whatever vessels could be obtained or improvised (including leather tent-covers stuffed with hay)—a superb piece of organization in the circumstances, and "a startling enough accomplishment today".[4]

Just before dawn broke Alexander advanced on the camp of the Getae, who expected nothing less than that the enemy would attempt to cross the Danube and hence were totally unprepared. Awoken, cut down and thrown into confusion by the sudden onslaught of the cavalry, they fled in panic to their settlement about three miles away. The phalanx of the Macedonians then came into action and stormed the settlement and razed it to the ground. The survivors of the Getae fled northwards; Alexander triumphantly recrossed the river in broad daylight. This "cutting-out" expedition had a tremendous effect on Syrmus and the Triballi, who immediately submitted; and the fame of the enterprise spread so rapidly across the Balkans that the Celts who lived on the east coast of the Adriatic sent an embassy to the King, seeking his friendship.

The army now turned back towards Macedonia, passing in a south-westerly direction through Agriania and Paeonia. En route disturbing news was received: an Illyrian chieftain, Cleitus, whose father had been defeated twenty-four years earlier by Philip, had risen in revolt; he was about to be joined by Glaucias, King of the Taulanti (an Illyrian tribe in the neighbourhood of Durazzo); and the Autariates, a tribe bordering on Paeonia, were intending to attack the army as it marched past. Cleitus and Glaucias threatened the whole western frontier of Macedonia and speed was vital. Fortunately Alexander had with him a good friend in the person of Langarus, King of the Agrian-ians, who offered to stop the threat from the Autariates by invading their country. His action effected a clear passage for the army; as his reward he received the hand of Alexander's half-sister, Cynna—whose husband had been murdered by Alexander a few months previously.

Alexander hastened across the breadth of his kingdom, following the course of the River Erigon (Tzerna). His object was the border fortress of Pelion, which had been occupied by Cleitus and was to be the meeting-place with Glaucias. Pelion lay on the River Apsus (Devol) and commanded the main route into western Macedonia. It was situated in a wide plain bordered by mountains. Cleitus had occupied the foothills of these mountains as well as the fortress, so that Alexander had first to drive him out of the hills before assaulting the fortress. When Alexander had achieved this and had begun to throw up earthworks against the fortress, Glaucias arrived to keep his rendezvous and, sizing up the situation, seized the foothills. Alexander was thus caught between two fires—Cleitus in Pelion and Glaucias in the hills—and was both outnumbered and cut off from supplies.

He saw that he must act quickly; that he had to draw Glaucias into the plain, where he could smash him with the phalanx, rather than try to dislodge him by means of mountain warfare and leave his rear open to attack by Cleitus. A highly complicated stratagem to achieve this is described by Arrian.[5] It was successful; Glaucias' men left the foothills for the plain, where they were suddenly charged and routed. They fled to join Cleitus in Pelion. Alexander himself, after thus securing his rear, retreated across the Apsus to replenish his supplies. The retreat was taken by the enemy for defeat. They grew careless and three days later Alexander heard that they had taken to camping outside the fortress without defence-works or sentries. That night he recrossed the river with the Hypaspists, Agrianians and archers and fell on the sleeping camp of the enemy. The panic-stricken mob were pursued as far as the Taulantian mountains. Cleitus, deserted by his allies, set fire to Pelion and made his escape to Glaucias in his confusion.

Alexander was given no more trouble by the Illyrian tribes during his reign. This, the earliest of his major campaigns, was one of his most brilliant. Executed in some of the most difficult terrain in Europe, it had shown that the new King possessed a sound grasp of strategy, a fierce determination to succeed and the ability to keep a cool head in a crisis, a firm control over his men—and, above all, the capacity (like Napoleon) to move with lightning rapidity. This latter quality was to stand him in good stead immediately after the successful conclusion of the campaign against Cleitus and Glaucias. For even whilst he was before Pelion, the news was brought that the city of Thebes had risen in revolt behind his back and had murdered the Macedonian garrison-commanders. They had been instigated by anti-Macedonian exiles, who had entered the city by night and spread the report that Alexander had been killed in Illyria. Moreover, the powerful Aetolians and certain Peloponnesian states were inclined towards the rebels; Sparta was wavering; and Athens had voted to supply the insurgents with arms. Demosthenes had already accepted a subsidy of 300 talents from the Persian government and was using this money to foment the revolution. The hollowness of the settlement of the previous year was clearly seen. On the eve of his departure for Persia Alexander was faced with the prospect of a general war with his Greek allies. Now, if ever, speed was essential to save the situation.

Marching with the mountains of Paravaea and Tymphaea on his right, Alexander reached Thessaly in seven days; a further six days and he had passed through Thermopylae, crossed the Phocian territory, gathering allies *en route*, and arrived at Oncestus in Boeotia, about twenty miles from Thebes. In thirteen days the army had covered nearly 250 miles. The Thebans were so amazed on hearing of his presence at Oncestus that it was believed that it must be Antipater with an army from Macedonia, or another Alexander—perhaps the Lyncestian.

The following day the King advanced and encamped near Thebes, where he was joined by contingents of soldiers from other Boeotian cities. His intention was to give the Thebans time to repent and make overtures of peace. They, however, continued their investment of the Macedonian garrison in the Cadmea (the citadel of Thebes) and actually sent out skirmishing troops to harass Alexander's outposts; and when the King demanded that they surrender Phoenix and Prothytes, two of the ring-leaders of the revolt, the Thebans countered with a demand that Alexander surrender Philotas and Antipater. Alexander now saw that there was no chance of the pro-Macedonian party in Thebes gaining the ascendancy and bringing about a peaceful settlement. He therefore gave orders to prepare to attack the city. But first, to emphasize that he was acting in the capacity as Hegemon of the League of Corinth, he caused a herald to proclaim to the Thebans that all who wished to share in the Common Peace were to leave the city and join him. The Thebans, it is said, issued a counter-proclamation that all who wished to join the Great King of Persia and the Thebans in freeing the Greeks and destroying the tyrant of Greece should come over to their side—a pronouncement which threw Alexander into a violent rage.

The actual attack on Thebes was brought on by accident—if we may believe the account of Ptolemy, who relates[6] that Perdiccas made an assault on the Theban palisade without awaiting Alexander's orders; that he was then followed by the battalion of Amyntas, son of Andromenes, when he saw Perdiccas within the palisade; and Alexander then ordered a general engagement with the rest of the army in order that Perdiccas and Amyntas might not be left stranded. But Ptolemy had good reason to dislike Perdiccas and it probably suited his purpose well to assign in this fashion to Perdiccas the ultimate responsibility for one of Alexander's most brutal acts. Diodorus mentions the same assault by Perdiccas as ordered by Alexander during the course of the fighting, when the Macedonian frontal attack on the Thebans was making no progress;[7] Perdiccas' task was to penetrate into the city behind the main Theban force. We may, in this instance, accept the evidence of Diodorus against that of Ptolemy (in Arrian). The responsibility for the attack on Thebes, as well as its sequel, is Alexander's.

The Thebans, though greatly inferior in numbers, resisted all attacks with a bravery and desperation that came from the knowledge that defeat meant one certain thing—the sack of their city. Gradually, however, they were forced by weariness and the sheer weight of the enemy's numbers, back into their city, where they were trampled down by their own cavalry in the narrow streets. As Alexander, the Hypaspists and the phalanx poured into the city through the gates and over the walls, the Thebans were simultaneously attacked by the detachment of Perdiccas and the Macedonian garrison which burst from the Cadmea.

The savagery of the final assault on Thebes goes almost beyond description. The Macedonians—semi-barbarian and maddened by battle-lust—were joined by Greeks who loathed Thebes with a bitter hatred: Phocians, whose land had been ravaged by the Thebans in a long and ruthless war; Plataeans, Thespians and Orchomenians—themselves Boeotians—whose cities had been destroyed by Thebes. Macedonian and Greek vied with each other in the butchery of the hapless Thebans; "in the end, when night finally intervened, the houses had been plundered and women and children and aged persons who had fled into the temples were torn from sanctuary and subjected to outrage without limit."[8] More than 6,000 Thebans were slaughtered in the final attack and more than 30,000 captured; of the Macedonians, 500 perished.

Alexander now summoned a meeting of the League of Corinth— or rather, such members as were on the spot—and put to the delegates the question of the punishment of the captured city. The decision was unanimous: Thebes, as a city, was to cease to exist, it was to suffer the terrible fate known to the Greeks as *andrapodismos*—the razing to the ground of the city and the selling into slavery of all its inhabitants.

Moreover, all Thebans who had managed to escape were outlawed from the territory of all League members. The city was destroyed in accordance with the decree. Only the priests, the hereditary guest-friends of the Macedonian royal family and the descendents of the poet Pindar were spared—these latter, not because of any love of the King's for the great poet's verses, but because he too had guest-ties with the ancestors of Alexander. From the sale of the prisoners 440 silver talents were realized—a welcome addition to the war-chest of the panhellenic crusader.

The capture and destruction of Thebes had a profound effect upon the Greek states, both immediately and in their future attitude towards their Hegemon. The enemies of Thebes said she had deserved her fate and brought up long-standing charges against her: her adherence to the Persian cause in the invasion of Darius; her enslavement of Plataea; and her attempts to have Athens razed to the ground in 404 B.C. The sower was reaping a just harvest. But the majority of Greeks viewed things differently; one of the "twin eyes of Hellas" had been extinguished with the utmost brutality by a savage from foreign Macedonia; it was to free the Greeks from the yoke of this same savage that the Thebans had taken up arms. Plutarch says that Alexander destroyed the city to cow the rest of the Greeks into submission;[9] they were cowed—but their hatred of the King was intensified. "The Macedonian" too was to reap a deserved harvest of hate.

The King himself had, it is true, acted in a perfectly constitutional manner throughout. By his proclamation before the attack began he had made the position quite clear: he was the Hegemon and General Plenipotentiary of the League of Corinth acting to bring back into line a rebellious member of the League. Quite proper too was his referring to the delegates of the League the question of Thebes' fate. But there is much truth in the statement that Alexander wanted to teach the Greeks a lesson that they would not forget in a hurry; and just as true the statement that he was urged on by a savage resentment against the city that had dared to defy him. Thebes was destroyed in accordance with a decree of the League; but the "League" on this occasion consisted only of representatives of such states as were on the spot—and these were the implacable enemies of Thebes. There was no doubt about the decision they would reach. Alexander himself, had he wished and had he possessed a fraction of the philhellenism so often attributed to him, could and would have reversed that brutal decree. But a mixture of cold-blooded political calculation and deep resentment made him destroy the city. It was probably the most revolting—and most inept—thing he ever did.

For the moment the terror of the act had its desired effect. The Aetolians sent ambassadors to beg forgiveness from the King; the Athenians, who had been celebrating the festival of the Mysteria (it was now September), abandoned the festival in dismay—and sent an embassy to Alexander congratulating him on his Illyrian campaign and his suppression of the Theban revolt. Alexander replied in a courteous tone, but demanded the surrender of the ten most prominent anti-Macedonian politicians at Athens, including Demosthenes. To their lasting credit, the people refused to agree and the pro-Macedonian Phocion was driven off the speaker's platform when he urged acquiescence in Alexander's demands. A second embassy succeeded in mollifying the King, who satisfied himself with securing the exile of certain prominent mercenary-leaders at Athens, including the famous Charidemus. These soldiers immediately went to Asia and took up service under the Persian standard—a most welcome accession of military skill for the Great King.

A full meeting of the Hellenic League was now summoned at Corinth and the King duly confirmed as Commander-in-Chief of the invasion of Persia, due to begin next spring. The size of contingents from the individual states was settled and all were ordered to convene at Amphipolis at a set date. Alexander could now return to Macedonia with the certain knowledge that one powerful Greek state, at least, would trouble him no more.

On his way back it is said that he stopped off at Delphi to consult the oracle. The priestess of Apollo refused to prophecy, for that particular day was not a lawful day. Alexander is said to have been overcome with impatience and to have seized her violently, intending to force her to prophesy. At this the priestess cried out "You cannot be overcome, my son". Alexander let her go, saying that he desired no further prophecy than this. From this ejaculation of the Delphian priestess arose the legend of "Alexandros Anicetos"—invincible Alexander.

Back in Macedonia, Alexander held a series of religious festivals with great magnificence; and, to emphasize his hegemony over the Greeks, organized and presided over the hundred and tenth celebration of the panhellenic Olympic Games. In a more serious vein, he attended to all the necessary details of administration and organization in preparation for the coming spring; general questions of strategy, too, were worked out with the senior generals. One thing only was left undone:

Parmenion and Antipater (whom Alexander was leaving behind in Macedonia as his Viceroy) advised him to produce a son and heir before embarking on such a perilous enterprise; thus, in the event of mishap, the succession to the throne would be clear-cut and civil war would not break out. It was sensible advice; but Alexander was not the man for amorous dalliance and rejected their counsel. "It would be a disgrace", he pointed out, "for one who had been appointed by Greece to command the war, and who had inherited his father's invincible forces, to sit at home celebrating a marriage and awaiting the birth of children".[10] A lofty utterance, which was to cost the Macedonian people dearly thirteen years later; in the meantime, for the new Agamemnon, the descendant of Achilles, the spring could not come quickly enough.

NOTES

1 Justin IX 7.10ff.
2 Diodorus XVII 5.2
3 Arrian 1.3.5.
4 J. F. C. Fuller, *Generalship*, p.223
5 Arrian 1.5ff.
6 Arrian 1.8.1ff.
7 Diodorus XVII 12.3
8 Diodorus XVII 13.6 (Loeb translation)
9 Plutarch, *Alexander 11*
10 Diodorus XVII 16.2

3

The Army of Invasion

The army which gathered at Amphipolis in 334 for the invasion of the Persian empire was not the small band of resolute heroes that popular imagination makes it out to be and it will not be out of place to interrupt the narrative at this point to describe it in some detail. It has been described, with justice, by a leading military expert as "probably the most wonderful ever devised by a single man, and one much more scientifically perfect than any existing today".[1] When the crossing of the Hellespont had been effected and a conjunction made with the advance-guard, the total land forces amounted to almost 50,000 men available for active service, of whom 43,000 were infantry, more than 6,000 cavalry,—a small figure, perhaps, when compared with the huge national mobilizations of modern times, but a most considerable one when compared with the armies of the Greek city-states.

The whole army was composed of four main units: native Macedonian soldiers; contingents from the cities of the League of Corinth; Greek mercenaries with no political affiliations; and divisions from the Balkan countries either directly subject to or in alliance with the Macedonian crown. The kernel of the army and the nucleus round which the rest of the force was built were the 15,000 or so Macedonians, subdivided into four main units, two each of infantry and cavalry.

Of the Macedonian horse, the best known are the troopers of the Companion Cavalry. 1,800 in number, they were organized in eight squadrons, or *ilae*, seven of which had a strength of slightly more than 200, while the eighth, called the Royal Squadron, numbered 300 men. The cavalry-troopers were all landowners of some considerable means, and most of them owed their land to the favour of the King. In return they gave him military service when required.

The Companions are usually referred to as heavy cavalry, but in using this term one should rid oneself of pictures of medieval knights or even Napoleonic dragoons. Their armour comprised a helmet, a shield, greaves and probably a breastplate. Their arms were a thrusting-spear of about six feet, and a short sword. Their mounts were small—little more than ponies—and the riders themselves used neither saddle nor stirrups, devices as yet unknown to the Greeks. When going into action the squadrons charged in a wedge-shaped formation, the thin edge penetrating the enemy's line and the sides of the wedge then exploding laterally. Though the whole force was under Philotas, the son of Parmenion, who had the title of Hipparch (or cavalry commander), Alexander himself always led the charge of the Companions in person, and this charge was usually the decisive moment in a battle.

The other Macedonian cavalry, the Sarissophori (Lancers), who also had the name of Prodromi (Scouts), were light horse whose job was either reconnaissance or skirmishing. About 900 strong, they were probably recruited from a lower social class than the Companions from whom they differed in armament. For they had no breastplate, and, instead of the thrusting-spear, they carried the long sarissa (see below), and used a smaller shield than the Companions.

Of the two Macedonian infantry units, the Hypaspists formed the King's personal corps and bodyguard. 3,000 in number, the Hypaspists were without a doubt the "crack" infantry division of the army, with a prestige and *esprit de corps* akin to that of Napoleon's Old Guard. All picked men, they constantly attended the King's person and the Hypaspist probably received higher rates of pay than his comrade in the phalanx. Their usual battle-station was on the left of the Companions and the right of the phalanx; and in this position they formed the connecting link between phalanx and cavalry. When the Companions had broken the enemy line at a certain point, it was the Hypaspists who probed and exploited the gap while the phalanx played a frontal holding role. In arms and armour they appear to have been identical with the soldiers of the phalanx. Their commander at the start of the expedition—whose title was Archihypaspistes—was yet another son of Parmenion, Nicanor.

The main body of Macedonian infantry was the phalanx, organized in at least fourteen battalions of 1,500 men each; of these Alexander took six battalions or 9,000 men and left eight with Antipater. These battalions represent the territorial peasant levies of the Macedonian kingdom, but, thanks to Philip's care and training, instead of being the badly armed and badly disciplined rabble that such levies often are, they were a superbly organized army of professional soldiers, toughened and trained by long years of warfare. They are frequently referred to as the Foot Companions (Pezhetaeri), an honorary title given them by Philip, who, by putting them on the same status as the Companions and Hypaspists, hoped to break down their allegiance to the baronial houses of the districts from which they were recruited and to put them in a closer and more personal relationship with the monarch.

Macedonia had never produced the hoplite, or heavily armed infantry-man, who formed the main fighting-force in the armies of the Greek city-states. This is probably because of the feudal conditions that still obtained over most of the country—an aristocracy of land-owning barons who fought on horseback, and a dependent peasantry, with little or nothing in between of what might be called a "middle-class", able to equip itself with the heavy body-armour that enabled a man to fight in the infantry-line. This social factor can be discerned in the equipment of the soldiers of the phalanx. They had none of the body-armour of the Greek hoplite; they had a helmet, greaves for the legs, a leather corselet in place of the breastplate of the hoplite, and whereas the hoplite protected himself with a large metalled shield, the phalangite possessed only a small round wicker shield. Philip, however, made up for this marked inferiority in defensive armour by giving his phalangites a superior offensive weapon, the sarissa, a pike of between twelve and fourteen feet in length. With this pike, which was twice the length of the thrusting-spear of the Greek hoplite, the phalanx gained the tremendous advantage of having the first strike and being able to keep the enemy out of range. The situation has neatly been compared to one side in modern warfare having field-guns with twice the range of the enemy. Such a long weapon was, of course, more difficult to handle than the shorter thrusting-spear, and to be effective the phalanx had to retain perfect dressing.

The battalions of the phalanx were purposely designed to be large enough to operate independently, if the need arose, and each was under the command of a *strategus*, an officer who might be compared in rank to the modern major-general. There was, however, no general commander of the combined battalions of the phalanx. Many of the most famous personalities of Alexander's reign started out with the expedition as battalion-leaders—Craterus, Perdiccas and Coenus, to name but three—and all were extremely competent, and in many cases brilliant soldiers.

These four purely Macedonian divisions of the army were skilfully designed to work in conjunction and to act in a complementary manner. The phalanx was the pivot from which the attack developed; its function was to engage the enemy and hold his advance, and, if possible, to create a break in his line. The Companion Cavalry with its wedge-shaped squadrons, was the decisive offensive arm, and was committed to the battle when the right conditions had been created for it by the phalanx. The Hypaspists formed the link between phalanx and Companions, protecting the right flank of the one, the left flank of the other. At the same time they were offensive infantry, whose function was to follow closely on the cavalry charge and exploit the havoc created by it. The lighter Prodromi, as well as having reconnaissance functions, were intended to prevent, in conjunction with light infantry, any attempt to encircle and outflank the right wing and to absorb and cushion any attack the enemy might make in the area of the Companions before these had been committed to battle.

Of the Greek troops in the army the Thessalian cavalry, though the Thessalian states were members of the League of Corinth, can be treated separately from the League contingents because of the special relationship that existed between the Thessalians and the Macedonian King. 1,800 in number in 334, the Thessalian cavalry was soon brought up to 2,000 in strength, making them the largest individual cavalry unit in the army. In arms and armour they appear to have been identical with the Companions, like whom they were organized in territorial squadrons, or *ilae*. The squadrons fought in a diamond or rhomboid formation and their regular battle-station was on the left wing of the line. Parmenion was the regular commander of the left wing and the Thessalian cavalry stationed there seem to have formed a particularly close relationship with that general; indeed it has been suggested that they virtually formed Parmenion's personal Companion Cavalry, with the Pharsalus squadron in a similar capacity to the Royal squadron of the Companions. The general command of the Thessalians—as was the case with all the non-Macedonian units—was in the hands of a senior Macedonian officer, in this case Calas, who had been closely associated with Parmenion in the operations of the advance-party in Asia.

The small number of troops—7,000 infantry and 600 cavalry—which Alexander, as Hegemon, had demanded from the League of Corinth both gives the lie to any propaganda of a Greek crusade and reflects the attitude, if not of the whole League, at least of powerful elements in it, to Macedonia in general, and the Macedonian King in particular. Indeed, as has already been remarked (see Introduction), perhaps the main reason why the Macedonian King took with him contingents from the League states was to ensure the good behaviour of these states during his absence; this was certainly the case with Athens, which reluctantly sent twenty ships and 200 cavalry as its contribution. It must, however, be borne in mind that the League did also provide the large part of the fleet of 160 ships on which the army crossed to Asia; and Alexander may well have decided that the Greeks could play a more useful, if not a more active, role on sea than on land. The infantry were nearly all hoplites, though it is likely that many of them were mercenaries, hired as substitutes for citizen-soldiers by the contributing city. The contingent of each state was under the command of its own officer, with the general command of the whole infantry in the hands of the great Macedonian, Antigonus, nicknamed Monophthalmus (the One-eyed). The cavalry likewise was under a separate Macedonian commander.

But by far the largest number of Greeks in the army were serving, not from any treaty obligations, but for pay as mercenaries. Alexander, it is estimated, had 15,000 in his service at the start of the expedition. The mercenary infantry were a mixture of hoplites and peltasts, the more mobile and lightly-armed missile troops that had been introduced with such success at the beginning of the century. The mercenaries had their own officers—two are known from Aetolia and Acarnania, favourite recruiting grounds—but, as usual, the general command was in the hands of a Macedonian, Menander. The presence of so many mercenaries at the start of the expedition, when the Macedonian treasury was so low, is a good indication that these skilled professionals at least expected the invasion of Asia to be both successful and lucrative.

In a slightly different category from these mercenary infantry and cavalry were the corps of archers from the island of Crete, whose native weapon had always been the bow. Philip seems to have made use of Cretan archers over a considerable period of time, so that the corps formed almost an integral part of the Macedonian army. The number of archers in 334 is not known with certainty, estimates varying between 300 and 1,000; but it is likely, in view of the known Persian strength in missile troops, that Alexander would take as many with him as possible.

The remaining combat-troops with the army—about 9,000

altogether—were recruited from the Balkan countries surrounding Macedonia and were without exception light-armed and with specialist qualifications; for Macedonia itself was deficient in such troops and hence forced to go outside her boundaries to find them. The Thracians, both cavalry and infantry, were the most numerous, amounting to 700 and 5,000 respectively. The cavalry were light horse, with functions similar to those of the Prodromi, and the infantry were mainly javelin-men. Grouped with these were contingents, similarly armed, of the warlike Triballi, Illyrians and Paeonians. As was normal, the individual contingents were under a native commander and the general command under a Macedonian, Ptolemaeus, called "general of the Thracians" and with responsibility for both infantry and cavalry.

A Balkan unit worthy of individual mention is that of the Agrianian javelin-men. Their King, Langarus, an old friend of Alexander, had attended him during the Balkan campaign of the previous year and his men were probably present with the army as a gesture of friendship to the King. The skill of the Agrianians with their javelins in all kinds of fighting—open, close or mountain-guerilla warfare—was exceptional, and they might well be called the Gurkhas of the Macedonian army. Perhaps 1,000 in number, their commander in 334 was the Macedonian noble, Attalus (not to be confused with Alexander's bitter enemy).

The fleet that accompanied the expedition was composed mainly of contingents from the League of Corinth and is hence usually referred to as "the Greek fleet". The 160 ships were all triremes—galleys rowed by crews sitting three to an oar—with a complement each of about 200 rowers, thus giving a total of over 30,000 mariners. The Aegean fleet of the Persians was very strong, said to be more than 400 sail and well-trained; and these two factors, combined with the known hostility of many of the Greek states to the Macedonian crown, reduced the fleet of the Greeks to little more than a transport role. For not only was it not competent to face the Persians, but there was a very real danger of large units deserting to the enemy during, or even before, battle. The system of command seems to be that each ship was under a captain from the contributing city; and where a city provided more than one ship, it also provided a commodore for the squadron; while the whole fleet was commanded by a Macedonian general, in 334 a certain Nicanor.

The army was accompanied by a large siege-train. Though the fourth century had seen great improvements in Greek siege techniques, there were still very few of the city-states who possessed a siege-train in their military establishment, possibly because of their prohibitive cost. Its possession was, in fact, a prestige-symbol. Philip had acquired a highly modern siege-train, which was in evidence in the sieges of Perinthus and Byzantium in 340–39, and Alexander had inherited this along with the army. The main siege-engines were immense battering-rams; mobile wooden towers, several storeys high, which were used to put the besiegers on a level with or above the walls of the besieged; and bridges and scaling-ladders by which the besiegers could pass into the enemy's fortress or town. The artillery was mainly catapults of the torsion variety, worked by twisted ropes (human hair being especially suitable for these). One type shot a long metal bolt, and, when using the maximum trajectory, could shoot a distance of 500 yards; another type shot a ball of stone, weighing up to twenty pounds, about 200 yards with accuracy. These catapults—especially the bolt-shooting type—came in various sizes and some could be mounted on board ships or on the platform of the moveable towers. The main use of artillery was to sweep the enemy's walls in order to give covering fire to the mining, sapping and battering activities of the besiegers. It was never used during a pitched battle because the hand-to-hand nature of the fighting meant that there was a strong possibility of hitting one's own men. In charge of the Macedonian siege-train was Diades, an expert, not from Macedonia but from Thessaly.

Opposing this army, the forces of the Persian empire, which could draw on a population of some fifty million people, seemed very impressive—on paper. The Aegean fleet, as has been seen, numbered perhaps 400 sail; but it was comprised of contingents from the maritime regions of the empire, many of which were disaffected from the Persian government. Thus Phoenicia, Egypt and Cyprus had all been in revolt in the comparatively recent past, and the Greek city-states of Asia Minor could not be trustworthy when matched against fellow-Greeks. On the military side, the Iranian cavalry was very numerous and could be very good; but for the most part, was lighter-armed than the Macedonians and faced with difficulties of mobilization because of the immense distances of the empire. The King had a standing body-guard of 2,000 horsemen; the rest of the cavalry consisted of the levies of the satrapies, raised from the large landowners and their retainers. Satrapal levies, raised only in times of need, also formed the bulk of the Persian infantry; and they were as badly armed and trained, and of as little use in battle, as the Macedonian territorial levies had been before the reforms of Philip. The only standing Persian infantry force were the Royal Bodyguard of 2,000, called Melophori ("Quince-Bearers", from the model of the quince on the blunt end of their spears); the body of 10,000 heavy armed infantry known as the "Immortals" appears to have been disbanded by this time. The Persian government had been experimenting with a force of 60,000 infantrymen called Cardaces. But they were probably armed in the fashion of the Greek peltast, not the much-needed hoplite, and could not stand up to the charge of heavy cavalry. The only worthwhile infantry on whom the Persian King could rely were, paradoxically, Greek mercenaries. 30,000 are said to have been in Persian pay at the time when the expedition began, a figure that is probably not too much of an exaggeration, and their loyalty to the Persian King is, if nothing else, a reflection on their attitude to the Macedonian King.

When one considers the difficulties of mobilization and the problems caused by the diversity of nationalities within the empire, it can be seen that the Persian Government had at its disposal much stronger forces on paper than it did in reality. About to invade their empire was the finest army of specialized troops that the ancient world had hitherto seen, commanded by officers of the highest calibre and veterans of many campaigns fought together. Provided he did not allow his impetuosity to get the better of him, there was no reason why Alexander should not win any battle he fought with the Persians; and providing he could keep the loyalty and support of his officers and men, there was no reason why he should not be able to advance, if he wanted to, to the farthest limits of the enemy's empire.

NOTE

1 J. F. C. Fuller in *Encyclopaedia Britannica*, s.v. "Macedonian Army"

4

The First Year in Asia

In the spring of 334 Alexander, King of Macedonia and Hegemon of the Greeks, set out with his army to invade the Persian empire, to free the Greeks of Asia Minor from their foreign masters and to exact vengeance for the wrongs done to Greece 150 years previously. Marching along the northern coast of the Aegean, the expedition reached Sestus on the Chersonesus (Gallipoli peninsula) in twenty days. Directly opposite Sestus, on the Asiatic shore, was Abydus, which was in the hands of the advance-force sent over by Philip two years before. Despite strong opposition from the Persian forces under the Greek mercenary general, Memnon of Rhodes, the advance-party had managed to retain control of the bridgehead. The Greek town of Grynium, which had refused to be liberated, had also been stormed and enslaved by this force.

Leaving Parmenion at Sestus to supervise the ferrying of the army, Alexander and his retinue went to Elaeus, at the tip of the peninsula and here the King sacrificed at the tomb of the Homeric hero Protesilaus, who, the first of the Greek host under Agamemnon to land on Asian soil, had been immediately killed by the Trojans. The new Agamemnon was trying, by his sacrifice, to avert such a bad omen for his own crossing. He then sailed across the narrow channel to the so-called "Achaean Harbour", where the Greeks were alleged to have beached their ships before Troy. Standing in the bows of his ship, Alexander threw his spear on to the shore so that it stuck into the ground: then "praying that those lands might not unwillingly receive him as their King",[1] he leapt ashore first of all the Macedonians and claimed to receive Asia from the gods "won by his spear", that is, as

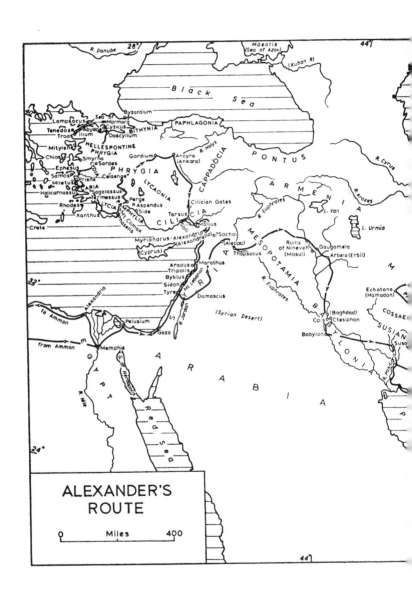

ALEXANDER'S ROUTE

0   Miles   400

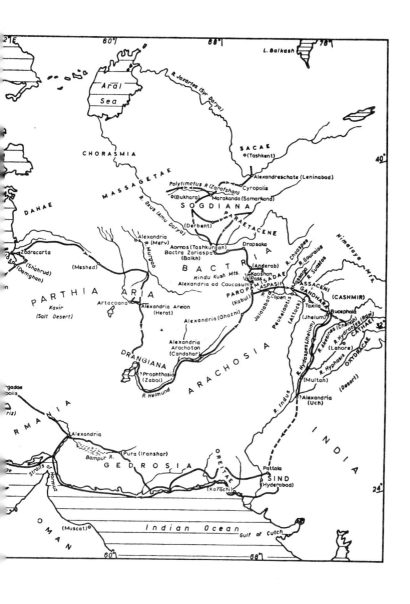

gained by right of conquest. This story, if true, would seem to indicate that from the very outset of the expedition Alexander entertained at least the idea of conquering the whole of the Persian empire, with which in the eyes of the ancients Asia was synonymous.

Troy was still foremost in the King's mind when he ascended to the small town of Ilium, built near the site of Homer's city. In the temple of Athena he dedicated his own armour and took down from the temple wall some armour allegedly dating from the Trojan War. At the tombs of Achilles and Patroclus, which the townsfolk displayed, he and Hephaestion laid wreaths. The King counted Achilles happy in having a Homer to preserve for posterity the record of his achievements. Arrian modestly claims to be acting as the King's Homer, "not judging myself unworthy to blazen before mankind the deeds of Alexander".[2] A sacrifice was also offered to Priam, the legendary King of Troy, praying him not to be wroth with the descendant of Neoptolemus. In the Trojan story it had been Neoptolemus, the ancestor of Alexander, who had sacrilegiously dragged the suppliant Priam from the altar during the sack of the city and had murdered him.

From Ilium Alexander rejoined the army, now ferried across the straits, at Abydus and marched northwards up the coast, past Lampsacus, making for the River Granicus (modern Tchan-tchai). The Persian satraps of Asia Minor—those of Lydia, Ionia and Hellespontine Phrygia—had taken up a position on the river, along with Memnon's Greek mercenaries, intending to try to stop Alexander there with the forces at their disposal. The Persian forces can hardly be dignified with the title of an imperial army. The Persian government, after the assassination of Philip, seems to have been confident that the expedition would be called off. This, combined with its preoccupation with a revolt in Egypt, meant that there was no major Persian army stationed in Asia Minor and no fleet patrolling its coast. The force on the Granicus consisted only of hastily raised satrapal levies; the native infantry was useless; and, although the armed retainers of the satraps made an efficient cavalry force, the backbone of the army were Memnon's Greeks. There were perhaps 30,000 men awaiting the invading army on the banks of the Granicus.

Since the Macedonians passed the small town of Priapus on the southern coast of the Sea of Marmora and since the Persian base-camp was at Zelea (modern Sari-Keia), it is probable that the two armies came into contact on the lower reaches of the Granicus. The Persians were stationed on the steep bank of the river to prevent the enemy crossing.

On the advice of Parmenion, since it was now late in the day, Alexander pitched camp for the night on the bank opposite. The Persians, because of their inferiority in infantry, retired from their bank to camp on the open plain some distance away. Next day, just before dawn, Alexander led the bulk of his cavalry across the narrow stream; the infantry then began to cross under their protection.

The Persians naturally countered this movement with their cavalry, and an engagement ensued, described by Arrian as "a cavalry battle, though more like an infantry fight. For horse was pressed against horse and man against man as they fought".[3] In the mêlée Alexander was nearly killed by the Ionian satrap, Spithridates, who attacked him from the rear with his battle-axe, but was cut down at the crucial moment by Cleitus, the leader of the Royal Squadron of the Companions.

Eventually Macedonian discipline and superior weapons—the stout thrusting-spear as compared with the light javelin—began to tell. The Persian cavalry was forced back and then broke, leaving the infantry at the mercy of the Macedonian cavalry and phalanx, which had now made the crossing. The Greek mercenaries retired in good order to the top of a nearby hill, whence they made offers of surrender in return for a safe conduct. Alexander refused and attacked the Greeks with both infantry and cavalry and slaughtered the unfortunate and helpless men until only 2,000 were left. These were granted their lives, but sent back to Macedonia in chains to work the mines there. As in the case of Thebes, the King's savagery can be justified on legal grounds, since the mercenaries in Persian service had probably been outlawed by the League of Corinth. He intended his brutal treatment of the mercenaries to act as a deterrent to other Greeks serving with the Persians. In fact, it had the opposite effect: the mercenaries realized that here was an opponent from whom they could expect no mercy and with whom it must be a fight to the bitter end. Nor could the act have increased his popularity with the states back in Greece, who felt more sympathy for their butchered kinsmen than for the alien conqueror.

The battle had been short and sharp, but it had cost the Persians dearly in terms of high-ranking cavalry officers; the Macedonian losses had been very light, not more than thirty infantry and sixty cavalry lost, according to Arrian.[4] His victory left Alexander free to operate in Asia Minor for some time without the need to face another Persian army; it also gave him control of the prosperous satrapy of Hellespontine Phrygia and its revenues—a welcome acquisition, if the stories told about the poverty of the Macedonian treasury in 334 are true. His action with regard to the satrapy indicates that Alexander—or his advisers—had in mind some more permanent settlement of Asia Minor than the official "liberation of the Greeks". For the Persian satrapal administration was taken over directly by the King and in place of the Persian Arsites, who had committed suicide after the battle, a Macedonian, Calas, was appointed as satrap. Calas had been one of the commanders of the advance-force and knew the area well; his place at the head of the Thessalian cavalry was taken over by Antipater's son-in-law, Alexander of Lyncestis.

Dascyleum (modern Eskili), the satrapal capital, had been evacuated by the Persian garrison and was occupied without trouble. The army then swung southwards to invade the neighbouring satrapy of Lydia, with its seat of government at Sardes. Sardes was the centre of Persian control of Asia Minor and is described by Plutarch as "the bulwark of the barbarian hegemony over the coast".[5] Strongly fortified and situated at the head of the Royal Road, the city was of great strategic importance, as is emphasized by the fact that the acropolis of the city (which also contained a royal mint) was held by a strong garrison whose commander was independent of the satrap.

This garrison-commandant, Mithrines, was now the senior Persian official at Sardes, the satrap Spithridates having died at the Granicus, and it was he who surrendered the city to Alexander. Lydia was now added to the Macedonian realm. Asander, a brother of Parmenion, was made satrap. The Lydians, because of their long tradition of civilization, were granted the privilege of being governed by their own laws. A modification was made in the administration, which indicates that the Macedonians had made a careful study of the weakness of the Persian system, namely the tendency of the peripheral satraps to break away from the central government, urged on by the distance of Susa and their own wide powers. For now in Lydia not only was the independent garrison-commander retained at Sardes, but a new official was appointed with control over finance. A major check was thus imposed on the satrap's powers. Mithrines, the former commandant, was taken along in the King's retinue and treated with honour—a useful piece of propaganda to encourage other Persian officials.

The large Greek city of Ephesus (near the modern Kusadasi), situated on the Lydian-Carian border, was the next objective. The city was entered without opposition, the garrison having evacuated the place after the Granicus. The democratic party at Ephesus was anti-Persian and therefore pro-Macedonian. The democrats had been in power at the end of Philip's reign and had instituted a cult of that monarch in the city. Just before the invasion began, the pro-Persian oligarchic party had seized power after summoning the aid of Memnon and his mercenaries. The now departed garrison had been a part of Memnon's force. Alexander naturally restored the democrats to power and the city was given its freedom, though it was to continue paying the tribute—the first signs of limitations on the "freedom of the Greeks". Party politics in Greek city-states were not conducted on the lines of modern Parliaments, with their Government and Opposition: the restored democrats immediately began to murder their oligarch opponents, dragging the leading oligarchs from asylum in the temple of Artemis and stoning them to death. Mob rule was not far away, when Alexander intervened and enforced an amnesty on both parties.

From Ephesus Alexander, pursuing the official propaganda of the expedition, despatched northwards up the coast an officer, with a detachment of troops, to free all the Greek cities which had been by-passed on the march from Dascyleum to Sardes. The officer, Alcimachus, was also to suppress oligarchies and set up democracies everywhere. This compulsory liberation and democratization of the cities raises the question of their legal status after liberation, a question that has been the subject of endless debate among historians. It must suffice to say that the Greek cities of Asia Minor were probably not enrolled in the League of Corinth; and that while they certainly became "free and autonomous", they became so as a result of Alexander's grant of these privileges and it lay within his discretion whether or not they were to pay the tribute or receive a Macedonian garrison for the sake of security. Each state probably entered into an alliance with the King, and though both sides were formally equal allies, the realities of power and the exigences of the war meant that from the outset the King was the dominant power. In reality, the liberated Greek states were little more than privileged parts of Alexander's growing Asiatic empire; and except for the institution of democracies and the remission, in most cases, of the tribute, their position was little different from what it had been under Persian rule. Nor should we view the imposition of democracies in these states as indicating Alexander's political bias. They were the result of pure expediency: the Persians favoured oligarchs, hence Alexander must support democracies. Back in Greece, where the democratic states were anti-Macedonian, it was the King's policy to support puppet-oligarchies.

The pronouncement of universal democracy was well timed. For a new factor was now about to enter the war—the Persian fleet, nearly 400-sail strong, heading northwards from Levantine waters and making for Miletus, the large harbour-city seventy miles south of Ephesus. Many of the crews in this fleet were Greeks from the states of Asia Minor and from the social class that naturally favoured the rule of the many. It was hoped that their loyalty to Persia would be shaken by Alexander's proclamation and that their native cities would deny the Persian fleet the use of their harbours.

There now began a race between the Macedonians and the Persian fleet to reach Miletus first. The city was in the hands of a garrison of mercenaries, whose commander had already made an offer of surrender to Alexander by letter. Now, however, encouraged by the proximity of the fleet, he underwent a change of heart. To both Persians and Macedonians the possession of the town was vital; to the former as a naval base, to the latter in order to deprive the enemy of such a base. The race was won by Alexander by about four days, but, because of the resistance of the garrison and the unco-operative spirit of the Milesians, he was compelled to invest the city by land and sea. The League fleet was used to block the narrow entrance of the harbour, so that despite its superior skill and numbers the Persian fleet could neither attack the League fleet nor enter the harbour.

After the Milesians had made an offer of neutrality to Alexander and had been refused, the assault on the city began. The Persian fleet and marines could bring no help and, says Arrian, were "almost like spectators watching their friends and allies in the city being besieged".[6] A breach was eventually made in the wall and the Macedonians began to pour into the city. The mercenaries, in desperation, made their escape to a small island in the harbour and there made ready to fight to the death. But Alexander had learned since the Granicus that it was a big mistake to leave these tough and skilful fighters with only the expectation of slavery if they surrendered. Hence he offered them a pardon, if they would join up with his forces; and all took the opportunity. Miletus, too, by the laws of war, had laid itself open to being sacked and plundered. But the King could hardly make an open farce of his official mission by making another Thebes of Miletus; and so the Milesians were pardoned and allowed their freedom.

Meanwhile the Persian fleet, which was stationed at Cape Mycale to the north of Miletus, kept on trying to provoke the League fleet to battle; but Alexander persistently declined. Already Parmenion had advised him, when the city was under attack, to let the fleet face the

Persians and Alexander had refused, above all because he feared that, in the event of a defeat, the whole of Greece would rise in revolt. The Persians were particularly eager for an engagement: their station at Mycale was uncomfortable and they were cut off from all nearby water supplies. Arrian neatly sums up their plight: "for want of water and other necessities, they were as good as besieged in their ships".[7] They even sailed to the island of Samos to obtain provisions; the island was an Athenian possession and if the provisioning was done with the consent of the Athenian government, it was a flagrant act of high treason against the League of Corinth and its Hegemon. Eventually the Persians sailed off to Halicarnassus (modern Bodrum), which was now the headquarters of resistance in Asia Minor.

Alexander now took the momentous step of disbanding the League fleet and sending home its contingents, retaining only the twenty Athenian ships, mainly to serve as hostages for their city's good behaviour. The reasons given for this decision are lack of money to pay the fleet and the realization that it was not, anyway, capable of tackling the Persian fleet. Moreover, he perceived that since he held Asia Minor with his land forces, he no longer needed a fleet; for he would bring about the dissolution of the Persian navy by cutting it off from all its coastal bases and recruitment areas. In the King's own words, he would "conquer the enemy fleet from the land".[8] Now while it is true that the League fleet was hardly equal to the Persian, it is hard to believe that money was a serious problem now that two wealthy provinces were under Macedonian control. Perhaps the King's main motives were his lack of faith in his naval allies and a typically Macedonian distrust of the sea. For like the Romans at a later date, the Macedonians never fully appreciated the value of sea-power and preferred to control the sea by controlling the sea-coast. Basically the new strategy was sound, though it did present dangers and problems. It meant that the Persian fleet was given a free hand in the Aegean, with the possibilities of its crossing to Greece and raising a general revolt there, or of its recapturing the coastal towns behind Alexander's back and cutting him off from his communications. It also meant that the whole of the eastern coast of the Mediterranean, as far as Egypt, had to be occupied to deprive the Persians of all their bases—and the task had to be done as quickly as possible.

From Miletus the advance continued over the border into Caria. Since the early years of the fourth century the satrapy had been a virtually independent monarchy in the hands of the family of

Hecatomnus. His son, Mausolus, famed for his magnificent tomb, the Mausoleum, had done much to develop a Hellenic type of civilization at his court at Halicarnassus. After the death of Mausolus and his sister-queen a complicated situation had developed, due to discord among the other children of Hecatomnus. Of the two surviving sons—Hidrieus and Pixodarus—Hidrieus succeeded to the throne and married his sister Ada. On Hidrieus' death, Ada was driven from power by Pixodarus; she took up residence in a castle at Alinda and fomented discontent against her brother, gaining in the process a strong following among the Carians. Pixodarus, to try to strengthen his position, had sought a marriage-alliance in 337 with the Macedonian royal family. When this failed he had sent to Susa asking for the assistance of a Persian satrap to maintain him in power. The satrap—Orontobates —was sent and married Pixodarus' daughter. Pixodarus died shortly before Alexander crossed into Asia and the satrap took over both the government and Halicarnassus. This was the situation when Alexander invaded Caria and it was natural that Ada should seek Macedonian help and equally natural that Alexander should favour the anti-Persian faction of Ada.

For this reason Alexander, instead of marching directly down the coast to Halicarnassus, made a large detour eastwards over the Latmus mountains in order to include Alinda and Ada in his journey. Ada received the King with great enthusiasm and turned over her fortress to him; to emphasize the sincerity of her friendship for the Macedonians, she adopted Alexander as her son. The King did not reject this mark of respect, which won him the goodwill of Ada's supporters and would show the rest of the Carians that he had come as something more than a mere conqueror. He returned Alinda to his adoptive mother and listened with favour to her plea for restoration as the rightful ruler of Caria, though he made no formal appointment as long as Halicarnassus was in enemy hands.

Halicarnassus, situated on the northern coast of the Ceramic Gulf, was a strongly fortified city, surrounded on three sides by high walls and on the fourth side by the sea. The spacious harbour was commanded by two citadel-fortresses, while a third acropolis was in the actual city. Since the city had been selected as the headquarters of the Persian fleet and the centre of resistance in Asia Minor, it had been well garrisoned with Greeks and Persians, stocked with arms and provisions and was ready to withstand a long siege. In command of the city's defence was Memnon, appointed by Darius after the Granicus as governor of the coastal regions of Asia Minor and admiral of the fleet. To appoint Memnon, a Greek, over the heads of the Persian nobility with whom he was not popular, must have required considerable courage on Darius' part. Memnon's intention was to hold Halicarnassus for his naval operations; alternatively, if the Macedonian pressure became too great, he intended to delay Alexander before the city as long as possible to give the central government time to raise and train an army.

Alexander for his part could not leave Halicarnassus in Persian hands behind his back. Hence, after making an abortive attack on the neighbouring town of Myndus, the Macedonians settled down to begin the first formal siege of the war. The point selected for the operations was the projecting northern tip of the city, and mining and sapping works were begun. When some progress had been made in this direction, the besieged made a sally one night. In the fierce engagement which ensued the Macedonians received a severe mauling, losing over 300 men and having many of their siege-engines burned.

Undeterred by this reverse, Alexander pressed on, and a few days later continual poundings with the battering-rams and sapping with mines caused the collapse of two towers and created a breach in the wall. The Persians, however, had foreseen that this would happen and had already erected a crescent-shaped demi-lune to seal the breach when it occurred. An assault on the breach resulted in a serious repulse for the Macedonians and Alexander was forced to acknowledge defeat by requesting a truce to gather up his dead. Ptolemy, as in the siege of Thebes, attempts to shift the responsibility for this reverse on to his enemy Perdiccas and at the same time to denigrate his abilities as a commander. For Arrian, drawing on Ptolemy, relates that the unsuccessful assault was brought on against the King's intentions by two drunken soldiers of Perdiccas: arguing as to which of the two was the braver, they decided to solve the question by attacking the enemy pickets at the breach; they were easily killed by the enemy, but as their comrades rushed up to help them, the engagement escalated till it became a general battle.

Despite the Persian successes, now that the breach had been made and the counter-wall was being battered steadily, it could only be a matter of time until the Macedonians broke into the city. One of the mercenary commanders in the city, the Athenian Ephialtes, devised and proposed to Memnon a daring plan: the besieged would make a surprise sally, in full force, in three divisions, one of which was to attack and burn the siege-train, while the other two were to take the Macedonians in the rear when they come to the rescue. It was hoped that the destruction of his engines and the loss of large numbers of his men would compel Alexander to abandon the siege.

The sally, which took place early one morning, was brilliantly executed. The Macedonian units that kept arriving to help repel the enemy from the siege-train were being hard-pressed; and when the main body of the Persians, under Memnon, took them in the rear, their position became desperate. The day was saved by the arrival of the veteran soldiers of the phalanx. Before their cool and steady discipline the Persians were gradually pushed back towards the city. The retreat turned to a rout as the gateway became blocked with men struggling to enter and the Persians were forced to close the gates and shut out many of their troops for fear that the Macedonians would force their way in with the Persians. More than 1,000 Persians and Greeks are said to have perished around the gateway.

The attack had been gallantly conducted, but its failure meant that the city would certainly fall soon. Memnon therefore decided to evacuate Halicarnassus, taking the fleet and remaining mercenaries to the nearby island of Cos and leaving a garrison only in the citadel. One night, when preparations were completed, the defence-works and arsenals were fired and Memnon effected his escape from the city. Alexander saw the flames and realized what was happening. After giving strict instructions that the citizens were not to be harmed, he entered the city unopposed.

The siege had been expensive to the Macedonians, both in time consumed and men killed, and their skill had been tested severely. But the results were well worth the labours. For apart from the fact that the Persians had now been deprived of their main naval base in the Aegean, it would have been a damaging blow to Macedonian prestige and morale if they had been forced to leave a hostile Halicarnassus in their rear. Ada was now formally appointed as satrap of Caria—the first non-Macedonian to receive such an honour, though the long established position of Ada's family in Caria made her appointment inevitable. She now took up her residence at Halicarnassus. But, as in Lydia, a strong garrison was left under an independent Macedonian officer who was given the task of reducing the Persians in the citadel.

Winter was now approaching and campaigning usually ceased at this time. The King made a very popular gesture when he sent home on leave for the winter all the men who had taken wives before leaving

Alexander the Great, ancient sculpture from Tivoli, now in the Louvre.

Coin of Philip II of Macedonia.

Cameo representation
of Alexander and
Olympias.

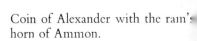

Coin of Alexander with the ram's
horn of Ammon.

Macedonia. Among their number was Coenus, who had himself married a daughter of Parmenion. Coenus' brother, Cleander, was sent to the Peloponnese to recruit mercenaries for the army. The married men and Cleander were instructed to rendezvous with the main body of the army the following spring, not at Halicarnassus, but at Gordium (modern Nallikan) in the centre of the Phrygian plateau.

For though it was winter and though much had been done in Asia Minor during the first season's campaigning, even more remained to be done and the winter months could be put to good use. Time was a vital factor in the policy of depriving the Persian fleet of its bases, and there still remained a large area of the coast-line of Asia Minor beyond Halicarnassus that had to be taken over before the Macedonians could descend on Phoenicia, the nerve-centre of Persia's naval organization. To wait till next spring before continuing the advance would mean using up much of that campaigning season on the rest of the coast of Asia Minor. Moreover, very little of the interior of Asia Minor had been touched in the first campaign, whose operations had been limited almost entirely to the coastal fringe. Alexander intended to use the winter months to reduce the rest of the coast-line and the main centres of Phrygia, so that he could begin his descent of the Levant next spring. Parmenion was given a large part of the army and the siege-train and ordered to take up winter-quarters in North Phrygia. Alexander himself, with his more mobile troops—the Companions, Hypaspists, most of the phalanx and the light-armed—would reduce the coastal areas as far as western Cilicia and then strike inland through the brigand-infested land of Pisidia to meet Parmenion early next spring.

Parmenion set off northwards to Phrygia, while Alexander entered Lycia, an ill-defined area adjacent to Caria and containing several Greek or partly-Greek cities on its coast. Of these the most important were Telmissus, Xanthus and Phaselis. Telmissus was the native-city of Alexander's most trusted seer, Aristander, and his influence may be behind the city's rapid submission. At Xanthus a favourable omen occurred when a spring near the city cast forth, after a violent up-heaval, a bronze tablet covered with ancient symbols. These, when deciphered, foretold the downfall of the Persian empire—or were said to foretell it. From Xanthus the King made a swift incursion into the Milyas, an area corresponding roughly to the northern part of the Bey mountains. His purpose was to harry the wild tribesmen, who lived in the mountains, while they were confined to the lower hills by the winter snows, and so deter them from their plundering raids on the coastal towns.

Phaselis had already come to terms with Alexander. Prosperous through its three harbours, it lay on the coast, enclosed to the north and east by high mountains, of which the most impressive is the Climax—the Greek word means "Ladder"—where the mountains came right down to the sea in an abrupt and steep series of shoulders. The northern neighbours of the Phaselites were the savage brigands of Pisidia, tribesmen, like those of the Milyas, prone to plundering the communities of the fertile central strip. The Pisidians had recently established a permanent stronghold on the plateau on top of the mountains overlooking Phaselis and used this as the main base for their raids. With the help of the Phaselites, Alexander undertook the destruction of this stronghold, in the course of which the Pisidian inhabitants, despairing of their safety, made an agreement among themselves and committed mass suicide.

Whilst the King was at Phaselis an incident took place which showed that the tensions of the beginning of the reign were still there. For Alexander of Lyncestis, at that time in command of the Thessalian cavalry and with Parmenion in Phrygia, was arrested on a suspicion of treason. The official version of the Lyncestian's disgrace, as given by Arrian[9] can hardly be called convincing: a Persian noble, it is said, had been intercepted carrying a proposal from Darius to the Lyncestian to assassinate Alexander; in return the Lyncestian would receive the Macedonian throne and 1,000 talents. No other evidence is adduced against him, and a touch of melodrama enters the story when Amphoterus, the brother of Craterus, is sent in disguise by the King to Parmenion with only a verbal message to arrest the Lyncestian. The real circumstances of the incident are beyond recovery, though the Lyncestian's strong claim to the throne was probably one of the main motives for the King's action. The arrest was a blow to Antipater, the Lyncestian's father-in-law; but it is a measure of the Regent's influence that the son-in-law was not immediately executed, but kept in custody for another three years. In the reshuffling of the commands that followed, the growing independence of the King can be seen in the appointment to the League of Corinth cavalry (whose commander had replaced the Lyncestian) of Erigyius, a Greek from Mitylene and a friend and supporter of Alexander under Philip.

From Phaselis the army pressed on into Pamphylia. The main body of the army was sent up the Climax gorge and over the mountain, a long detour but the only possible route for a large force. Alexander and his retinue had decided to take the shorter coastal route, which necessitated passing the Climax by travelling along the sea-shore. At high tide the water reaches high up the base of the mountain; southerly winds also produce the same effect, making the route completely impassable. When Alexander's party was leaving Phaselis there was a strong southerly blowing, but by good luck it changed direction before they reached the Climax, so that they were able to make the passage without undue difficulty.

Such a stroke of good fortune could hardly be without the element of divine intervention. The official historian, Callisthenes, surrounded the incident with an aura of the supernatural: Alexander and his mission were under special divine favour and protection; the sea, recognizing its invincible lord, had withdrawn and made obeisance to him. This miraculous interpretation was made with the approval and encouragement of the King; its effect on a cultured Athenian poet, Menander, is seen in the following verses:

> How Alexander-like, indeed, this is; and if I seek someone,
> Spontaneous he'll present himself; and if I clearly must
> Pass through some place by the sea, this will open to my steps.[10]

Little trouble was encountered in Pamphylia, which bordered on the wild and little inhabited coast of western Cilicia, known to Greeks and Romans alike as "Cicilia the Rough". Only at Aspendus, perched on the heights over-looking the River Eurymedon (modern Köprü Chay), was a show of force necessary, and then only after the Aspendians had revoked their agreement with the King. As a punishment this Greek city was made to pay double the tribute it had paid to the Persians, to surrender hostages and to place themselves under the supervision of the new satrap of Lycia and Pamphylia—another friend of the King's youth, Nearchus of Crete, a man with some connections in the area.

With the garrisoning of Side, the last large port before Cilicia, the occupation of the coast of Asia Minor was complete. Spring was approaching and Alexander could now strike northwards into Phrygia to join up with Parmenion. The march took the army through Pisidia, where the opportunity was taken of making a show of force to the barbarous natives. By-passing the fortress of Termessus, the Macedonians assaulted Sagalassus (modern Aglasum), inhabited by men who were reputed to be the most warlike of all the warlike Pisidians. After a hard fight the town was stormed and razed to the ground. Its destruction was followed by the surrender of many other Persian strongholds. Such as did not surrender were destroyed and the area was brought to some form of subjection.

It was almost a year since the army had landed on Asiatic soil and from both a military and political point of view it had been a highly successful year. The Greek cities had all received their liberation from Persian rule; a Persian army had been destroyed, their fleet deprived of bases in Asia Minor and four of their satrapies taken over (counting Lydia-Ionia and Lycia-Pamphylia as single units). But the enemy fleet was still a potent factor to be reckoned with and the Macedonians still had to be tested against a full-scale Imperial army. Whether Alexander's intentions were to extend his conquests beyond Asia Minor or merely to hold what he had won, the next season's campaign would be vital.

NOTES

1 Justin XI 5.10
2 Arrian I 12.4
3 Arrian I 15.4
4 Arrian I 16.4
5 Plutarch, *Alexander 17*
6 Arrian I 19.2
7 Arrian I 19.8
8 Arrian I 20.1
9 Arrian I 25
10 Quoted by Plutarch, *Alexander 17*, and translated in the Loeb edition by B. Perrin.

5

Darius Takes the Field

Skirting Lake Baldur, Alexander made for the satrapal seat of Phrygia, Celaenae, which was still in the hands of a Persian garrison. The Commander of the garrison offered to surrender to the King, if relief did not arrive before a certain date. Alexander, eager to join up with Parmenion, agreed. A blockading force was left behind at the city and a high-ranking Macedonian appointed as satrap.

The strategic importance of Phrygia, which straddles the main military roads through Asia Minor to the East, can be seen from the man selected as satrap—Antigonus, known as "the one-eyed", who figures in the wars following the King's death as one of the most brilliant generals among the "Successors". The fact that he was the bitter enemy of Ptolemy, the main source used by Arrian, may explain the lack of prominence given to him in the accounts of Alexander's reign.

At Gordium, once the capital of the former Kings of Phrygia, the divisions of Alexander and Parmenion reunited. Here also there arrived from Macedonia the married men, who had spent the winter on furlough, and reinforcements amounting to 5,000 infantry and 650 cavalry. They were perhaps accompanied by an Athenian embassy, which had been instructed by the Assembly to request from their ally and Hegemon the release of the Athenian citizens captured fighting on the Persian side at the Granicus and now serving hard labour in the Macedonian mines. They were disappointed, for Alexander would not give up at that moment such valuable hostages for Athenian good behaviour. The ambassadors were told to approach the King again when conditions were more settled.

The acropolis of the city contained a temple of Zeus "the King". Near this temple was an ancient wagon, whose yoke was tied in a complicated knot by means of thongs made of cornel-bark. The wagon was believed to have belonged to Gordius, the father of Midas, one of the old Kings of Phrygia. It had been dedicated to Zeus by Midas after he had become ruler of Phrygia in the following strange manner: the Phrygians, it is said, were in a state of civil war; an oracle was given which said that a wagon would bring them a King and this man would put an end to the civil discord. Whilst the citizens were discerning this oracle in their assembly, Midas and his parents—then poor tillers of the soil—drove up in a wagon. The coincidence was taken to signify the fulfilment of the oracle and Midas was made King. The wagon was dedicated on the acropolis and a prophecy made that whoever should undo the knot on the yoke would become ruler of Asia.

Now the Macedonians had a tradition of their own, which can be tied up with this legend, that the Phrygians had once been neighbours of the Macedonians, living around the Bermium mountain-range; then they were called Brigians and had a King, called Midas, who was famed for the beauty of his gardens near Bermium, where—so the story goes—he once captured the satyr Silenus and had a long conversation with him on the meaning of life. The tradition continues that the Brigians and their King Midas migrated to Asia, where they settled down and became the people known as the Phrygians.

The two traditions about Midas—Phrygian and Macedonian—perhaps refer back to an original conquest of the country and people of Phrygia by foreign invaders. That Alexander was aquainted with the Macedonian form of the legend is highly likely. For Mieza, where he received his tuition from Aristotle, was situated at the place where, in the legend, Silenus had been captured by Midas; and a fragment of a lost work by Aristotle, which contains an imaginary conversation between the satyr and Midas, shows that Aristotle himself was interested in the story.[1]

Alexander, then, with his knowledge of the legend, must have believed that the wagon dedicated at Gordium by Midas was the very one in which he had made the journey from Macedonia to Phrygia; and the fact that Zeus, in his capacity as the King of the Gods, was a deity much cultivated by the Macedonian royal family would have invested with considerable credibility in Alexander's eyes the prophecy regarding the wagon that had been dedicated to Zeus.

Superstition, curiosity and the possibility of a useful piece of propaganda to follow on the incident at the Climax, impelled Alexander to attempt the undoing of the Gordian knot; according to Arrian, he was motivated by his *"pothos"*—that burning desire to achieve something never before performed by any mortal.[2] Accompanied by his retinue, he ascended to the acropolis. The knot on the wagon had been tied so cunningly that no loose ends at all were visible. Alexander studied it for some time, though he could not see where he was to begin. He then made an attempt on the knot, but—not surprisingly—met with no success. Tension mounted among the courtiers; Alexander, afraid of having to admit defeat and of the loss of prestige that such an admission would entail, drew his sword, and with the words "It doesn't really matter how it's undone" slashed through the knot, "thus either tricking or fulfilling the oracle".[3] In fact, the King's action appears to have been perfectly legitimate; for the wording of the prophecy contained a typically oracular ambiguity, in that the Greek verb *luein* can have both a specific meaning of "untie" and a more general meaning of "undo, sunder, resolve". Thus the words of the prophecy could be interpreted as saying that the knot must be untied or merely that it must be undone or resolved. The natural way of interpreting it is the former, and so everybody up to that time had interpreted it; but Alexander, perhaps prompted by the seer, Aristander, adopted the second meaning.

If any of the spectators were filled with the same doubts as Curtius on the legitimacy of the solution, these must have been quickly dispelled. For that very night there occurred a violent thunder-storm, with frequent flashes of lightning. Thunder and lightning were the two personal possessions of Zeus, King of the Gods, and the seers interpreted their occurrence as a sign that Zeus was pleased with the action of his protégé. The oracle had indeed been fulfilled; the King of Heaven had promised rule over the whole of Asia to Alexander.

The next important town after Gordium was Ancyra (modern Ankara), less than fifty miles from the River Halys and on the eastern border of Phrygia. Beyond the frontier, to the east, was the large, though ill-defined, satrapy of Cappadocia; to the north, and equally ill-defined, lay Paphlagonia, an area where the natives had virtually no city-life and made at the most but a formal acknowledgement of Persian suzerainty. The Paphlagonians sent envoys to Alexander at Ancyra, making some token submission and requesting the King not to invade their territory. Alexander, who had no intention, anyway, of wasting time and effort in the mountains of Paphlagonia, agreed to their request, and, as a special privilege, granted them exemption from the tribute which they had not even paid to the Persians.

Just as nominal was the "reduction" which followed of Cappadocia. After marching a short distance into the satrapy, the King entrusted it to a certain Sabictas, who was probably a local baron. The following year Cappadocia was to become the centre of Persian resistance in Asia Minor; and when, ten years later, Eumenes of Cardia, the royal secretary, received Cappadocia as his province after Alexander's death, he immediately had to begin to subdue the area.

Southwards of Cappadocia and over the Taurus mountain range was the eastern half of the satrapy of Cilicia, known to the Greeks as Cilicia Pedias, "Plainland Cilicia". A glance at a map easily demonstrates the appropriateness of this designation. For the satrapy consists of a large coastal plain surrounded on three sides by high mountains. From the north the only practical entrance to the plain from the mountains are the so-called Cilician Gates, a pass situated at over 3,000 feet above sea-level and allegedly so narrow that no more than four men could pass through when marching abreast; from the east, the only pass is that which runs through the Amanic range of hills and hence known as the Amanic Gates (modern Bogtche Pass). The satrapal seat was at the city of Tarsus; the satrap in 333 was Arsames, who had fought at the Granicus, and it was he who now organized the defence of Cilicia as the Macedonian army headed towards the province.

As was to be expected, Arsames decided to try to hold the Cilician Gates, through which the invaders must pass, and a strong force was despatched there. These, however, proved of little use. For Alexander, on finding the pass blocked, waited till night had fallen and then, taking his most mobile infantry, made a surprise attack on the defenders. These were thrown into a panic at his approach and took to flight. The next day the Macedonian army passed through the Gates and began the descent into the Cilician plain.

Arsames, whose preparations against the invasion seem to have been of the sketchiest, now decided to adopt the policy that he had previously opposed so vigorously before the Granicus—to retreat before the Macedonian advance, burning and destroying everything that might be of use to the enemy. It was also resolved to evacuate Tarsus and, after removing all available money and treasure, to set fire to the city.

This was the news that reached Alexander at the head of his column. The King immediately pressed on ahead with his cavalry and the hard-working Agrianians to forestall the intended incendiarism. The forced march was successful, since Arsames, learning of the King's rapid approach, withdrew hastily before he could carry out his plan and made his way eastward to join Darius. For the information had reached him that the Great King, alarmed by the failure of his satraps and commanders to halt the invasion, was himself on the way to meet Alexander, advancing with his army from Babylon up through Mesopotamia. It can hardly be doubted that Alexander too was informed by deserters of Darius' approach as soon as he reached Tarsus. He must have calculated, however, that the slowness with which Persian imperial armies were accustomed to march would leave him with ample time to accomplish the reduction of Cilicia before he made ready to meet the Persian army.

His calculations were slightly upset by an unforeseeable chance. It was now midsummer and the weather was very hot at Tarsus, situated in the middle of the plain where the summer heat is contained and intensified by the encircling mountains. Through the city runs the River Cydnus, whose waters were said by ancient writers to be extremely cold because of the quantities of melted snow they receive from the mountains. Alexander, dusty and sweating copiously after his journey, is said to have bathed in the river, as a result of which he caught a chill which soon turned into raging fever.

So violent was the illness that all but one of the doctors either gave Alexander up for lost or feared to attempt to cure him, lest they fall under suspicion in the event of his death. The one exception was a certain Philippus, a doctor from Acarnania, who appears to have been on somewhat close terms with the King. Philippus' panacea was to administer a very strong purge to the system, and Alexander agreed to submit himself to this treatment.

While Philippus was preparing his draught, a note was brought in from Parmenion, warning the King to beware of the doctor, who had been bribed by the Persians to poison his master. Alexander read the note in silence; and when Philippus handed him the potion, he in turn gave the note to the doctor to read. At one and the same time, says Arrian, Alexander drank the medicine and Philippus read Parmenion's message.[4] The doctor possessed a cool head. He merely bade the King to follow the rest of his instructions, if he wished to recover. The purge worked, and three days later Alexander was able to show himself to the army. As for Philippus, his professional stature was increased and he henceforth lived in great honour at the court. The story of the warning note and Alexander's reaction is a charming one, meant to demonstrate that the King was "totally void of suspicion where his friends were concerned";[5] it was also intended to show Parmenion in a bad light and probably stemmed several years later from the pen of Callisthenes, when that historian was putting forward the "official" story of how the family of Parmenion had abused their trust.

The illness and period of convalescence must have thrown Alexander's plans somewhat out. Darius was drawing closer and eastern Cilicia had not yet been pacified. There followed a period of great activity among the army. Parmenion was sent with a strong force, which included all the League troops and the Thessalian cavalry, to occupy the mountain passes leading into northern Syria (the so-called Pillar of Jonah and the Syrian Gates, or Beilan Pass); it was by this route that it was expected that Darius would come after leaving the Euphrates. Whether through ignorance or over-confidence, Alexander neglected to occupy the Amanic Gates to the north of the Gulf of Alexandretta.

He himself, meanwhile, took over the towns of Anchialus and Soli. At the former place was an indecent statue of the ancient Assyrian King, Sardanapalus, which Arrian found quite fascinating; at the latter a garrison had to be imposed because of the pro-Persian sympathies of the citizens. Here too news reached Alexander that the Persian force at Halicarnassus had been brought to battle and defeated by the Macedonian force there. At Mallus there was civil discord; the King put an end to this, as he had done at Ephesus, and, because the Mallians could claim a common descent from his ancestor Heracles, he remitted their payments of tribute.

Now came the news that everybody, from Alexander down to the humblest private, had anxiously been awaiting: Darius and his army had at last arrived and were encamped at Sochi, about two days' march from the Syrian Gates. The exact position of Sochi is not known; but it is somewhere to the east of the Amanus range and to the west of the city of Aleppo, on the edge of the Syrian desert. Thinking that Darius intended to bring him to battle near Sochi, Alexander hastened to join up with Parmenion with a view to approaching Darius through the Syrian Gates. Leaving any sick and wounded *en route* at Issus, at the head of the Gulf of Alexandretta, and marching at top speed, Alexander covered seventy miles in two days, passing through the Pillar of Jonah and arriving at evening on the second day at Myriandrus (near the modern Alexandretta), the first town in Phoenicia and a few miles to the west of the Syrian Gates. Here the two army-groups joined forces.

But, whether through over-confidence or lack of time, Alexander's reconnaissance had been very poor and he was led into a serious strategic blunder. For Darius had not remained at Sochi. After waiting there for some time, the Great King had grown impatient and, despite the advice of the refugee Macedonian, Amyntas, son of Antiochus, to stay where he was and make the most of the open spaces around Sochi for his cavalry, he had decided to strike camp and go in pursuit of Alexander in Cilicia. First, however, he sent his baggage-train and most of the non-combatants to Damascus, about 130 miles to the south.

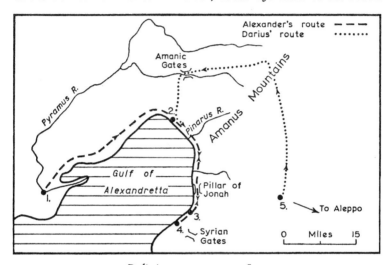

Preliminary manoeuvres to Issus

1	Mallus	4	Myriandrus
2	Issus (?)	5	Sochi (?)
3	Alexandretta		

There had been serious unrest in Phoenicia and Egypt and it seems that Darius, confident of victory, was intending to pay these satrapies a personal visit after the battle.

The Great King then passed, with his army, over the Amanus mountains—but not by any of the occupied passes, but through the Amanic Gates, descending on Issus about one day after Alexander had left the town. After slaughtering the Macedonian sick and wounded, he pressed on southwards as far as the River Pinarus (modern Deli), about twenty-three miles to the north of Myriandrus, and here took up a defensive position on the left bank. Either by good luck or superb

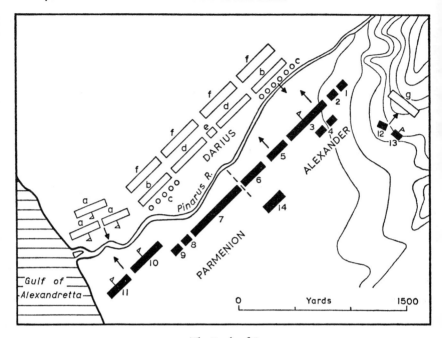

The Battle of Issus

strategy—and the timing seems to indicate the latter—Darius had gained the position that all generals in warfare before the twentieth century dreamed of gaining: he had come down behind his enemy's army, cutting him off from his line of communications. Alexander was completely bottled up in the narrow coastal plain of northern Phoenicia. Darius has frequently been blamed by military critics for halting on the Pinarus and not pressing on in pursuit after catching Alexander in the rear; but it has rightly been said by one of Alexander's greatest admirers that Darius needed only to hold his position on the river and fight a drawn battle and Alexander's career was over.[6]

Alexander was resting his weary troops at Myriandrus, when he received the startling news that Darius was across his rear and not at Sochi. It is not difficult to imagine the consternation and despondency that the report must have created in the King, officers and men alike. For "there is nothing soldiers dread more than to feel that their line of retreat has been blocked".[7] A ship was sent along the coast to verify

ALEXANDER		DARIUS	
1	Agrianian detachment	a	Cavalry under Nabarzanes
2	Archer detachment	b	Cardaces
3	Companion Cavalry	c	Archers
4	Prodromi or Sarissophori	d	Greek mercenaries
5	Hypaspists	e	Darius and bodyguard
6	Two battalions of phalanx	f	Satrapal levies
7	Four battalions of phalanx (under Craterus)	g	Light armed detachment
8	Archer detachment		
9	Thracian javelin-men		
10	Thessalian cavalry		
11	League of Corinth cavalry		
12	Agrianian detachment		
13	Detachment of light cavalry		
14	Greek mercenaries and League of Corinth infantry		

the report and when it had returned, after inspecting the Persian forces and position, Alexander decided that, the situation being as it was, the best form of defence was to attack as quickly as possible. Weary though his men must have been after their long march, he roused them again and returned as far as the Pillar of Jonah, where they made bivouac at about midnight. The next morning they set out again in column towards the Pinarus, descending into the plain of Issus. About three miles from the river, and in the middle of the afternoon, Alexander began his deployment from column into line of battle.

The small plain of Issus, where the battle was to be fought, was bisected by the River Pinarus, which flowed from the Amanus mountains to enter the Gulf of Alexandretta. From the foot of the mountains to the sea the width of the plain was hardly more than a mile and a half. The banks of the river were steep and uneven, but the river itself was fordable along its length. Where the crossings were easiest, Darius had erected wooden palisades on his side of the stream.

Of the two forces, the Macedonian army was at much the same strength as it had been at the Granicus—about 50,000 altogether. The army of their opponents was probably not much larger (in fact, it is possible that the Persians were outnumbered) and was far from being the full imperial levy, which Darius had not had time to call up and train. Its main strength lay in the native Iranian cavalry, the Greek mercenaries under Amyntas, son of Antiochus—over 10,000 in number—and in the so-called Cardaces, of whom mention has already been made (see chapter 3). They were said to number 60,000 at Issus, but this figure is almost certainly greatly exaggerated in this instance. The ludicrous total for the Persian army of 600,000 men, which Arrian found in his "official" source, may be treated with the contempt it deserves.[8]

As Alexander began his deployment, the infantry, who were at the head of the column, moved into their positions first. On the far right were the Hypaspists and next to them two battalions of the phalanx; these formed the front-line infantry of the right wing. The other four battalions of the phalanx under the general command of Craterus, formed the infantry of the left wing. The whole left wing, when deployment was completed by the posting of the Thracian javelin-men and Cretan archers as the flank-guard, was put under Parmenion. Behind the first line the mercenaries and League of Corinth infantry were stationed as a reserve. The cavalry was not immediately deployed, but it was intended that it should all mass with Alexander on the right wing, leaving Parmenion to rest his left flank against the sea.

As the Macedonians began to move into position, Darius too began to draw up his line of battle. First he sent all of his cavalry and some light infantry across the river to act as a screen. Then, in the post of honour at the centre of his line he placed the Greek mercenaries; on their flanks were the Cardaces, with a strong force of archers in front of each of the two divisions. The weaker satrapal levies were posted as a second line of infantry. On the far left of his line, and in advance of and at a right angle to it, he stationed a detachment of light armed troops in the foothills across the river. Their function was to protect Darius' left flank and to harass Alexander's right flank, if the opportunity presented itself. Having drawn up his infantry, Darius recalled the cavalry, under the command of Nabarzanes the Vizier, and posted it on his far right wing, near the sea-shore and opposite Parmenion. Then he himself took up his regular position in the centre.

Alexander had originally allocated the cavalry of the League of

Corinth to Parmenion. But when he saw that all the Persian cavalry was opposed to his left wing, he detached from himself the Thessalians and sent them to reinforce Parmenion. To protect the right flank of his own cavalry he posted detachments of the archers and Agrianians; the rest of the Agrianians and some light cavalry were stationed at a right angle to the rest of the line to guard against the Persians in the foothills. These were, in fact, sent before the battle opened on a "cutting out" expedition and easily cleared the enemy from the hills. As at the Granicus, the spearhead of Alexander's attack was to be the squadrons of the Companion cavalry, supported by the Prodromi. The general plan of both Alexander and Darius seems to have been very similar: to concentrate and then throw the mass of their cavalry against what was thought to be the enemy's weak spot.

Alexander slowly continued his advance towards Darius with his army in line, making frequent halts to rest the men and to maintain the dressing of the line. Before he came within bowshot of the Persians, he called a halt and then rode along the line, exhorting the soldiers in general and calling upon individuals by name; Napoleon too endeared himself to his men by this ability to remember the names and faces of his private soldiers. The time was now about four o'clock in the afternoon, which, in late October or early November, meant that little of the afternoon was left.

The Macedonians again began their slow and methodical advance, until they were just within range of the Persian bowmen. Suddenly, with terrifying force and rapidity, Alexander charged across the river with all his cavalry, followed closely by the Hypaspists and infantry of the right wing. The Persian archers panicked as the Companions smashed into them and turned to flight. They ran straight into the ranks of the Cardaces, immediately behind them, closely followed by the stabbing spears and trampling horses of the Macedonian cavalry. In a short time the whole of the Persian left wing, as far as the mercenaries, had been thrown into confusion; and when the Cardaces, helpless before their mounted and more heavily armed adversaries, crumpled, confusion of the left wing quickly became a rout.

But the speed of Alexander's charge, and the closeness with which he had been followed by the infantry of the right wing, had opened up a gap in the centre of the Macedonian line. Darius' Greeks—every man a professional soldier—were quick to exploit this gap and charged into it as the left wing of the phalanx was still struggling in the river. It

was here that the hardest part of the fight took place and the Greeks
gave the phalanx battalions a severe mauling; the Macedonians lost
120 officers alone in the engagement. The bitterness of the fighting at
this point is emphasized by Arrian[9] and is explained as stemming from
the hatred which the two peoples—Greeks and Macedonians—felt for
each other. It was Chaeronea all over again; and this time the mercenaries were determined to make it a Greek victory. The outcome,
indeed, looked black for the phalanx, until the Hypaspists and battalions
of the right wing turned their attentions from the Persian left and
crashed into the flank and rear of the mercenaries, dashing any hopes
of a Greek revenge.

It was probably now that Darius turned his chariot and fled from the
battle-field. He has frequently been accused of cowardice for this, but
his action was a sensible one and in all probability had been agreed upon
before the battle, in the event of things going badly. The fight was now
obviously lost, with the left wing smashed and the mercenaries
surrounded; Darius himself was now in an isolated and exposed position and Alexander, with the victorious Companions, was free to
wheel to the centre to kill or capture the King. Darius must be saved to
organize and lead the defence of the empire in the future; his safety
would more than counterbalance the loss of the rest of the army at
Issus. These motives, not cowardice, were behind the flight of Darius.
Pursued by Alexander and the Companions, the Great King fled in his
chariot till he reached more broken ground, when he took to horseback, discarding his gorgeous cloak and weapons to make himself less
conspicuous. Alexander kept up the pursuit till darkness fell and then
was forced to abandon his hopes of capturing Darius and make his
way back to the battle-field.

Meanwhile, on the far left of the Macedonian line another battle had
been taking place. Here the Persian heavy cavalry, all massed on this
wing, had made their charge and had been received by the Thessalians.
It was fortunate for the Macedonians that Alexander had sent the
Thessalians to Parmenion before the battle began, since the Persians
pressed them hard and did not break off the engagement until they saw
Darius in flight and the mercenaries being cut down. They then began
to retreat, pursued by the Thessalians. In the course of the withdrawal
many of the infantry of the Persian right wing were killed, either
trampled to death by their own cavalry or cut down by the jubilant
Thessalians.

Thus ended the battle of Issus, the first direct confrontation between

Aristotle. Ancient sculpture in the National Museum, Rome.

Ptolemy I. Ancient bronze in the National Museum, Naples.

Statue of Alexander executed by the sculptor Menas in the second century B.C. Now in the Archaeological Museum, Istanbul.

the two Kings. The whole engagement probably took less than two hours, though it would be fair to say that it had been won in the first few minutes by the ferocity of Alexander's cavalry charge. The Persian losses were heavy, including the deaths of two satraps at least, though the figure given by Arrian (and drawn from Ptolemy) of 100,000 dead is merely laughable. It was also Ptolemy who narrated that, in the pursuit of Darius, Alexander and his men came to a deep gully and crossed it on the bodies of the dead piled within.[10] Indeed, most of the Persian cavalry escaped unscathed and made its way to Cappadocia, where it participated, the following year, in the counter-attack that developed in Asia Minor; while of the mercenaries at least 10,000 made an orderly retreat from the battle-field and most of them renewed the struggle against the Macedonian King, some joining up again with Darius, others taking service with the Spartan King, Agis, then busy with stirring up a war of liberation in the Peloponnese. The figures given for the Macedonian losses—450 killed and 4,500 seriously wounded—show that the Greeks at least had inflicted serious damage. The victory at Issus had been spectacular, but far from decisive.

Perhaps the battle made its greatest impact, not in Asia, but back in mainland Greece, where in many quarters a Persian victory would have sparked off a revolt against Macedonian domination. Tension had been mounting on the mainland during the summer of 333 as the result of the activities of the Persian navy in the Aegean. We may here briefly sketch in these activities in order to bring the picture of the war up to date on both its major fronts.

In the spring, Memnon had begun his expected counter-attack in the Aegean. He hoped to achieve three things: to capture the islands of the Aegean and retake the cities of the Asia Minor coast; to try and raise a revolt in mainland Greece; and, at the same time, to gain control of the Dardanelles and so cut Alexander off from his communications with home. Chios was betrayed to him by the pro-Persian faction; at Lesbos, after overrunning the island, he was forced to blockade and lay siege to the main town, Mitylene. During the course of the siege, Memnon fell ill and soon died, a piece of good fortune for Alexander and "the most damaging blow at that time to the Great King's affairs".[11] Pharnabazus, the nephew of Memnon and himself a high-ranking Persian, took over the command of the fleet and pressed on with the siege of Mitylene, which was compelled to capitulate. Mitylene's treaty with Alexander was cancelled, a tyrant set up and a Persian garrison imposed.

It was now that Darius, preparing for the Issus campaign, sent instructions to Pharnabazus to send the body of Memnon's Greeks to the land-army. This was a serious blow to Pharnabazus' war-effort, though he still pressed on with his operations in the Aegean with such success that Tenedos, at the entrance to the Dardanelles, was brought into Persian hands and Lampsacus, on the Asian shore, was captured. This direct threat to his communications with Europe compelled Alexander to send two senior officers, Hegelochus and 'Amphoterus—the latter being the brother of Craterus—back to the coast to raise a new fleet to oppose the Persian fleet and attempt to recover the islands.

Hegelochus hastily raised a fleet from the Greek cities on the coast and managed, after the Persians had sailed off southwards, to regain control of Tenedos and the Dardanelles area. This same officer soon afterwards seized the Athenian corn-fleet coming from the Black Sea and detained it for a while at Tenedos. He had rightly gauged the feeling of the majority at Athens and his detention of the corn-ships was intended to ensure that Athens made no hostile move at this critical time. Open war, in fact, did almost erupt over this incident; for the Athenians voted the fitting out and immediate sailing of a hundred triremes, though the crisis seems to have passed over before the dilatory citizens had time to put their motion into effect. A minor victory was also gained by another Macedonian naval officer, Proteas, who in a daring night attack destroyed a Persian squadron at Siphnos in the Cyclades.

Despite the successes of Hegelochus and Proteas, at the end of the summer of 333 the Persian fleet was still in a commanding and threatening position in the Aegean. The Persians were in possession of most of the islands and their proximity to the mainland aroused in many of the Greek states the hopes of an invasion of Greece and liberation from Macedonian domination. At Athens, which was still smarting from the incident of the corn-fleet, the people were in an ugly mood; and when the news came through, late in October, that Darius and his army had reached the coast and Alexander was cut off in Cilicia, Demosthenes, openly displaying letters from the Great King, exulted that the Macedonian "was on the point of being trampled underfoot by the Persian cavalry".[12] In the Peloponnese the Spartan King, Agis, was preparing to lead a revolt against the Macedonians and was in touch with the Persian admirals for aid with men, money and ships.

The news of the Persian disaster at Issus dashed these hopes to the ground, though in some cases only temporarily. At Siphnos Agis was actually in conference with the Persian commanders when the report came through. The conference immediately dissolved, since the Persians feared the outbreak of revolts in the islands occupied by their garrisons. Agis was forced to be content for the moment with a small subsidy in money; later he took into service the mercenaries who had made their escape from Issus. Athens too was stricken by the Macedonian victory and gave up any intentions of immediate action. On the Persian navy, also, the battle had an effect which was soon to manifest itself. For the victory at Issus had opened up Phoenicia to Alexander and the possibility of Macedonian action in the near future around their native-cities dangerously weakened the loyalty of the various Phoenician contingents with the Persian navy; it was from this time that the dissolution of the Persian fleet began.

NOTES

1   Aristotle, Fragment 44 (Rose); Plutarch, *Moralia* 115 b-e
2   Arrian II 3.1
3   Curtius III 1.18
4   Arrian II 4.10
5   Arrian II 4.11
6   W. W. Tarn, *Cambridge Ancient History* VI, p.367; *Alexander the Great* I, p.24
7   J. F. C. Fuller, *Generalship*, p.156
8   Arrian II 8.8
9   Arrian II 10.7
10 Arrian II 11.8
11 Arrian II 1.3
12 Aeschines, in *Ctesiphontem* 164

6

Phoenicia and the Siege of Tyre

For Alexander himself, his Staff and the army the immediate sequel to the battle was a night spent in celebration of the victory amidst the spoils of the captured Persian camp. It was here that the King received his first taste of oriental luxury and splendour. The sight of the royal quarters and of the magnificent dining-pavilion adjoining them, and the exotic foods and wines laid out there, elicited from Alexander a cry of astonishment and admiration: "This, it seems, is what it means to be a King!"[1] The court of Philip had been lavish by Greek standards, but it bore no comparison with that of the Persian monarch.

The story is told that during the course of the celebrations in the dining-pavilion the sound of wailing and lamentation suddenly arose from a nearby tent. It came from the mother, wife and two daughters of Darius, who together with the Persian's six-year-old son had been captured along with the camp. A eunuch-slave had just informed them that Darius was dead; for he had seen a Macedonian soldier carrying the cloak worn by Darius in the battle, but cast off during his flight. Alexander, it is said, immediately sent the Bodyguard* Leonnatus to inform the captive women of the true situation: Darius was not, in fact, dead, but had made his escape; they were not to fear, since Alexander granted them all their accustomed prerogatives; he had no personal quarrel with Darius and the battle had been fought in lawful

---

*The Bodyguards were a group of seven or eight high nobles, intimate friends of the King, who were expected to be in attendance on him at all times. They were thus debarred from holding independent offices necessitating absence from court over a long time; thus neither Parmenion nor Harpalus were Bodyguards. The part was very prestigious and honorific.

fashion for the rule of Asia. To support these statements, the King next day allowed the royal women to choose out whom they wished from the Persian dead to be buried with full honours.

Alexander's treatment of the Persian women won him nothing but applause from the ancient writers. "If only he could have continued to practise such moderation to the end of his life", laments Curtius;[2] "I have nothing but praise for Alexander for his compassion towards these women", is the opinion of Arrian;[3] and Plutarch states that these ladies—the queen-mother, Sisigambis, the queen, Statira, and the beautiful pair of daughters—lived during their captivity, not as though they were in an enemy's camp, but as if guarded in holy and inviolable maidens' chambers, apart from the speech and sight of men.[4] It would be perhaps churlish to add to these laudatory remarks that, as Alexander's plans widened in their scope and purpose, such considerate treatment afforded good material for propaganda, reflecting well on Alexander, and badly on Darius, who had left his family at the tender mercies of the conqueror while he himself took to disgraceful flight.

Parmenion was now despatched to Damascus to secure the Persian baggage and treasury which had been sent there by Darius before the battle. He was accompanied on this mission by the Thessalian cavalry, allegedly as a reward to these troopers for their valour in the fight. For it was expected that there was much booty to be gained at Damascus. Alexander himself appointed as satrap of Cilicia Balacrus, a relative of Antipater, and then began his descent into Phoenicia.

Surprise has sometimes been expressed that Alexander, after his resounding victory, did not press on into the heart of the empire in pursuit of the stricken Darius, but chose instead to continue his original policy of securing the coastal areas and towns. But perhaps there is no cause for such surprise. For the Persian fleet was still active and would continue to be a menace as long as it had bases from which to operate. Besides, Alexander must have realized that what he had defeated at Issus was far from being the full levy of the Persian empire. The resources of the Far Eastern satrapies were as yet untapped and if Darius should be pursued now, there was the danger that he would retreat with his followers into the vast spaces of the East and carry on a war of attrition that could last for years and require a huge army of occupation to hold down the various satrapies as they were overrun. It was a far better policy to give Darius time to mobilize an army that was truly representative of the empire and then smash this in a pitched battle; and Issus had shown Alexander that there was a good chance that he could beat any Persian force that opposed him. Alexander's strategy, then, was to allow Darius to raise a new army and in the meantime himself to continue neutralizing the enemy's fleet. Perhaps, too, at this stage not a few of the men and officers would have refused to follow him into the great unknown heart of the Persian empire.

Phoenicia, a narrow coastal strip extending southwards almost to Egypt, was a land of many city-states, all acknowledging Persian suzerainty and all, with the exception of Tyre, doing so with great reluctance. Sidon especially hated the Persians. For after heading a Phoenician revolt early in the 340s, from which Tyre, the age-old rival of Sidon, had stood aloof, the city had been treacherously captured and most of its inhabitants sold into slavery. The inhospitable nature of the Phoenician hinterland had made the cities dependent on maritime commerce; and their naval skill made the Phoenicians a vital part of the Persian fleet, each state supplying a contingent. Monarchy—usually Persian supported—was the normal form of government.

Aradus (modern Arwad) was the first Phoenician state as one approached from the north. It was situated, not on the coast, but on a small island about two and a half miles from the mainland. Several small towns on the mainland seem at this time to have been under the control of the ruler of Aradus, a certain Gerostratus. The most important of these was Marathus, and it was here that Gerostratus' son came to meet Alexander, offering him his submission and congratulations on the victory at Issus. The son was acting as viceroy for his father, who was then absent with the Persian fleet in the Aegean. Alexander confirmed Gerostratus in his rule at Aradus—a gesture which would hasten that prince's departure from the fleet and encourage the other Phoenician dynasts to do the same.

News came through at Marathus that Parmenion had taken over Damascus from its Persian governor without a fight; that the Persian field-treasury, amounting to more than 3,000 talents, had been captured, along with the families of several of the highest ranking Persian nobility; and that there had been found in Damascus and with the Persian retinue ambassadors to the Great King from the exiled Thebans, from Sparta and from Alexander's supposed ally, Athens. These ambassadors had reached Darius before the battle and had been sent by him with the baggage-train to Damascus.

In reply to Parmenion, Alexander instructed him to send the Greeks to Marathus. Parmenion himself was to remain at Damascus and to supervise the military organization of northern Syria, known to the ancients as "Hollow Syria". His commission also included the occupation and garrisoning of the small countries southwards of Damascus, such as Judaea and Samaria. Parmenion's task was purely military and of a temporary nature; he was to rejoin the army as soon as possible. The normal administration of Syria was put in the hands of a Macedonian satrap, Menon. His Persian predecessor, Mazaeus, had fled to Babylon after Issus and, in view of his long and distinguished career, was appointed to the vacant satrapy of Babylonia.

Still at Marathus, the King received a letter from Darius himself, containing offers of peace. Its contents showed that Darius "was not cast down from his pride, though he had met with great disaster".[5] Haughty arrogance befitting the King of Kings ran all through the letter, which included a condemnation of the Macedonian's unprovoked aggression and a demand for the return of his family. More in keeping with the realities of the situation, the letter also offered a large ransom for the captives and a statement of Darius' willingness to cede Asia Minor westwards of the Halys river, if Alexander entered upon a treaty of friendship and alliance.

The proposals placed Alexander in a difficult position. In all probability the occupation of Asia Minor "within the Halys" had been the territorial objective of Philip, shared by his senior officers. Now Darius was offering to acknowledge all this territory as Macedonian. Alexander may have felt that any attempt to reject such an offer in the council of his officers would be so strongly opposed by the older and more influential of them that he would be forced to agree to limit his conquests to Asia Minor. Thus, when he assembled his council, he read out to his officers the body of Darius' letter, but omitted the section containing the territorial offer. The apparent lack of concessions and the generally haughty tone of the letter made it appear obvious to the generals that they would have to continue the fight against Darius and all urged Alexander to press on with the execution of the war.

The deception had succeeded and a Macedonian envoy conveyed to the Great King Alexander's reply. The letter began with an outright rejection of Darius' offer of peace and continued with a detailed account of Persian wrongs to both Greeks and Macedonians: Darius had been responsible for Philip's murder; Darius had tried to incite the Greeks to wage war on their legally elected Hegemon; moreover, the same Darius was an usurper, who had seized the throne through violence. Alexander's actions, if continued, were purely in self-defence; and if Darius wanted his family back, he must come to Alexander and ask for them. "And in future", it concluded, "when you send letters to me, send them as to the King of Asia; and do not write to me as though on equal terms, but, if you want anything, ask me as being master of all your affairs. Otherwise, I shall treat you as a criminal. If you lay claim to the kingdom, stand and fight for it; and do not run away, for I shall march against you, wherever you may be."⁶

This highly provocative and insulting letter was intended to serve two purposes: to demonstrate to the Greeks, among whom it would be circulated, that Alexander had just and compelling reasons for extending the war beyond the liberation of the Greeks of Asia Minor; and to sting Darius into committing himself to fighting a set battle which would decide the fate of his empire. In this latter purpose Alexander was successful. For Darius, on receipt of the letter, saw that there was no hope of a peaceful settlement and began to make plans for a counter-attack in Asia Minor with the forces which had escaped from Issus; and at the same time he began the slow process of summoning the levies of the eastern satrapies and training a new army.

Early in January, 332, the army left Marathus and advanced down the coast, past Byblus, as far as Sidon (modern Saida). The Sidonian ruler, Straton, was supported and maintained in his position by Persian influence. The majority of the people, however, loathed the Persian domination because of their treatment in 345 and consequently forced the hated Persian puppet-ruler to surrender to the Macedonians. He was deposed by Alexander and a successor appointed who was acceptable to the populace as a whole. As in the Greek cities of Asia Minor, Alexander is here pursuing the deliberate policy of replacing Persian-imposed governments by a more popular ruler and so winning for himself local support.

About twenty-five miles southwards of Sidon was the great city of Tyre, the largest and most powerful of the Phoenician states. Like all the other coastal cities, Tyre lived by commerce, its main trading commodity being the beautiful and highly-prized purple dye, which could only be extracted from the shellfish *murex*. The far-ranging activities of the Tyrian merchant sailors is apparent from the many Tyrian colonies scattered the length and breadth of the Mediterranean, the most renowned being Carthage in North Africa and Gades (Cadiz) in southern Spain. The political attitude of Tyre at this time tended to be one of acquiescence in the rule of Persia: in the great revolt of the 340s Tyre alone of the Phoenician cities had remained loyal to Persia; and now, when all the other cities had so far welcomed Alexander, it was highly unlikely that he would meet with a similar reception at Tyre.

However, any apprehensions Alexander may have felt were temporarily dispelled. For as he approached the city, a deputation of the citizens set out to meet him. They were headed by the son of the Tyrian King, Azemilk, who was acting as viceroy. For Azemilk was absent in the Aegean, commanding the bulk of the city's fleet, which formed the largest contingent in the Persian navy. The absence of most of their fleet, together with the willing surrender of the other Phoenician cities, had left the Tyrians in a somewhat isolated position early in 332; and it was probably these two factors that impelled their envoys to adopt a conciliatory manner with the King. For after presenting Alexander with a golden crown, they announced that the Tyrians had decided that they would obey Alexander's orders. They hoped that he would be content with this show of submission.

Alexander decided to test the sincerity of their professions. The Tyrians worshipped above all the god Melcarth, identified by the Greeks with Heracles. The god's temple was situated on the island known as New Tyre. Alexander instructed the envoys to report to the Tyrians that, since Heracles was a god especially close to the Macedonian royal house, he wished to offer sacrifice to the famous Tyrian Heracles. This was merely a diplomatic way of saying that the King wanted the Tyrians to open up their gates to himself and his army, and both sides realized this. But the request had an even deeper significance. For it was the time of the great annual feast of Melcarth; and during this feast only the Tyrian King, who was also the Chief Priest, had the right to offer sacrifice to the god in his main temple on the island. If Alexander knew of this custom—and it is highly likely that he did—his request amounts to a demand that the Tyrians acknowledge him as their King and rightful ruler.

Alexander was perhaps not surprised when the envoys returned with the decision of the Tyrians: there was a temple of Heracles in mainland—or Old—Tyre, and the King may sacrifice in that if he wished; furthermore, though they were willing to obey all Alexander's other orders, they would admit neither Macedonians nor Persians within their walls. Such a pretence at neutrality deceived nobody, least of all Alexander. Throwing aside all friendly pretentions, he sent the envoys back to inform the Tyrians that, since he was refused admittance, he would lay siege to their city.

The Tyrians too must have expected such a reply from the King and they resolved to put his siege-craft to the test. Apart from the strength of their fortifications, they were given confidence by representatives of Carthage, present for the feast of Melcarth, who promised that the colony would send aid to the mother-city. Moreover, their loyalty to Darius was really a deep one; and they realized that to hold Alexander up by means of a protracted siege would be a tremendous service to the Persian monarch in the plans he was now maturing for a counter-attack in Alexander's rear. After formally declaring war on Alexander, they pressed on with their preparations to resist his assault.

The Tyrians had every reason to believe that their city was impregnable especially to a besieger without a fleet. Old Tyre—the original city—had been built on the mainland. At some date the Tyrians had moved their abode to the largest of a group of rocky islets about half a mile from the shore. The new city they built there had a circuit of more than two miles and was completely surrounded by a high wall, said to be 150 feet high on the side facing the coast. The island-city had two fine harbours, one facing northwards towards Sidon and hence called the Sidonian harbour, the other facing towards Egypt, known as the Egyptian harbour. Between the island and the shore the water was for the most part shallow, though near the island itself it reached a depth of twenty feet.

The siege of such a city was undoubtedly a formidable undertaking and, in view of the morale-sapping effects of a long investment, not to be begun lightly. It does seem that Alexander encountered opposition from certain officers in his Staff, who would have preferred him to press on, leaving a strong garrison in Old Tyre and relying on the other Phoenician states to counterbalance the Tyrian naval power. However, the King prevailed and the army settled down to begin what was to be one of the longest and most famous sieges of antiquity.

Alexander's main problem, arising from the sea-girt position of Tyre and his own lack of ships, was how to get within range of the city to commence operations. He decided to build a mole from the shore out to the island and so enable his men to bring up their engines against the wall. The mole was designed to be 200 feet wide and material for it was obtained by demolishing Old Tyre and using the bricks and rubble. Timber was obtained by cutting down trees—the famous cedars—in the nearby forests of Lebanon. For labour, the inhabitants of the local towns and villages were pressed into service.

While the mole was being pushed forward through the shallow water, good progress was made. But when it reached the deeper waters near the city, the workers came within range of missiles discharged from the walls, and the Tyrian fleet, which had left the Persian navy and returned to Tyre soon after the opening of the siege, was able to sail round the mole and attack it from the sides. Alexander, having no fleet, was unable to prevent these demoralizing attacks by sea. He therefore had two huge towers constructed, which were moved on rollers to the end of the wall. The towers were built in several storeys and each storey had artillery mounted on it, so that the top storeys could sweep the walls, while those at the bottom fired on the enemy ships as they sailed past.

The towers were highly successful until the Tyrians hit upon the idea of using a fire-ship, filled with combustibles, to destroy them. The fire-ship was towed out of the harbour by two triremes, and, when near the mole, was ignited and set free. It crashed into the mole and the wooden towers quickly caught fire. The crews of the triremes, which had heaved to nearby, kept the besiegers away from the flames with a constant hail of missiles. Suddenly they were joined by a party of their fellow-citizens in small boats. These, covered by fire from the triremes, jumped on to the mole, pulled down the protective palisades and burned any engine not yet ablaze.

The sally had been executed with great skill and success. Alexander, seeing that without a fleet of his own little progress could be made, now decided to go to Sidon to collect ships. (The contingents of most of the Phoenician cities had left the Persian fleet at the news of Alexander's operations in the area and the fleet was in a state of rapid dissolution). At Sidon the King assembled eighty warships from Aradus, Byblus and Sidon itself. A welcome addition to this number was made by the arrival of another twenty-three ships from Lycia, Cilicia and Rhodes. This last state had hitherto been on the Persian side; it now made its peace with Alexander and was perhaps enrolled in the League of Corinth. Soon after this, there put in at Sidon a further 120 warships, the contingents of the dynasts of the Cyprian cities. They too had thrown off their allegiance to Darius and had come to make their submission. The King's fleet now amounted to more than 220 warships, easily outnumbering the Tyrian navy.

Alexander returned to Tyre by sea with the fleet, which was drawn up in battle-order. Alexander himself commanded the right wing, Craterus and Pnytagoras, a Cyprian prince, the left. The Tyrians being unaware that the King had collected so large a fleet, Alexander sent on ahead a small squadron, hoping thus to draw the whole Tyrian fleet out into an ambush. The ruse nearly succeeded; but when the Tyrians saw—with an unpleasant shock—how large a fleet Alexander now had, they turned and fled back to the safety of their harbours, whose mouths they blocked with a line of ships.

The next day the Cyprian squadrons were sent to blockade the Sidonian harbour, while the Phoenicians attended to the Egyptian harbour. The Tyrian fleet was now effectively bottled up and sallies were no longer possible on any large scale.

Soon after the mole reached the city-wall and the siege engines began their steady pounding. But it became evident after a while that the wall at this point was too solid to be breached and that another place would have to be found. To extend the mole in a lateral direction would take too much time and labour, and so Alexander adopted the novel plan of mounting his battering-rams on ships, which could float round the walls and select the weak points in the fortifications. Because the walls were so strong, a much larger ram than usual had to be employed—it was perhaps as long as 150 feet—and this meant that a second ship had to be fastened securely behind the ship on which the ram was mounted to give the ram the space necessary for its swing. The ships were, however, safe from the Tyrian artillery, which could not train on them because the angle of depression was too great.

In reply the Tyrians sank great blocks of masonry into the sea at the foot of the wall opposite the mole; for it was here that the ram-ships first took up position. These blocks, intended to prevent the ships from coming close enough to the walls to use the ram, were only removed with great difficulty by means of cranes set up on the mole. Then the ram-ships resumed their positions at anchor. The pounding on the walls began again.

In Tyre morale was now sinking: despite his reverses and despite the length of time—now several months—spent before the city, Alexander showed no sign of giving up the siege; they themselves had lost command of the sea and could only wait as their walls were continually battered; and, a final blow, envoys from Carthage, having evaded the blockade, announced that the colony, distracted by civil war, could not send aid to its mother-city. After debating whether to revive the obsolete religious rite of sacrificing a young boy to propitiate the god Moloch,[7] they adopted a more practical plan, whereby they hoped to reduce the naval odds and perhaps induce the King to raise the siege.

The blockading fleets, grown careless through long inactivity, were in the habit of putting their crews ashore at midday for a siesta, in which Alexander himself usually participated. The Tyrians carefully observed this routine and made their plans accordingly. Filling their ten fastest ships with picked crews, they made a sudden sortie one midday on the Cyprians at the entrance to the Sidonian harbour. The surprise attack was successful at first and four Cyprian vessels were quickly sunk. Unfortunately, however, for the Tyrians, Alexander this particular day had foregone his siesta and was in his usual station with the Phoenician squadrons at the Egyptian harbour. When the news of the Tyrian sortie was flashed to him from the shore, he immediately took a strong detachment of ships and sailed round the north of the island to take the Tyrians in the rear. Despite desperate warnings from the walls, the Tyrian ships were unable to break off their engagement in time to escape and most of them were sunk or disabled.

The siege was now pressed on more fiercely by Alexander who perhaps saw in his own troops a decline in morale similar to that within the city. The ram-ships, finding the walls near the mole too strong, were moved around the city's circumference until a weak point was found to the south of the Egyptian harbour; and now the constant battering brought its reward. For a breach was gradually opened in the wall; and it was here, after the gap had been widened, that Alexander decided to attempt the assault and storming of Tyre.

The spearhead of the assault was to be the Hypaspists and the battalion of Coenus. These troops were put on board two vessels equipped with boarding-bridges and the ram-ships were withdrawn to allow them to get into position by the breach. To distract the attention of the Tyrians from the breach once the assault began the Cyprian and Phoenician fleets were ordered to attempt to force their way into the harbours, while a squadron equipped with artillery and archers would sail round the island, shooting wherever they saw the enemy. Alexander himself would be with the Hypaspists, heading the attack.

The order was given to attack; the bridges were thrown over the breach, the Hypaspists poured forward, followed by Coenus' battalion. Gradually the Tyrians were pushed back from the breach into the streets, when suddenly triumphant cries and trumpet-calls from the harbour-areas proclaimed that both the Cyprians and the Phoenicians had broken through the barriers and were entering the city at those points. The destruction of Tyre was imminent.

The Tyrians, now being attacked from all sides, were pressed into a tight throng and retreating slowly through the streets, they took up a last-stand position at the shrine of the hero Agenor. Here, as panic and desperation increased, they were attacked and routed by the Macedonians and their allies in full force. A sickening slaughter of the unfortunate Tyrian soldiers ensued, with the battle-mad Macedonians giving no quarter. 8,000 were butchered after the last-stand had broken and the whole city was given over to the horrors of a sack. So brutal and savage were the Macedonian victors that even the Sidonians, enemies of the Tyrians and themselves having suffered a similar fate thirteen years before, smuggled many Tyrians away to Sidon in their ships during the sacking of the city.

The only males to be spared were those who had taken refuge in the temple of Melcarth; among them were Azemilk, the King and the Carthaginian envoys. 2,000 men of military age are said to have been crucified after the capture of the city. The survivors, nearly all women and children, were sold into slavery; their number was 30,000. The city was not razed to the ground; there was little need to do this, since there were hardly any Tyrians left to make it a future danger.

Tyre fell to Alexander in the month of July, 332, after a seven months' siege. As a purely military feat, it was perhaps Alexander's greatest achievement. The trained army and the modern siege-train Alexander had inherited from his father; the drive, obstinacy and determination to carry through such a lengthy and difficult operation and the ability to keep up the morale of his soldiers was the King's own special contribution. The success was somewhat marred by the savage treatment of the defeated enemy after the city had been stormed, though allowances should be made for the effects that a protracted siege has on the temper of the besiegers. The punishment administered to the non-combatants was harsh in the extreme, but it served as a warning to all other would-be Persian supporters of the folly of resistance.

The main immediate military result of the siege and capture of Tyre was the final dissolution of the Persian navy in the Aegean and the collapse of the Persian threat in Alexander's rear in Asia Minor. For, as was stated earlier in this chapter, the willingness of the Tyrians to undergo a long siege was the result of the part they were to play, by holding up Alexander's advance, in Darius' grand strategy. The essence of this strategy was that the Persian army, which had escaped from Issus to Cappadocia and Paphlagonia, should attempt to reconquer Lydia and Ionia, thus regaining contact with the Aegean fleet. The Royal Road could then be used again for the conveyance of troops and money to the coast and there would thus be the hope and possibility, with Alexander cut off from Asia Minor and his land communications, of keeping alive in the Greeks the spirit of resistance.

The plan was a good one and potentially dangerous to the Macedonians. The Persian land-forces had established a firm control over Cappadocia and Paphlagonia; and the naval successes of the fleet in the Aegean in 333 have already been noticed. It does seem that, after Issus, further naval successes had been gained by Pharnabazus and his deputy, Autophradates, at the all-important towns of Halicarnassus and Miletus, so that the army had two excellent points of embarkation, if and when they broke through to the coast.

The crisis for Alexander began in the early part of 332, when the Persian army began its thrust westwards. It is tantalizing that the only account left to us of the ensuing operations is a brief and passing reference in the narrative of Curtius.[8] In the silence of the sources it is perhaps possible to discern the partiality of Ptolemy, since the man responsible for stopping the Persian spearhead was his great enemy, Antigonus, satrap of Phrygia. Three pitched battles were required before the Persian army was finally smashed, and in this, if ever, Antigonus deserved well of his King. At the same time Alexander's operations in Phoenicia and at Tyre, while they did keep him pinned down, were having their effect on the Persian navy, which (as has been seen) began rapidly to break up as the individual Phoenician contingents returned to their native cities. By late spring the crisis was over for Alexander. On land the satraps Antigonus, Calas and Balacrus could begin mopping-up operations against isolated groups of Persians in Asia Minor; while at sea the reorganized Macedonian fleet under Hegelochus and Amphoterus swept down the Aegean against the remnants of the enemy's navy, winning back island after island. Later in the year Hegelochus was able to report to Alexander the total destruction of Pharnabazus' fleet. The Persian admiral had suffered the indignity of being taken prisoner, but had managed to elude his guards and make his escape.

The total failure of the counter-offensive is reflected in the second offer of peace which Darius made to Alexander, sometime near the end of the siege of Tyre. Darius was now in a most unenviable position, since his preparations for raising a new army seem hardly to have been set in motion; he had been relying deeply on the success of his forces in Asia Minor. The offers of peace were thus considerably more generous than those made at Marathus: Darius would give a ransom of 10,000 talents for the release of his family and would cede to Alexander all the territory to the west of the River Euphrates; in return Alexander was to marry Darius' daughter and become the friend and ally of the Persian King.

The imminent success of the siege of Tyre gave Alexander greater confidence in dealing with his senior officers, and this time the full letter was read out to the Staff. Parmenion, now back from Damascus, counselled acceptance of the offers, but his advice was rejected by the King with a sarcastic jibe. The reply to Darius was yet another refusal to negotiate, couched in terms just as provocative as the first letter: Alexander had no need of money from Darius; he would not accept part of the Persian empire in place of the whole; if he wanted to marry Darius' daughter, he would do so, with or without Darius' permission; and if Darius desired friendship and alliance, he must come to Alexander and ask for it. Darius, realizing that he must fight again with the Macedonian invader, abandoned all hopes of a negotiated settlement and hurried on his military preparations.

From Tyre the King continued his southwards advance down the coast, making for Egypt, the last area left open for a Persian revival by sea. After passing through Palestine the army came to a halt, about the beginning of September, before the walls of Gaza, the last of the coastal cities of the eastern Mediterranean, standing on the edge of the long stretch of desert that extends as far as the Nile delta. The Persian commander of the garrison, Batis, had made ready to resist the invader and Alexander's demand to surrender was contemptuously refused. For the second time this year the army was subjected to the wearying task of besieging a large and well fortified city.

To relate the details of the subsequent operations would be tedious. It need only be remarked that the task facing Alexander's engineers was made almost as formidable as at Tyre by the fine, shifting desert sand— a material which filled in the mines as they were dug out and which made the construction of siege-works almost an impossibility; that the resistance of Batis and the beleaguered garrison was of the bravest and held up the Macedonian advance by a further two months; and that when a breach had been made in the wall and the city was stormed the carnage and destruction rivalled that at Tyre. 10,000 soldiers and civilians were indiscriminately slaughtered; the survivors—mainly women and children—were sold into slavery; and Gaza was re-populated from friendly tribes in the neighbourhood. Curtius relates that Batis, who was taken captive, was bound by the ankles, tied to the rear end of a chariot and then dragged to his death by the King round the walls of Gaza; thus, boasted Alexander, he was following the example set by his ancestor Achilles, who had dragged the body of Hector round the walls of Troy.[9] Homer, at least, represents Hector as dead before he was dragged behind his victorious enemy's chariot.

With the fall of Gaza the way now lay open for the invasion and occupation of Egypt, the south-western bastion of the Persian empire, the home of one of the oldest of the world's civilizations, a land which had reluctantly endured the rule of foreigners for 200 years.

NOTES

1 Plutarch, *Alexander 20*
2 Curtius III 12.17
3 Arrian II 12.8 (Loeb translation)
4 Plutarch, *Alexander 21*
5 Diodorus XVII 39.1
6 Arrian II 14.9
7 See Milton, *Paradise Lost* I 329ff. for human sacrifices to Moloch
8 Curtius IV 1.34ff.
9 Curtius IV 6.29

7

Egypt

Egypt in ancient times was a country on which foreign empire-builders cast covetous eyes for two main reasons—its wealth and its strategic impregnability; this latter quality, indeed, it has only recently lost with the advent of mechanized transport and the aeroplane. It is surrounded on three sides by desert; to the south, the Nubian desert; to the east, by the barren land of the Sinai peninsula and the Arabian desert; and to the west, the Lybian desert. The approaches by land were guarded in the east by the fortress of Pelusium (near modern El Qantara on the Suez Canal); in the west by Paraetonium (modern Matrich, 100 miles west of El Alamein). To an invader by sea the marshes and sandbanks of the Nile Delta's mouths presented their dangers, as was discovered by an Athenian fleet in 454, which was trapped by the Persians at the island of Prosopitis and destroyed.

The wealth of Egypt then, as now, depended on the annual flooding of the Nile to irrigate the land and deposit a rich, productive silt; "corn in Egypt" has become a proverbial expression, and 300 years after the death of Alexander the country, annexed by the Romans, was to become the granary of the Imperial City. Some idea of the wealth of Egypt can be gained from the tribute-list of the Persian empire as given by Herodotus in the middle of the fifth century.[1] Egypt is assessed at the second highest total in all the empire, with an annual tribute of 700 talents, besides the provision of corn for the garrison troops; this figure is 100 talents higher than the total tribute of the Athenian empire at the same time. Alexander himself observed a keen appreciation of the possibilities of the country for economic exploitation, and of its strategic advantages, as will be seen. Ptolemy, son of

Lagus, was also aware of these factors; for seizing Egypt as his own province when the empire was carved up after Alexander's death, he organized the country as a private estate of the ruling family, thus setting a precedent and model for the Ptolemies' Roman successors.

The Persians had annexed Egypt in 525 B.C., when Cambyses established it as the south-western bastion of his realm. But the Persian government had one of its rare failures in its administration of Egypt and the Persian name was generally hated throughout the land. Much of this hatred seems to stem from Persian attempts to break down the power of the Egyptian priesthood, whereby they exercised a strong and potentially dangerous influence over the peasantry.

Cambyses had tried to break the priests' power by showing contempt for the irreligious beliefs they represented. With his own sword he is said to have slain the sacred bull-calf, Apis; he destroyed the temples of the gods and violently abused the priests.

His actions, however, had exactly the opposite effect, for the Egyptian peasants would stand any oppression providing the oppressor honoured their gods. The result was Egyptian hatred of their Persian rulers and frequent attempts to throw off the yoke; attempts which sharply reminded the Persian government of Egypt's strategic solidity. Indeed, the revolt which began at the end of the 5th century was not crushed for sixty years, during which time Egypt remained—and was regarded by the outside world—an independent country. Four attempts were made at reconquest—in 385; 374 (when over 200,000 soldiers and 300 ships took part); 358; and 343, when the energetic but brutal Artaxerxes Ochus, aided by the Rhodian Mentor, succeeded finally in crushing the rebellious province. To celebrate his victory, Ochus—perhaps in conscious imitation of the original conqueror of Egypt—had caused the Apis bull to be slain and roasted for a banquet, and had stabled an ass in the temple of Ptah, acts of sacrilege which aroused for the Persians even greater hatred on the part of the Egyptians, who nursed their bitterness for six years before breaking out in rebellion again shortly before the accession of Darius III. This revolt was not crushed until late 335 to early 334, and—as has already been suggested—is probably responsible for the tardy entry of the Persian fleet in the war against Alexander (and it is notable that there is no record of any Egyptian vessels serving with the Persian fleet in all of its operations between 334 and 332).

Egypt then was ready, as Curtius observes,[2] for a change of masters; how ready can be seen from the affair of Amyntas, son of Antiochus, the renegade Macedonian, turned mercenary leader. After the battle of Issus he had effected an orderly retreat from the battlefield with the 4,000 Greek mercenaries he had brought from the Persian fleet to Darius. Making their way to the Phoenician town of Tripolis, where they had disembarked from their ships, and finding the vessels still there, they set sail for Cyprus. Here Amyntas hit upon the plan of seizing Egypt, taking advantage of the weakness of the Persian garrison—the satrap, Sabaces, had been killed at Issus—and forestalling Alexander's advance on the country. His object was probably to attract the mercenaries to Egypt to serve under his flag. After building up a large army, the country could be firmly held down and exploited as Amyntas' personal *Reich*. A strong defensive line at Pelusium would bar Alexander from entry and, it was hoped, force the Macedonian to leave Egypt and turn his attention to Darius.

The enterprise began well. Pelusium came into the Greeks' hands without a blow, since Amyntas claimed to have been appointed satrap by Darius in place of the dead Sabaces—a story the garrison had no means of checking. He then began to move his force against Memphis (near Cairo), the capital of the old Pharaohs of Egypt, and since the assumption of this title by the Persian ruler, the seat of his Viceroy, the satrap. News of his advance put Amyntas in the light of a deliverer from the Persian oppression in the eyes of the Egyptians, who began a series of local revolts, slaughtering the garrisons in the towns and villages.

Mazaces, the garrison commander at Memphis, who had taken over the satrapal functions, led his troops out to meet Amyntas. A pitched battle was fought outside the walls of Memphis, in which the Persians were defeated and driven back into the town—an indication of how weak their number was at this time. Amyntas then foolishly allowed his men to begin plundering and looting the estates surrounding the city. Whilst they were scattered about and disorganized, Mazaces suddenly led his men out again and cut down the mercenaries to the last man. "And that", says Diodorus, "was the end of Amyntas, who had attempted great things and had failed contrary to his expectations".[3]

The affair of Amyntas, as well as displaying the hatred felt by the Egyptians for their Persian overlords, shows too how hopeless resistance to Alexander would have been by the Egyptian garrison. Pelusium was not even reoccupied by the Persians, who seem merely to have sat in Memphis awaiting the arrival of Alexander.

Thus the King had a clear road into Egypt. The distance from Gaza into Pelusium is approximately 130 miles, and the army covered the distance in just short of 7 days—a remarkable effort. At Pelusium, where Alexander's fleet had already arrived, a large crowd of Egyptians had gathered to welcome the liberator. A garrison was left in the fortress, and the fleet ordered to sail up the most easterly branch of the Delta towards Memphis, a distance of about 150 miles.

Alexander himself and the army kept pace with the fleet along the right bank of the river till he reached Heliopolis—the City of the Sun— just below the apex of the Delta. Here he crossed the river and continued southward along the left bank towards Memphis. Mazaces surrendered the city without a fight, together with the satrapal treasury of 800 talents, and was received with honour into the King's suite.

How long the expedition stayed at Memphis is not recorded. It must, however, have been at least a month, extending well past the New Year of 331, since it did not reach the coast again till the end of January. The stay was marked by an event of deep significance both politically and with regard to Alexander's personal development. For it was here that he was crowned Pharaoh of Egypt, with all the traditional ritual, by the priesthood. It has already been mentioned that the Persian Kings were also Pharaohs of Egypt (when the country was in their possession); the unpopular Darius was thus considered to be deposed and Alexander to be his legitimate successor. Indeed, popular imagination was doing even more to establish his legitimacy, for the story soon became current that Alexander was none other than the natural son of the last native Egyptian ruler, Nectanebo, who had visited Olympias in the form of a snake. Hieroglyphic texts show that Alexander had all the traditional titles conferred upon him, amongst them "Horus, the strong prince, the protector of Egypt", "King of Upper and Lower Egypt, the beloved of Ammon and selected of Rē." Unlike his Persian predecessors, Alexander was very careful to win over Egyptian opinion by a display of piety towards their gods, sacrificing to them all, but especially the bull-calf Apis. The goodwill thus secured was to last Alexander throughout his reign and form a valuable reserve for his successors in Egypt, the Ptolemaic dynasty.

But the new Pharaoh was also King of the Macedonians, son by adoption of the Queen of Caria, and Hegemon of the Greeks; and as if to emphasize this multiplicity of roles as well as affording a holiday for the army, he also held at Memphis athletic and literary contests in the

Greek manner, to which athletes and men of letters were invited from Greece.

Then, about the middle of January, 331, the Pharaoh set out to inspect the lower part of his realm. Sailing down the most westerly part of the Delta, he reached the coastal region at Canopus (near Rosetta), on the north-eastern end of Lake Mareotis (Maryut). From here he sailed round the lake, and disembarking on the isthmus of land opposite the island of Pharos, "he thought", says Arrian, "that the place was most excellent to found a city on, and that the city would become prosperous. He was, accordingly, seized with a desire for the enterprise."⁴

The city that was founded took its name from its founder, and still goes by that name today—Alexandria. That the decision to found a city on the coast was so sudden as Arrian implies is hardly likely; it may have been made at Memphis, but was quite likely made even earlier. For the care given to choosing the site and the attention lavished on the new city implies that Alexander was intending that it should replace Tyre as the main commercial centre of the eastern Mediterranean. Nor must the foundation be used as evidence of Alexander's philhellenism, as has often been done. For his opinion that the city would prosper quickly proved correct, and Alexandria in the next generation became the acknowledged capital of the Mediterranean. It replaced Athens as the intellectual centre of Greek thought and its university, the Museum,—founded by Ptolemy, son of Lagus— attracted the leading scholars, scientists and artists; the Museum's great library eventually held 700,000 volumes. But more important from a Greek point of view, the city rapidly displaced Athens and Rhodes as the greatest trading-city of the Mediterranean, and the old Greek mart of Naucratis in Egypt sank into insignificance before the new emporium.

At this point it will not be out of place to give a brief description of the original city. Alexander himself is said to have marked out the site of the agora—the civic centre—and the various temples, which included one for the Egyptian Isis—another concession to native sentiment—and the city-wall. The site was marked out with barley-meal, in accordance with the old Macedonian custom, in the shape of a *chlamys* or military cloak. Whilst this ceremony was being performed, birds suddenly gathered and devoured all the meal. The omen distressed the King, but the obliging Aristander interpreted it to mean that the city would be completely self-sufficient and the nursing-mother of many races of men (and, in fact, Alexandria became distinguished for the cosmopolitan character of its population). The foundation-date, as is shown from contemporary documents, was 30th January, 331.

The site was indeed an excellent one. Located on the narrow isthmus between the sea and Lake Maryut, directly opposite the island of Pharos, it embraced in its circuit the old village of Rhacotis, which had long been the resort of Greek and Phoenician sailors. By land the city was easily defensible, being approachable only by the narrow strips of land to the north and south of the isthmus. The position left the city open to the cooling north-westerly winds in the summertime, so that the inhabitants enjoyed a comparatively moderate climate and freedom from the marsh-diseases so prevalent in the Delta.

The town-planning was left in the hands of Deinocrates, who had designed the new town of Ephesus. Deinocrates employed the design so prevalent in Australian cities of a rectangular grid system. The city was bisected from north to south and from east to west by two large roads, each 200 feet wide. These quarters were then subdivided into blocks, with the streets crossing each other at right angles. The streets were wide enough to take both wheeled carriages and pedestrians.

The coastline opposite Pharos—a natural break for the north winds—was the harbour and dockland area. Pharos itself was joined to the mainland by a great mole, seven-eighths of a mile long and called because of this the Heptastadion.* On the north-eastern side of the mole was the Greater Harbour; on the south-western was the harbour of Eunostus, or the Haven of Happy Return. The Eunostus was connected through the basin of Cibotus (the Chest) with Lake Maryut by means of a canal, and by means of another canal, linking up with this, to the Canopic branch of the Nile. Under the rule of Alexander's successor in Egypt, Ptolemy, son of Lagus, work was to begin on Pharos on the huge lighthouse, 400 feet high, which became one of the marvels of the ancient world.

The historian Diodorus visited Alexandria in the middle of the first century B.C., and saw the city with his own eyes. "By many", he says, "it is reckoned to be the first city of the world; and it surpasses all others in its elegance, extent, riches and luxury. For all the Kings from Alexander onwards were lavish in the additions they made in the city". In Diodorus' day, the number of free inhabitants, according to the census returns, were more than 300,000; one can safely assume a total

* The Greek *stadion* was approximately equivalent to our furlong.

population of nearly half a million if Diodorus' figure refers to male citizens, their wives and children.[5]

There now followed one of the most perplexing incidents in the King's career—the visit to the oasis at Siwah—perplexing because of the sensational reportage of it by all ancient writers without exception; who, recognizing the importance of the incident for Alexander's psychological development, freely invented details designed to emphasize the miraculous nature of the visit.

The oasis at Siwah, situated almost due south of Sidi-Barrani and less than fifty miles from the western border of the United Arab Republic, is still an important centre for caravans crossing the Lybian desert. In antiquity it was even more famous for the temple and oracle there of the Egyptian god Ammon. The god and his oracle had for long been well known to the Greek world, being equated by them with Zeus (as Ptah was equated with Hephaestus). The Theban poet Pindar had written a hymn on Ammon; the Athenians had sent a sacred embassy to consult the oracle during the great war with Sparta and had very recently built and dedicated a temple to the god at Athens; to the people of Cyrene Ammon was the chief deity whose portrait appears on their coinage. The oracle's responses were looked upon as being very reliable and it was placed by the Greeks on a par with Delphi and Dodona as an oracular seat.

It was to Siwah and Ammon that Alexander set off after the foundation of Alexandria, early in February, 331. The question immediately arises as to why he undertook this long and arduous journey to a place that was hundreds of miles off the beaten track at such a stage in the expedition. Arrian says that he was seized (as at Alexandria) with a passionate desire to consult the oracle, partly because of its reputation for infallibility, partly because mythology stated that both Perseus and Heracles had visited it; and Alexander was filled with a desire to outdo these heroes, both of whom the Macedonian royal family numbered amongst its ancestors.[6] The influence of mythology on Alexander has already been seen at Ilium. Alexander obviously believed implicitly in the veracity of the old stories and, as his career advances, will be seen more and more to try to emulate the gods and heroes of mythology and show himself their superior. The Heracles–Perseus motive would be a strong one.

One modern authority has suggested that the sole purpose of the journey was a politico–military one; that the new Pharaoh of Egypt and avowed successor to the Great King of Persia was beating the boundaries of his new domain and checking on its military security. But, though an alliance was made *en route* with the ambassadors from the Greek state of Cyrene, this solution appears to be too secular and too prosaic to be the only reason.

It does seem that two motives can be added to those given by Arrian. Alexander was shortly to enter upon what he hoped would be the final campaign against Darius. Just as he had received—and caused to be spread—at the beginning of the campaign that led to Issus a prophecy promising him the rule of Asia, so now he would go to one of the ancient world's most reliable sources and receive a confirmation of this prophecy, whose propaganda value would be inestimable; there would be, there is little doubt, only answers that were, in Arrian's words,"to his heart's desire". Moreover, as Pharaoh, Alexander automatically became the son of Amon-Rē, of which Ammon is the Greek form. This new relationship was not unwelcome to Alexander and confirmation of it from the Siwah oracle, with its close connections with the Greek world and the equation by the Greeks of the god with Zeus, would be highly satisfying to his ego, and again tremendous propaganda.

The King set out on the journey. Who his companions were we do not know. Ptolemy may have been with the suite; Callisthenes, as official historian, probably was. The route taken was along the coast, through El Alamein and Fuka, as far as the border fortress of Paraetonium (modern Matruk), a distance of nearly 200 miles. From Paraetonium the party swung south-westwards into the desert, following the traditional caravan-route to Siwah, almost 180 miles from Paraetonium. Now the miraculous elements begin to intrude into our ancient accounts. The heat of the desert and thirst of the travellers was allayed by a copious downpour of rain. Then the guides lost their way amidst the shifting sand dunes and went astray in the desert. Ptolemy— a writer much praised by Arrian for his veracity—soberly narrates that they were recalled to the proper route by two snakes, who preceded the party uttering human speech and guided them to the oracle and back again! Almost as fantastic is the account of Callisthenes and Aristobulus that two ravens appeared as guides to the party, flying ahead of it then waiting for it to catch up.[7]

The whole journey from Alexandria to Siwah seems to have taken about twenty days, so that it was late February when the party reached the oasis, then entering upon early spring. Ancient descriptions of the oasis, which nowadays is surrounded to the east and west by salt marshes, give it a length and breadth each of about six miles. Within this area, which was full of cultivated trees, olive and date palms, the people dwelt in small villages, enjoying a milder climate than the dry heat of the surrounding desert (Diodorus compares it with the climate of Greece in spring).[8] In the centre of the oasis was a citadel-fortress surrounded by triple-walls, formerly the abode of the ruling sheik of Siwah. This fortress contained a temple of Ammon, though the main temple was outside the fortress and a short distance away. Close by the main temple was a spring of water, called the Spring of the Sun from its behaviour: at midday its waters were icy-cold; as the sun sinks lower in the evening, the water becomes warmer, until at midnight it is hot; then it begins to cool off again, being already cold by sunrise and reaching its maximum coldness again by midday. That the salt marshes surrounded the oasis $2\frac{1}{2}$ millenia ago is implied by the local practice of digging for salt, which was "exported" to Egypt by the priests and used in sacrificial rites, being much purer than the salt gained from the sea by dehydration.

When the Macedonian party reached the oasis, news of their coming had obviously gone on before them. For the chief priest of Ammon had come out in person to meet the King and conduct him into the temple. The priest met Alexander with the traditional greeting to the Pharaoh of Egypt and "Son of Ammon". The two then entered the temple alone to consult the oracle whilst the rest of the party waited outside in the temple precincts.

The answers of the oracle to the King's questions—given by the god's image in the form of nods and signs which were interpreted by the priest—must remain a mystery, since nobody was allowed in the inner sanctuary with Alexander. Arrian, professing to report Alexander's own account, simply states that he heard what his heart desired.[9] Plutarch quotes what purports to be a letter of Alexander to his mother in which he says that he received certain secret replies that he would disclose to her alone when he returned.[10] The account of the official historian, Callisthenes, must be given credit for showing at least what Alexander wanted to be divulged about the replies. He says that the priest openly said that Alexander was the son of Zeus (that is, Ammon, his Egyptian equivalent).[11] It is probably also from Callisthenes that the additional information is derived that the god promised Alexander the rule over all mankind—the very prophecy he desired; and the assurance that all the murderers of Philip—now no longer called Alexander's father—had been punished.

What exactly was said in the inner sanctum is beyond recall. That Alexander was informed that he was the god's son seems beyond doubt; that he was promised empire over all the world is also highly likely. That the whole affair was invested with a definite aura of the miraculous is obvious from our sources, all of which probably stem back to Callisthenes. This latter gives as an additional detail to emphasize this "rebirth" of Alexander from a loftier parent the fact that the oracle of the Branchidae at Miletus, which had been silent from the days of Xerxes, had suddenly produced prophecies that were brought to Alexander at Memphis: the god Apollo declared that Alexander was the son of Zeus; that he would win a great victory at Arbela, which would be followed by the death of Darius; and that the Spartans would rebel against the Macedonians. It is certain, too, that the oracular responses at Siwah had a profound effect on Alexander personally. This new and special relationship with Ammon can be looked upon as an important stage in the discarding of Alexander's Philippic heritage and entrance upon a more Oriental way of life. But it also had a deep meaning for Alexander who took his divine sonship seriously and eventually caused a great resentment among the Macedonians by it. Henceforth Ammon was especially dear to Alexander's heart, and any suggestion of scepticism or mockery of the King's descent from the god would provoke a violent outburst of rage. The oracular responses given at Siwah, whether traditional in form or intended to flatter, put the King a long way along the road that was to lead to his demand for deification in 324.

From Siwah the party returned to Memphis across the desert, following the path of the modern road that leads through Qara and El Maghra—a distance of nearly 350 miles. Some estimate of the importance of the journey to the oracle can be gained from the fact that the whole round trip entailed a journey of nearly 750 miles, almost all through desert. At Memphis the Pharaoh of Egypt, the King of the Macedonians and the Hegemon of the League of Corinth held court. Envoys from the Greek states assembled with requests and athletic and artistic contests were held. Reinforcements also arrived from Europe as part of a general build-up of forces for the coming campaign—400 Greek mercenaries from Antipater and 500 Thracian cavalry.

The administration of Egypt was also reorganized. In place of the former satrapal system, with its danger of investing too much power in one man (an especial danger in Egypt), a policy of division of power was tried. Egypt was divided into two administrative areas, Upper and

Lower; the civil administration of these areas was entrusted, not to Macedonians, but to two noble Egyptians—a remarkable concession to native sentiment. One of them, however, declined the honour and the administration of the whole country was given to the other, Doloaspis. Two independent garrisons were left, mainly mercenaries, though perhaps with a stiffening of Macedonians; one was at Memphis, under Pantaleon of Pydna, the other at Pelusium, under Polemon of Pella. Both men were Macedonians; their forces totalled a mere 4,000 men. The military command was even further sub-divided, since the troops were made immediately responsible to two other Macedonian commanders; what the power relationship of these two men was to the garrison commander is not known. A fleet of 30 warships was assigned to the defence of the Delta, again under a Macedonian officer. The districts to the east and west of the Delta, called vaguely by the ancients Lybia and Arabia-by-Heroopolis respectively, were also given separate governors. To the latter was appointed a Greek, Cleomenes, from the Greek settlement of Naucratis. Cleomenes' speciality was finance, and he was given the additional responsibility of seeing to the collection of the tribute for all Egypt. His sharp practices in this office were to win for him great notoriety among the Greeks.

This system, designed to prevent the illicit seizure of power by one man in this natural fortress, wins the praise of Arrian who compares it to the Roman system obtaining in his day. It was not entirely successful, since only a few years later we find that Cleomenes—how, it is not known—had taken the entire reins of government into his own hands and was acting as a full-blown satrap. However, Cleomenes' methods of governing seem to have been efficient and—more to the point—lucrative; and Alexander was content to leave things as they were.

It was now April and, the security of Egypt having been assured, time for the expedition to leave the country and move eastwards to meet Darius and his newly raised army for the decisive battle. The Nile was bridged at Memphis and the Macedonians set off northwards, along the route by which they had entered Egypt, towards Syria, there to assemble all their forces and to pick up the supplies and munitions which the Syrian satrap had been ordered to prepare for the coming campaign.

NOTES

1   Herodotus III 89ff.
2   Curtius VI 7.1

3 Diodorus XVII 48.5
4 Arrian III 1.5. Here again is the King's famous *pothos*
5 Diodorus XVII 52
6 Cf. Arrian III 3.1. Note again the King's *pothos*
7 See Arrian III 3.5ff.; Plutarch, *Alexander* 27
8 Diodorus XVII 50.1
9 Arrian III 4.5
10 Plutarch, *Alexander* 27, showing that Callisthenes is the source of Aristobulus' version
11 At Strabo XVII 1.43

8

Gaugamela

In the spring of 331 the Macedonian army, after leaving Egypt, returned to Phoenicia to make the final preparations for the invasion of the heart of the Persian empire. Tyre was selected as the headquarters of the expedition, and here, to give the army a holiday before the strenuous march ahead of them, more games were held. Envoys from Athens who arrived at Tyre were granted their wishes: the Athenian prisoners taken at the Granicus three years ago were all released.

Whilst reinforcements were being contracted to Tyre from the western satrapies, Alexander busied himself with several important administrative matters. The original Macedonian satrap, Menon, had apparently died soon after his appointment. His successor, Arimmas, had been given the responsibility of arranging for the supplies and equipment of the army of invasion, but had failed to complete his task on time. He was dismissed from his post and replaced by Asclepiodorus, son of Eunicus, an officer who had only recently joined the expedition. In Samaria, too, there had been trouble: Andromachus, who had been appointed district military commander the previous year, had apparently offended Samarian religious sentiment in some way; the Samarians took their revenge by capturing him and burning him alive. Alexander had the ringleaders rounded up and executed.

Trouble was also brewing in the Peloponnese with the Spartans. To assist Antipater, Amphoterus was sent to the Peloponnese with a squadron to rally the anti-Spartan element there. The Phoenicians and Cyprians were also ordered to despatch a hundred warships to the Peloponnese. Amphoterus was given the additional task of clearing

Crete of the remnants of the Persian navy, who were using the island as a base for piracy.

An important innovation was made at this time in the financial administration of the growing Asiatic empire: Philoxenus, a high-ranking Macedonian, was given control of the whole of Asia Minor, westwards of the Taurus range; another Macedonian, Coeranus, was given a similar post in Phoenicia, Syria and Cilicia. Satrapal finance-officers were now appointed in all the satrapies where the system had not yet been introduced. They were, of course, subordinate to Philoxenus and Coeranus, depending on their satrapy.

Among the duties of Philoxenus and Coeranus was that of supervising the ever growing lines of communications with the west; for this reason Philoxenus had his headquarters at Ephesus, at the head of the Royal Road, and Coeranus had his at Tyre. They had the task of seeing that troops coming from Europe were properly equipped and paid before they began the long march inland to join the main army; and in this capacity they enjoyed wide powers over the movements of shipping and control of harbours. Their subordinates in each satrapy carried out the routine collection of taxes, and, after deducting the annual expenses of the satrap's administration, remitted the balance to the area-officer, who then forwarded it to the central treasury.

That Alexander had been meditating some financial reorganization for a long time is suggested by the affair known as the "first flight of Harpalus". Harpalus, an old friend of Alexander's, had been exiled by Philip at the time of the Pixodarus affair. He received his reward for his loyalty at the start of the expedition, when he was appointed treasurer (being lame, he could not command an army group). Then just before the battle of Issus, Harpalus fled from the camp with a certain Tauriscus, who was suspected of being involved in a plot against the King. Tauriscus went to join the fighting in Italy under Alexander's brother-in-law, the King of Epirus; Harpalus took up residence at Megara, where he stayed till the King begged him to return in the spring of 331. It seems that the cause of Harpalus' "flight" was pique at Alexander's decision even before Issus to divide up his financial realm between subordinate officers. Philoxenus and Coeranus performed Harpalus' functions until this new reorganization at Tyre, when the King, perhaps feeling remorse for his treatment of his old follower, perhaps missing Harpalus' financial acumen, invited him to return to his old post as Treasurer-in-chief; the subordination of Philoxenus and

Coeranus was expressly acknowledged. Harpalus returned, but with exaggerated ideas of his own importance and influence.

When all these arrangements had been completed and the army divisions brought up to maximum strength, the advance into central Asia began. From Tyre the army moved northwards through Syria to Thapsacus on the river Euphrates. The site of this city was probably near the modern Deir ez Zor. The river at Thapsacus had already been almost bridged in two places by Hephaestion, who had been sent ahead by Alexander for this purpose. The work had not quite reached completion because the left bank of the river was being held by a strong force of 3,000 Persian cavalry under the command of one of Darius' best cavalry officers, Mazaeus, the satrap of Babylonia. However, on the approach of the main army, Mazaeus decided not to contest the crossing further, but retreated into the interior of Mesopotamia. The bridges were completed and the army crossed the Euphrates in the Athenian month of Hecatombeion (between 10th July and 8th August). It was then allowed a few days' rest in preparation for the march that would lead to Darius.

Darius had gathered his Grand Army on the Euphrates at Babylon, the capital of the Mesopotamian satrapy, the seat of the Great King's winter residence and one of the largest cities in the empire. He expected that, when the Macedonian invasion came, the route that Alexander would follow would be along the eastern bank of the Euphrates, down through Mesopotamia in an almost straight line for Babylon, the economic nerve-centre of the empire and the key to the other great cities that lay to the east, such as Susa and Persepolis. The Mesopotamian valley was a natural route for an invader and Darius, bearing in mind the campaign of the younger Cyrus at the end of the fifth century, would be almost certain that Alexander would follow it. He intended therefore, to make the Macedonians fight a battle on ground of his own choosing, suitable for his cavalry; such a place would be Cunaxa, to the north of Babylon, where in 401 B.C. the younger Cyrus had been defeated by Artaxerxes II. Mazaeus was sent north to the Thapsacus crossing with orders to report on Alexander's progress and to devastate Mesopotamia before the enemy's advance. Alexander would thus arrive at Cunaxa with his men and cavalry mounts in a weakened state from weariness and lack of provisions and meet with Darius' own fresh troops.

The plan was a good one, provided Alexander did what he was expected to do. Alexander, for his part, seems at Thapsacus to have reasoned as follows: Darius was known to be at Babylon; the Euphrates valley, though fertile in comparison with the desert lands to the west, did not contain as much fodder or provisions as the land to the east to the Tigris; moreover, the Mesopotamian valley is one of the hottest places in the world in midsummer (it has a mean maximum daily temperature of over 110 degrees Fahrenheit in July); Mazaeus' force across the Euphrates was too large to be a mere scouting-force and too small to be a combat-division—its function was probably to ravage the land before the army. He would therefore not advance on Babylon by the direct route, but would advance across northern Mesopotamia, cross the Tigris upstream and then move at his leisure down the eastern bank of that river. Such a move would badly upset the Persian's plans. For the additional time that Alexander's route would entail would be a severe strain for the area round Babylon in the matter of provisioning the army; the troops of Darius also would tend to lose spirit if they were kept hanging about for a long time, waiting for the enemy to appear. Moreover, Darius himself would be most reluctant to allow the fertile area east of the Tigris to go unprotected. These considerations, thought Alexander, would probably cause Darius to move his army away from Babylon to meet him. The initiative would then pass to Alexander's hands, for Darius' polyglot host would certainly be disorganized by any lengthy marching, nor would Darius have a strong town like Babylon to fall back on in the event of defeat. The army was therefore turned in a north-easterly direction when it began its march again.

News of this unexpected choice of route was immediately despatched by Mazaeus to Babylon, 440 miles south of Thapsacus. This intelligence threw the Persian High Command into something of a panic and brought about the hoped-for change of plan. It was decided to move the army north to try to catch Alexander as he was crossing the Tigris and ambush him there—an ambitious plan in view of the distances involved and the normally slow rate of progress of a Persian Grand Army. For though he was marching at a leisurely pace, Alexander had nearly a week's start on Darius; and the most southerly of the Tigris fords, Mosul, was almost equidistant from Thapsacus and Babylon.

To ambush Alexander as he crossed the Tigris necessitated, of course, knowing exactly where he intended to cross—though the Mosul ford seemed the most likely place. For this purpose an elaborate screen of scouts was despatched northwards; these were to keep an advance-party of 6,000 cavalry under Mazaeus informed of Alexander's movements and this information was to be communicated to the main army, whose headquarters would be at Arbela (modern Erbil), situated on the Royal Road. Once it could definitely be established where Alexander was intending to cross, the whole army could then make its way there and be in concealment. Mazaeus would then engage the Macedonians with his cavalry force as they crossed the river; when the enemy was firmly joined in battle, the main army would leave its ambush and sweep the Macedonians into the Tigris.

Again the plan was well conceived, provided that Darius could reach Arbela—and then the Tigris—before Alexander's arrival and provided also that the plan could be kept a close secret from the Macedonians. The first of the provisions seems to have been satisfactorily fulfilled and Darius reached Arbela, a largish town, with time to spare; then, assuming that the Mosul ford must be Alexander's intended crossing place, he advanced towards it, moving across the Lycus river (Greater Zab). It was from the security angle that the plan broke down and the element of surprise was lost. For Alexander, who was in all likelihood making for the Mosul ford, as Darius had anticipated, had the good fortune to capture some of the Persian scouts, who informed him that Darius was on the Tigris, where he intended to oppose his crossing. This information showed Alexander that he had succeeded in driving Darius away from Babylon; he must, however, have received a shock to realize that the Great King was so close. Accordingly he turned north and accelerated his rate of march from the leisurely ten or so miles per day that he had been making across Mesopotamia and crossed the Tigris unopposed in the area of Abu Wajnam, about forty miles north of Mosul, on the 18th September. Curtius gives a vivid description of the difficulties the army encountered in crossing the swiftly-flowing river[1]—in Persian the word Tigris means an arrow—and there can be little doubt that if Darius could have caught the Macedonians as they were emerging from the river, things would have gone badly with them.

Mazaeus for a second time had the unpleasant task of informing his King, now heading for Mosul, that his plan was in ruins; and now there was little time to draw up a new strategy with Alexander less than a hundred miles away. The best that could be done in the time available was to find a new battle-field suitable for the cavalry. A quick reconnaissance led to the plain near the village of Gaugamela (modern Tel Gomal), a name which means "The Camel's Grazing Place". The village is situated on the west bank of the River Khazir,

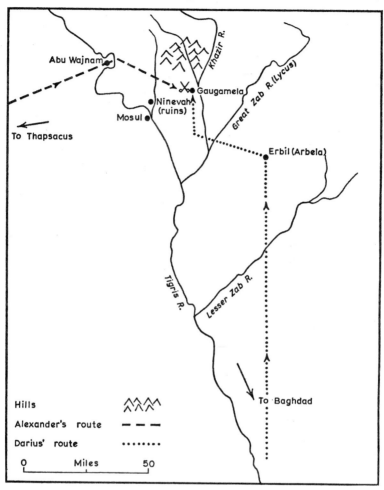

Approach marches to Gaugamela

about fifty miles from Arbela and forms, as it were, the apex of an isosceles triangle, whose base is the line from Abu Wajnam to Arbela. Here the Persians decided to bring Alexander to battle and accordingly set about levelling any uneven ground for the benefit of their cavalry and scythed-chariots. Darius, however, made a mistake in neglecting to occupy a low range of hills about three miles to the north-west of the field, which Alexander was able to seize and use as an observation-post to examine Darius' intended dispositions for the battle.

Alexander for his part rested his army for two days after crossing the Tigris. A minor cavalry skirmish took place on either the 18th or 19th of September with the cavalry brigade of Mazaeus who had been sent after his interview with Darius to keep the Macedonians under observation. The Persians, inauspiciously, were severely mauled in the running fight that took place. On the night of the 20th–21st the Macedonian camp was thrown into near panic by an eclipse of the moon, which filled the soldiers with superstitious fears. Aristander's interpretation that the eclipse foretold a Macedonian victory assuaged their terrors.

At daybreak the Macedonians broke camp and began their march down the Tigris. On the fourth day of marching (the 24th) Persian cavalry was seen in the distance. The army was drawn up in battle order, but the cavalry turned out to be merely a large Persian scouting-force (probably Mazaeus' group). The Macedonian cavalry was sent out to attack and the Persians took to flight; they were probably under orders not to engage the enemy. A few prisoners were taken and from these Alexander learned that Darius was only eight miles away at Gaugamela; the two armies could not see each other because of the range of hills to the north-west of Gaugamela. He therefore pitched camp on the spot to give the troops a rest before the battle and remained there from the 25th to the 28th inclusive.

While Alexander was encamped there, tragedy overtook Darius again. For his wife, a prisoner in Alexander's camp but a few miles away, fell ill and died (if Plutarch's statement is true[2] that she died in childbirth, there can be but one candidate for the child's paternity, since Darius himself had not seen his wife since November, 333). The news was conveyed to Darius by one of the Queen's eunuchs, who escaped from the Macedonian camp—an unfair blow of Fate to the unhappy man who was shortly to do battle for his kingdom and his life. According to Curtius, his wife's death impelled Darius to seek a peaceful settlement even at this late hour, making the same offers as at Tyre, but trebling the ransom-money offered for the remaining members of the family. The offer was rejected, in Curtius' narrative, with the same arrogance as had been displayed at Tyre.[3]

In the early hours of the 29th Alexander ordered the Macedonians to break camp and advance in battle-order towards the enemy, intending to make contact at dawn. Darius, when he heard that Alexander was approaching, drew up his army in battle-order too. The two armies came into sight of each other for the first time about dawn as the

Macedonians were descending from the range of hills; the intervening distance was about three and a half miles.

Alexander now halted his army and summoned a war council of all the divisional commanders. The question put before them was: should an attack be made immediately or only after a thorough reconnaissance of the battle-field? In favour of the former was the fact that the troops were keyed up to battle-pitch and delay might affect their morale; in favour of the latter, that any potential dangers, such as minefields sown with caltrops, could be discovered and the enemy's tactical dispositions observed carefully. The latter plan—urged, it is said, by Parmenion—prevailed.

Alexander then took a powerful mobile force with him and made a thorough reconnaissance of the battle-field; no opposition was met from the Persians. The officers were then reconvened and given a thorough briefing on the tactics to be followed the following day. The men were ordered to relax and rest themselves. Parmenion is reputed to have had second thoughts after the briefing and to have come to Alexander advising him to make a surprise attack by night on the enemy as a means of reducing the huge Persian numerical superiority. He received yet another snub for his pains; for Alexander replied that "it is a cheap trick to steal a victory; Alexander must conquer openly and without resort to guile".[4] The King's refusal, though it could have been expressed more pleasantly, was strategically justified, since it was impossible to direct a large battle in the dark and, as Arrian says, "at night many unforeseen occurrences have happened as much to those who are adequately prepared as to those who are badly prepared".[5]

The two armies, then, spent the night of the 29th camped within sight of each other's camp-fires—the Macedonians at rest in their bivouacs, but the Persians standing at arms in the battle-stations; Parmenion's plan had suggested itself to Darius also and he was afraid to dismiss his men from action-stations, with the result that the Persian troops entered the battle the following day weary and with shattered nerves.

On the morning of the 30th, when the soldiers had breakfasted, both commanders led their armies out to battle. Darius had used well the time available to him and had gathered the levies from all the eastern parts of the empire, including strong contingents from Bactria and Sogdiana, the two most easterly outposts of the empire.

He had in all about 34,000 cavalry, most of whom were very fine horsemen indeed. Improvements had been made in the cavalry's

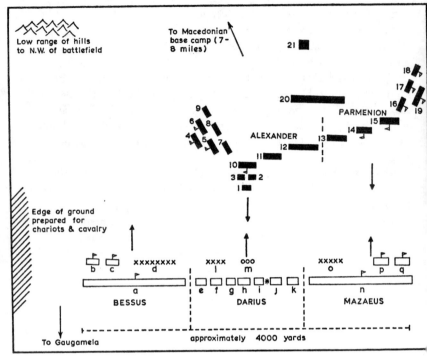

Tactical disposition at Gaugamela

equipment since Issus; each trooper was equipped with a coat of chain mail and a shield, while his offensive weapons had been adapted to the Macedonian model by giving each man a short sword and a stout thrusting-spear to replace the javelin.

The numbers of the Persian infantry cannot be determined with anything approaching accuracy; there may well have been as many as 100,000 foot-soldiers on the field, but very few of these were of value, the majority being ill-trained and ill-equipped satrapal levies. The infantry's backbone was a core of 2,000 Greek mercenaries and 2,000 heavy-armed Persians who formed the Royal bodyguard; there is no mention of the Cardaces who had been used at Issus—presumably the experiment had not been repeated. Darius was obviously basing all

ALEXANDER

1 Detachment of Agrianians
2 Detachment of archers
3 Thracian javelin-men
4 Greek mercenary cavalry under Menidas
5 Prodromi or Sarissophori
6 Paeonian cavalry
7 Detachment of Agrianians
8 Detachment of archers
9 Greek mercenary infantry
10 Companion Cavalry (Alexander)
11 Hypaspists
12 Four battalions of phalanx
13 Two battalions of phalanx (under Craterus)
14 Detachment of League of Corinth cavalry
15 Thessalian cavalry
16 Thracian cavalry
17 Detachment of League of Corinth cavalry
18 Odrysian cavalry
19 Greek mercenary cavalry not with Menidas
20 League of Corinth infantry and Greek mercenaries
21 Baggage and Thracian light infantry

DARIUS

a Left-wing cavalry—main body, from Bactria, Dahae, Arachoria, Persis, Susiana and Cadusia
b Scythian cavalry
c Detachment of Bactrian cavalry
d A hundred scythed chariots
e Archers
f Indian cavalry
g Carian cavalry
h A thousand Greek mercenaries
i A thousand Royal Bodyguards
j A thousand Royal Bodyguards
k A thousand Greek mercenaries
l Fifty scythed chariots
m Fifteen war elephants
n Right-wing cavalry—main body, from Syria, Mesopotamia, Media, Parthia, Albania and the Sacesini
o Fifty scythed chariots
p Cappadocian cavalry
q Armenian cavalry
★ Position of Darius

his hopes of victory on his cavalry. In addition, his Ordnance department had dragged out from the inner recesses of the Imperial arsenals 200 scythed chariots, a vehicle long since obsolete. Finally fifteen war-elephants had been procured; these could be most effective against horses not accustomed to them. They do not, however, appear to have had any influence on the course of the battle.

The order of battle adopted by Darius was discovered after the fight among captured Persian documents. The army was drawn up in two lines: the front line, with the exception of the Greek mercenaries and the Persian bodyguard, was entirely composed of cavalry; the back-line was almost entirely infantry. This arrangement was dictated by the poor quality of the infantry, whose function can hardly be described as anything more than that of "cheer-leaders". Darius himself was in general command in the centre; Mazaeus, satrap of Babylonia, commanded the right; and Bessus, satrap of Bactria, the left, which would have the task of containing Alexander himself.

From left to right, the left-wing front line was composed of Bactrian, Dahan, Arachosian, Persian and Susian, and Cadusian cavalry contingents. The Dahae were cataphracts, or troopers fully covered in chain mail. In front of these were two brigades of Scythian and Bactrian cavalry and a hundred scythed chariots. The left wing contained a total of almost 19,000 cavalry.

The centre, from left to right, comprised a detachment of Mardian archers; brigades of Indian and Carian cavalry (these latter had been "transplanted" by the government from Asia Minor to Central Asia); and then the troops in the immediate vicinity of the King—2,000 Greek mercenaries and 2,000 Royal Bodyguards. In front of the centre were posted fifty chariots and fifteen elephants.

The extremity of the right wing was held by the Syrian cavalry, who had next to them the horsemen from Mesopotamia, Media and Parthia—these latter were destined to become the scourge of Rome's eastern empire. The right-centre was held by the Albanian and Sacesinian horse. In front of the line were the cavalry of Cappadocia and Armenia, with fifty chariots. Nearly 15,000 horsemen were massed under Mazaeus' command.

Alexander had drawn up his main line in the usual order: the Companion cavalry, with its squadrons drawn up in column, held the extreme right wing under the command of Philotas; next to them and linking them to the centre were the Hypaspists under Philotas' brother, Nicanor; the six battalions of the phalanx formed the centre, with the first four battalions attached to the right wing, the last two, under Craterus, being ordered to co-operate with Parmenion on the left wing. After the phalanx, the left wing was held by the main body of the League of Corinth cavalry, and, holding the extremity of the left wing, the Thessalian cavalry.

In front of the right wing were the 500 Agrianians, 500 archers and 1,000 Thracian javelin-men. Their purpose was to keep the battle away from the Companions' front, to enable the Companions, at the right moment, to make their charge with unimpaired and unimpeded force. The left wing, being purely defensive, had no need of such a protection.

The line of battle had, however, a subtle difference from normal.

At Issus, once the battle had begun, the sea on the left and the hills on the right relieved Alexander of the fear of a turning-movement on his flanks. Here, at Gaugamela on the wide-open plain, with nothing on which either flank could be rested, the danger of a turning-movement by the Persians became very real, especially in view of their great numerical superiority in cavalry. In the lack, therefore, of natural protection for the flanks, artificial protection had to be made. This was done by stationing troops at an angle bending backwards on both wings so that both covered the flanks and formed, as it were, a wall to prevent a turning-movement. The troops beginning the angle on the right wing and stationed next to the Royal squadron of the Companions were the remaining 500 Agrianians, on whose right were the other 500 archers, followed by the Greek mercenary infantry of Cleander. In front of this line were positioned the Prodromi and Paeonian cavalry; and in front of these, as a third line, the main body of the mercenary cavalry under Menidas. A similar line was formed on the left wing, where the Thracian cavalry began the angle, covering the Thessalians' flank, followed by the remainder of the League cavalry, with the Odrysian horse on the outside. In front of this flank-guard were the rest of the mercenary cavalry not with Menidas.

Behind the main line, and forming the fourth side of the quadrilateral, were the infantry of the League of Corinth and the rest of the mercenary infantry. Their function was both to form a reserve for the front line and to wheel round to form a hollow square should the flanks be turned. The soldiers' packs and the transport-animals were left behind the battle-area, guarded by the Thracian light-infantry. The main camp was seven to eight miles behind the Macedonian line.

The tactics of the two Kings were dictated by the forces they commanded. The Persian army was essentially an attacking force; Darius' tactics, therefore, were to use its tremendous numerical superiority and the prepared ground to envelope Alexander's army in a pincer movement and overwhelm it by sheer weight of numbers. Should Alexander charge with the Companions, his attack could easily be absorbed by the mass of cavalry opposing him.

Alexander's tactical planning was more complicated. Because he was outnumbered five to one in cavalry, he had to plan a defensive battle at the beginning, tempting Darius into committing more and more cavalry into the attack. These would be held by gradually "feeding" into the fight the units of the flank guards. When most of Darius' cavalry was engaged on the flanks, trying to break through the holding lines, Alexander would launch his attack with the Companions at the now thinly defended Persian left centre. For this manoeuvre to succeed two things were essential: Darius had to be tempted into making the first move; and this achieved, there had to be perfect timing for the charge of the Companions—too early and the force of the attack would be blunted, too late and the flank guard might collapse and the Companions themselves be taken from the rear.

This tactical thinking explains Alexander's procedure as the two armies advanced to meet each other. The Macedonian line moved forward with its left wing "refused", its aim being to draw the Persian right towards it and throw the enemy out of gear. At the same time, Alexander, who was facing Darius in the Persian centre—so great was the overlap at this side—edged his line towards the fight. Darius, to counter this, began to edge his line to the left. As the advance continued in this oblique direction, both lines began to approach the edge of the prepared ground. Fear of moving off this ground had exactly the effect upon Darius that Alexander hoped it would. He rose to the bait and made the first move, ordering Bessus to send the Bactrian and Scythian front brigades to wheel round Alexander's right flank and so stop the movement towards the right.

This move was countered by Alexander with the mercenary cavalry, and when these were—not surprisingly—driven back, he fed more cavalry from the flank guard into the engagement, so that Bessus was forced to bring more of his wing into the engagement; whereupon the Persians began to press the flank guard hard.

At this point Darius decided to exploit the pressure being applied by Bessus by sending the scythed chariots against the phalanx. As the chariots thundered forward, they were met by a hail of javelins from the Agrianians and Thracians posted in front of the line and thrown into confusion, which was made worse by the nimble Agrianians darting between the chariots and stabbing the drivers. A few chariots penetrated as far as the phalanx, which now displayed its perfect drill by opening up broad lanes in its ranks through which the chariots clattered harmlessly, to be overpowered behind the lines.

At the same time as the chariots were launched—like a preliminary artillery bombardment—Darius ordered a general advance of his whole line. Bessus, however, was pouring more and more men into the Macedonian flank guard to try to penetrate it and turn Alexander's flank. As more units of Persian cavalry began to swing round the Macedonian right wing, Alexander drew on his remaining cavalry reserves and sent the Prodromi to attack them. The Persian cavalry on the left was by now nearly all engaged with the right flank and their left centre was looking very thin—a gap may even have developed there.

Alexander now decided that the critical moment had arrived and, at the head of the Companions, drawn up in a wedge-shaped formation, launched his charge against the Persian left centre, followed by the Hypaspists and the four phalanx battalions of the right. The feelings of Darius and his centre can be well imagined as "out of the dust-cloud rising from the fighting on their left . . . [they] beheld the dreaded Macedonian heavy cavalry, emerging in perfect and impressive order as, with unmistakable *élan*, they commenced their formidable charge".[6] The Companions crashed through the Persian line to the left of Darius, then swung leftwards and began to roll up and encircle the line towards the Persian King, while at the same time the Hypaspists and phalanx began to batter and thrust back the front of the line. Darius was now in great danger of complete encirclement and capture. Seeing that the battle was now completely out of his control, he did the only possible thing he could do in the circumstances—he turned and fled the battle-field.

Alexander was too good a general to let this local success go to his head when the battle was by no means over. Instead of setting off on a pursuit of Darius, he broke off the fight at the centre, leaving it to the phalanx, and wheeled the Companions to the right to relieve his hard-pressed right flank by taking Bessus in the rear and flank. The advent of the victorious Companions quickly altered the balance on the Macedonian right, and a general rout of the Persians there began to ensue. A big gap was thus gradually opened up between the Persian centre (being pushed back by the phalanx) and the left wing. To under-stand the next episode, we must first look at the course of the battle on the left wing under Parmenion.

At the opening of the struggle Parmenion had been engaged by Mazaeus at the same time as Bessus was attacking the Macedonian right. 3,000 cavalry had been sent immediately by Mazaeus round the Macedonian wing to ride beyond the battle-field to the Macedonian camp. It was hoped that these would, firstly force Parmenion to detach against them some of the much-needed cavalry and secondly, rescue the Persian royal family. In both they were unsuccessful. Parmenion refused to weaken his line: and when the cavalry stormed into the lightly guarded camp, they could not prevail upon the Queen Mother to leave Alexander. After plundering the camp, the troopers then returned to Mazaeus, and, since their operation must have taken at least two hours, can have played little part in the battle.

By the time that Alexander and the Companions made their charge, Parmenion was facing the full Persian right wing of 16,000 cavalry under Mazaeus, and was being very hard-pressed indeed. The brunt of the defence was borne by the Thessalians. It was essential that Parmenion should not let his wing collapse; however, the forwards movement of the right hand part of the phalanx brought about a gap between the fourth battalion (operating with the right) and the fifth (operating with the left). Through this gap there charged a strong body of Indian and Persian cavalry, sent probably by Darius to try to take Parmenion in the rear.

Fortunately for Alexander—now engaged with the enemy centre—this cavalry group, instead of obeying orders, crashed straight through the second line of infantry, made their way to the Macedonian baggage-camp, and began to loot it and release Persian prisoners taken in the battle. The infantry of the second line, recovering from their surprise, wheeled about and rallied to the defence of the baggage.

There were now four separate engagements going on simultaneously on the field: on the Macedonian left, Parmenion was struggling to prevent a break through by Mazaeus; behind the Macedonian line, the second line infantry were engaged with the cavalry force at the baggage-camp; in the centre, the Hypaspists and phalanx were pushing back the Persians; and on the right, Alexander was rolling up the Persian left wing.

At this juncture Parmenion felt he could hold out no longer and despatched a messenger to Alexander begging reinforcements. The messenger galloped behind the Macedonian line till he reached Alexander just as or just after Bessus' wing had broken and taken to flight. Alexander immediately wheeled the Companions to the left and, taking Menidas' command with him, made for the gap between his right and centre. As he was passing through this gap on the way to Parmenion, he ran straight into the Indian and Persian cavalry who had been ejected from the baggage by the second line infantry and were trying to escape through the gap. In the engagement that followed the Indians and Persians fought with the courage of desperation, and the fight is said to have been the fiercest of the whole battle. In it sixty of the Companion cavalry died, and Hephaestion, Menidas and Coenus (who had broken off the fight at the centre to help here) were wounded before the Persians managed to escape.

On arrival at the left wing, Alexander found that since the receipt of Parmenion's message the situation there had changed. Mazaeus, seeing how the rest of the battle was going, had broken off the engagement and was retreating fast, pursued by the Thessalians. His presence no longer being necessary, Alexander set off in pursuit of Darius, while Parmenion seized the Persian field-camp and baggage-animals.

Darius and his immediate retinue, after fleeing from the battle-field, had crossed the Greater Zab, not even breaking down the bridge in their haste, and made their way back to the base-camp at Arbela, where they arrived about midnight. To his council Darius announced his intention to continue his flight towards the north, rather than southwards back to Babylon. He believed—rightly, it turned out—that his opponent would naturally make for the rich and populous heart of the empire—Susa and Babylon, the prizes of war. He himself would thus be able to effect his escape, make for the Far Eastern provinces of the empire, which were still untouched by the war, and renew the struggle from the deserts of East Iran and the mountains of Afghanistan. He was joined as he set out by Bessus and the remnants of his Bactrian cavalry and the 2,000 Greek mercenaries, who seem to have escaped from the battle with remarkably light casualties. Their loyalty to their foreign paymaster in his hour of distress is at least a tribute to Darius' power of leadership.

It was late in the day when Alexander left Gaugamela in pursuit of Darius and his cavalry-troopers were weary from the battle. Therefore on crossing the Greater Zab at nightfall, he gave men and horses a few hours' rest till midnight, then pressed on to Arbela, arriving about dawn. He found Darius gone, but—a sign of the Great King's haste—captured his chariot and weapons, as well as the Persian field-treasury, amounting to 4,000 talents.

The battle fought at Gaugamela on the 31st September, 331 B.C., was perhaps Alexander's greatest military achievement and one of the most decisive battles in the world in its influence on its course of history. Under his brilliant generalship the highly trained and disciplined Macedonian army had defeated a force many times its own size, on ground of the enemy's choosing, and with amazingly light losses—the highest recorded figure being 1,000 infantry and 200 cavalry dead.[7] For the Persian losses no reliable figures exist, though the total of 40,000 dead given by Curtius[8] may not be too wide of the mark in view of the butchery that took place during the rout of their army, where the infantry in particular would have suffered. Darius too was now only Great King in name, with little or no hope of raising another army that he could put into the field against Alexander. His downfall was complete and the vast monolith of Achaemenid Persia had been split from top to bottom. The Persian empire, which had seemed to people of the time as eternal and invincible as did hundreds of years later the Roman empire, had collapsed, never to be revived in its old form. All of Asia as far east as the Hindu Kush had passed into the hands of the Macedonian King in one day's fighting and was his to use as he pleased—as foreign conqueror or as successor to the Achaemenid throne.

NOTES

1   Curtius IV 9.15ff.
2   Plutarch, *Alexander 30*
3   Curtius IV 9.1ff
4   Arrian III 9.1ff
5   Ibid., section 3
6   Marsden, *The Campaign of Gaugamela* p.57
7   Papyrus Oxyrhyncus 1798
8   Curtius IV 16.16

9

The Heart of the Empire

Darius' conjecture on Alexander's course of action was correct. Alexander lingered in the area of Arbela only long enough to bury his own dead. The thousands of Persian corpses, scattered for miles around the battle area, were left to rot. Indeed, one reason for the King's rapid departure from the region is the fear of plague arising from the corpses. He set out at the head of his victorious army in a southward direction, after crossing the Tigris, and made for the nerve-centre of the empire, Babylon, 300 miles distant from Arbela.

The area through which the army was now passing—Mesopotamia —was famed in antiquity for the fertility of its soil, brought about by its position between the two great rivers. Curtius says that the natives do not allow their flocks to pasture there for fear that they may die of satiety.[1] Near modern Kirkuk Alexander was shown a spring of bitumen, with which the walls of Babylon had been cemented, and a well of crude oil. He was later treated to a demonstration of the properties of this marvellous substance: at dusk one evening, the road leading to his quarters was sprinkled by the natives with a line of petroleum; a torch was then applied to it at the far end and "with the speed of thought the flame darted to the other end, and the street was one continuous fire".[2]

This was the area of the old Babylonian empire, at its height under the reign of Nebuchadnezzar. Since its conquest by the Persians in 538 it had been a Persian province, whose satrap resided at Babylon, which was also used by the Great King as his capital for several months of the year.

The city itself—the Babel of the Old Testament—whose ruins lie between the modern towns of Khan Mahawil and Hilla, was still the largest and most important in the Persian empire. Not only was it the Great King's capital for a large part of each year, but it was the very hub of the empire's economic life and contained the main royal mint. Tradition makes Queen Semiramis, wife of an Assyrian King, the city's foundress and credits the builders with completing the circuit-wall in exactly one year at the rate of a furlong a day. This wall was made of small baked bricks, covered and cemented with bitumen. Herodotus, who claims to have visited the city in the fifth century, states that the four sides of the wall formed a perfect square, each side being fifteen miles long. The river Euphrates cut the city in two and as a precaution against flooding huge embankments had been raised, each having large overflow basins on the landward side. The two parts of the city were connected by a stone bridge.

Among the city's many marvels were the ruins of the enormous temple of the chief Babylonian god, Bel, which had been destroyed by the Persian King, Xerxes, early in the fifth century and never rebuilt. But most famous of all were the Hanging Gardens, numbered by the ancients among the Seven Wonders of the World. Curtius gives a full description of them:[3] the buildings on which the gardens were planted were two and a half miles round and eighty feet high; the gardens themselves were as high again as the walls and planted with great trees which yielded as much fruit as though they were growing in their native soil. Rivulets of water irrigated the gardens continually. Legend says that they were built by a King of Assyria for his wife who longed for woods and groves which were not to be found in the Babylonian plain.

As Alexander approached the city, the populace came out *en masse* to meet him, led by the priests, the Magi and the Chaldaeans. There also came to make their peace with the King and to surrender the city and its citadel Mazaeus, the satrap, and his family, and Bagophanes, the garrison commander. They were received with courtesy by the King, as were all the other dignitaries.

Alexander had advanced on Babylon in the expectation that he would have to lay siege to it; he entered the city in triumph over a road strewn with flowers, surrounded by huge crowds eager to catch a glimpse of the new master of their destinies. Alexander himself was obviously surprised by the enthusiasm of his welcome and made somewhat suspicious; for he entered the city with his army drawn up in battle-order ready to combat any ambush.

For a month the army rested and revelled at Babylon, while the people showed that their reception was based on solid goodwill. The Babylonians had always had a reputation for luxurious living, and now they went out of their way to make the Macedonians' sojourn a memorable one. Neither wine nor women were lacking for the soldiers —indeed, it is said that the heads of families were by no means reluctant to give the troops, as part of their hospitality, the opportunity to enjoy the favours of their wives and daughters. Curtius[4] describes with puritanical disapproval a torrid dance performed by the women, and states that "nowhere else did Alexander do more harm to the discipline of his soldiers. For nothing is more corrupt than the habits of that city".[5]

But not every member of the expedition was seduced by the delights of the flesh. Callisthenes spent his time in collecting and transcribing the astronomical observations of the Chaldaeans, which were said to go back over a period of 31,000 years. The data thus compiled was sent off to his uncle at Athens, and there utilized by the great Greek astronomer, Callippus, who was working with Aristotle at the Lyceum.

Alexander, too, though doubtless not untouched by Babylonian conviviality, was kept busy with affairs of state. To try and win over the influential caste of the Chaldaeans, he gave instructions that the great temple of Bel was to be rebuilt from the ruins that Xerxes had left 150 years ago—a decision that found great favour with the common people; as usual, Alexander was most scrupulous in respecting local religious sentiment.

The appointment of the satrap for Babylonia must have come as a great surprise for all outside the King's immediate entourage. For Mazaeus was reinstated in the position he had held since Issus. Native satraps or governors had already been appointed in Caria and Egypt, but these areas were hostile to Persian rule; now in the heart of the Persian realm, in the richest province, a Persian was being confirmed by the conqueror in his office—a Persian, moreover, who but a month previously had almost defeated that conqueror in set battle.

The King's action is perhaps not so reckless or quixotic as it appears. In the provinces of the west, both Persians and Macedonians were foreigners to the native populations and a change of rulers was a matter of indifference to them, provided taxation was not too oppressive and their local institutions were not interfered with; hence the complete absence of national uprisings in the rear of the advancing army. But in the lands across the Euphrates Iranian national feelings had to be taken into consideration; and if Alexander wished to win acceptance among these people he would have to show them that he had come not merely as a foreign freebooter and conqueror. What better way to demonstrate this than by appointing an Iranian to one of the posts traditionally occupied by the Iranian aristocracy? Mazaeus was a highly distinguished Iranian, whose adherence to the victor of Gaugamela and whose willingness to serve him would do much to conciliate the rest of the Persian governing class. Mazaeus is invariably spoken of in laudatory terms by both ancient and modern writers for his abandoning the cause of Darius; only Curtius has the honesty to call him by his proper name—a deserter.[6] Henceforth Iranian satraps were to become the regular practice in the East as far as India.

But the appointment did contain a strong element of risk, and Alexander showed that he recognized this. For Mazaeus' functions were limited purely to the field of civilian administration; and strong checks were put upon him by the appointment of an independent Macedonian officer to command the military forces of the satrapy and another to command the citadel-garrison at Babylon. Finance was also taken out of the satrap's hands by the appointment of a Macedonian finance-officer, directly responsible to Harpalus, though Mazaeus was allowed to continue issuing coinage from the mint in his own name—a unique privilege. The Persian was given little opportunity to change horses a second time.

The army now left Babylon to continue its march eastwards, Alexander having overcome any reluctance towards a further advance by means of a lavish distribution of largesses, which in the case of the Macedonian cavalry troopers amounted to almost a year's pay each.

The object of the march was the great city of Susa, capital of the fertile and well-watered province of Susiana—"Elam" of the Old Testament. Susa lay slightly to the south-east of Babylon, at a distance of about 375 miles, and the two cities were directly linked by the Royal Road. To make the journey today the traveller must cross from Iraq to Iran. Alexander covered the distance in twenty days—a fair marching speed helped by the men's freshness, the excellent road and the flatness of the terrain.

The ruins of Susa lie just to the south of modern Shush, which preserves the old Persian name meaning "abounding in lilies". The city, founded by the first Darius, became, thanks to its central position, the most important of the centres of imperial administration. It was to Susa that all foreign embassies made their way; in the great palace of the Persian King, in 387, had been dictated the terms of the treaty, known after the Spartan diplomat, as the Peace of Antalcidas, which the Great King sent down to the city-states of Greece—perhaps the greatest diplomatic triumph in Greco–Persian relations. Built on the left bank of the Karkheh River, Susa was surrounded by a wall of burnt brick and housed the palace of the King, a large and easily defended citadel and one of the main treasuries of the empire. A modern analogy is justifiable here: if Babylon was the New York of the empire, Susa was its Washington.

An officer had already been sent ahead to persuade the governor to surrender. The mission had been successful and whilst Alexander was still marching towards Susa he was met by a messenger informing him that the city had surrendered and its treasuries were in safe hands. The satrap of Susiana, Abulites, had not fought at Gaugamela, his satrapal levy being led in the battle by his son. His decision would have been influenced by the news from Babylon of Mazaeus' treatment; and his son must have informed him about the warlike efficiency of the Macedonians.

The wealth confiscated at Susa was fabulous. The smallest estimate, exclusive of the furniture, plate and jewellery of the Royal Palace, gives 40,000 talents of silver and 9,000 talents of gold coin,[7] which "many King's over a long period of years had amassed . . . for their children and their posterity, as they thought, but a single hour delivered it into the hands of a foreign King".[8] Other loot found in the treasury included almost a quarter million pounds weight of purple dyed cloth from the city of Hermione, which had been stored there 190 years without its colour fading.

Less valuable materially, but highly impressive as evidence of the former might of Persia, were jars of water which earlier Kings had had sent from as far as the Nile and the Danube as tokens of subjection. There were also found the bronze statues of the tyrannicides, Harmonidus and Aristogeiton, which Xerxes had carried off from Athens. They were restored to that city by Alexander and Arrian saw them standing in the Potter's Quarters more than 500 years later.

A minor incident which almost had much wider repercussions took place at Susa. Alexander had received from his mother a quantity of cloth woven in Macedonia, together with the women who had woven it. He ordered the cloth and the women to be given over to Sisigambis, with the recommendation that she have her granddaughters taught by the women to spin. In Persia it was considered a great disgrace for any noble-woman, but especially those of royal blood, to engage in any form of manual toil; and Sisigambis, who was such an excellent piece of propaganda for Alexander, was deeply insulted and only mollified by Alexander with great difficulty. Nevertheless, when he departed from Susa, Alexander left behind the Persian Royal family in the city with tutors to teach them Greek. It is likely that he already had some idea forming of what he was going to do at Persepolis, and did not want the Queen mother and her family as witnesses.

Shortly before his arrival at Susa, Alexander had been rejoined, after an absence of a year, by the battalion-leader Amyntas, son of Andromenes, who had been despatched to Macedonia to levy reinforcements for the army. Amyntas' commission had been highly successful, for the troops he brought with him totalled 13,500 infantry and 1500 cavalry, of whom 6,000 infantry and 500 cavalry were Macedonians. These reinforcements represent a total equivalent to half of the original Macedonian infantry strength and a quarter of the Companion cavalry strength at the start of the expedition; and, in view of the storm that was brewing in the Peloponnese, their departure must have been watched most reluctantly by Antipater.

The infantry soldiers were divided up among the phalanx battalions according to the usual territorial principle and a new battalion—the seventh—was now instituted. The new Companions, however, were divided among the squadrons not on a territorial basis, but indiscriminately. Alexander was continuing his father's policy of making the Companions and Hypaspists loyal only to the person of the King by breaking down their old regional loyalties.

The tactical formations of the Macedonian cavalry—both Companions and Lancers—was now modified. Each squadron was subdivided into two separate companies (*lochi*) each under its own *lochagus* (company commander), so that the Companions now contained seventeen companies altogether. The reason for this was probably to give the cavalry greater tactical flexibility by forming semi-independent sub-units.

Administrative arrangements at Susa followed much the same pattern as at Babylon. Abulites was left as satrap of Susiana, but with a Macedonian finance-officer and two Macedonian military officers—one as commandant of the citadel, the other as general military officer of the satrapy.

It was now January of the year 330 B.C., a time when the troops of both protagonists could reasonably expect to go into winter-quarters till the arrival of spring. For Susiana was bordered to the east by the massive Zagros chain of mountains, forming a backbone separating the Near East from the Iranian plateau. To the south-east of Susiana lay the province of Persis (Persia proper), the very cradle of the Persian race with its capital cities of Persepolis and Pasargadae; to the north-east lay Media, with its capital of Ecbatana, which was now sheltering Darius. To reach either of these two provinces from Susa it was necessary to cross the Zagros range, whose peaks tower up in places to 15,000 feet and whose passes are frequently blocked by snow in winter. Darius might well be excused if he reached the conclusion that Alexander would now rest his men at Susa before continuing his eastward advance in spring. During this time the forces of Media, Persis and the eastern provinces might be rallied and defences organized to use this mountain barrier as a wall to keep the Macedonian out of the eastern half of the empire. Persis and Media especially could be relied on to defend its King against the invader.

Alexander, however, had learned two very important principles of strategy from his father and from his own experience: campaigns can be conducted by a well-trained force equally as well in winter as in summer—to the great disadvantage of an enemy who believes the opposite; and a victory must be exploited to the full and as swiftly as possible. Thus, he now decided, greatly to the enemy's consternation, to continue his advance south-eastwards and invade Persis, thus securing the Persian homeland and opening for himself an easier road northwards against Darius. This would be grand strategy of the highest order; for the occupation of Persis meant the turning of the southern flank of Darius' mountain defences and the capture of Persepolis the loss to Darius of the most venerated of Persian cities. There now began what one modern scholar has described as "one of the most tremendous pieces of exploitation of a victory in the history of warfare".[9]

Persepolis lay about 370 miles to the south-east of Susa, near the modern city of Sheraz and on the River Araxes (modern Kur). There were two possible roads to the city: the Royal Road, which skirted the mountains to the south, following the modern main road from Behbehan, through Kazerun and Shiraz, then turning to the north; and a more direct route across the mountains, again starting from Behbehan, through Fahlian and over the plains of Ardakan. This route passed through a deep and narrow defile in the mountains, known as the Persian Gates.

Ariobarzanes, the loyalist satrap of Persis, had raised the levy of his satrapy after Gaugamela and had gathered an army of at least 25,000

Persian infantry and 700 cavalry. Now on the news of Alexander's advance from Susa, he moved his forces and took up his position at the Persian Gates, building a wall across the defile. The position was well chosen; for if, as seemed most likely, Alexander came by the quicker route across the mountains, he would find the Gates an impossible obstacle; if he chose the easier route to the south, then Ariobarzanes, though unable to prevent his penetration to Persepolis, would have ample time to withdraw his army, remove the treasury from the city and escape northwards.

As Alexander moved southwards from Susa, he entered the territory of the Uxii, a tribe who inhabited the border areas of Persis. Whichever road the King decided to take to Persepolis, he had first of all to pass through the Uxian territory. The lowland Uxians surrendered without trouble; but the highlanders, whom the Persians had never managed to subdue, sent envoys to Alexander demanding the payment of the toll they had been accustomed to levy on the Persian Kings when passing through their lands. Alexander bade them meet him at the pass through which the way led, there to receive payment at his hands.

When the envoys had departed, Alexander took the Hypaspists and 8,000 other troops and with the help of Susian guides made a night march by a little-known mountain path to the Uxian villages. Falling on them, he massacred the inhabitants. He then pressed on at top speed towards the pass that the Uxii intended to occupy to prevent the army's passage, detaching *en route* Craterus to seize some heights which lay on the likely line of retreat of the mountaineers. Arriving first at the pass, he occupied it and on the appearance of the Uxians led a surprise attack on them. The Uxians were dismayed and panic-stricken; turning about, they fled to the heights where they thought to find safety, only to fall into Craterus' ambushing force which almost annihilated them. "These", says Arrian with grim irony, "were the gifts they received at Alexander's hands".[10]

In a short and brilliantly executed mountain campaign of not more than a day and a night's duration, the road between Susiana and Persis was at long last made safe for travel. The tribe, saved from extermination only by the intervention of Sisigambis, was compelled to pay a tribute of horses, oxen and sheep each year.

It now remained to deal with Ariobarzanes. Parmenion was sent off with the Thessalians, mercenaries and League troops and baggage along the easier southern route. Alexander had decided to take his "shock" troops—the Macedonian part of the army, with the Agrianians and archers—and make a surprise march over the mountains before Ariobarzanes could effect a withdrawal to Persepolis.

Setting out along the mountain road, the King marched at top speed for five days, camping on the sixth night out of sight of the Gates. The next day he moved his troops forward for the assault—and walked straight into an unpleasant surprise. For Ariobarzanes had built his wall between two sheer cliff faces and had mounted artillery on it. A frontal assault only was possible, and when Alexander sent his men against the wall, they were repulsed with great loss. A retreat was sounded and the dead were left in the defile.

The wall obviously could not be taken by frontal attack only; it had to be turned from the flank. By a stroke of good fortune some prisoners had been taken, one of whom, a local shepherd, offered to guide Alexander by a path that would bring him out behind the Persian wall; the path, however, was rough and dangerous, but Alexander decided to make the attempt. Craterus was left at the entrance to the defile with two brigades of the phalanx, 500 cavalry and some archers. He was ordered to create the impression that the full force was there by burning the usual number of camp-fires, until Alexander's detachment appeared behind the enemy. Then, at a given signal, he was to attack the wall again from the front, while Alexander fell on the Persians from behind.

The path along which the guide led Alexander's group was about twelve miles in length and took them eastwards of the Gates. The journey was made by night. *En route*, three senior officers, Amyntas, Philotas and Coenus, were detached with a force of cavalry and infantry to make their way to the Araxes river and throw a bridge over it. Alexander's purpose in this was to enable himself, should the surprise attack on the Gates fail, to turn about, rejoin Amyntas and occupy Persepolis before Ariobarzanes. He could then move against Ariobarzanes from the north, while Parmenion came up in a pincer-movement from the south. The move was strategically sound, though it entailed a weakening of his own forces.

At midday Alexander halted and gave his men some rest. At dusk the march began again and just before dawn the first Persian outposts were encountered and overpowered. How rough the going was can be seen from the fact that it took two nights and a morning to cover the twelve mile path. Alexander then threw his men straight into the attack on the unsuspecting Persian camp. At the sound of Alexander's trumpet, Craterus also began his assault on the wall.

Taken by surprise and hemmed in on both sides, the Persian levies panicked and took to flight the only way they could—up the steep walls of the defile. Here they ran straight into a detachment of 3,000, posted on top of the cliffs for this very purpose; its commander was Ptolemy, son of Lagus, appearing for the first time in a position of responsibility. A great massacre took place, and, according to Arrian,[11] only Ario-barzanes accompanied by a few horsemen managed to escape into the hills.

Without pausing to rest his troops, Alexander pressed on to the Araxes and crossed the bridge that Amyntas had thrown over the river. The whole force, now reunited, moved on at full speed to Persepolis, entering the city perhaps on the 31st January, before the Persian troops left behind had time to plunder the treasury—a danger of which the turncoat garrison commander, Tiridates, had warned Alexander by letter. The tactical brilliance of this assault on the well-guarded entry to Persis—its rapidity, boldness and forceful execution—cannot be overemphasized; to use the words of a modern scholar, it was "one of the most hazardous, audacious and certainly most profitable of mountain campaigns in the annals of history".[12]

Persepolis—the Persian Parsa—had been built by Darius I as the capital of his empire. Its citadel contained two magnificent palaces and the royal treasury; the nobility had built their palaces round those of the King. For the last century, however, the city had lost ground—perhaps because of its remoteness—to Susa and Babylon as the main imperial capital. It seems to have been little known in the West, whereas Susa was a household word among the Greeks. But it was still the capital of Persis and the chief repository for the wealth that flowed into the empire; and, because of its ancestral associations, all the Kings of Persia were buried there.

As Alexander and his army were approaching the city, they were met by a sight that was both horrible and pitiable. A crowd of Greeks came out to meet them. They were prisoners of war and mostly of advanced age—probably mercenaries taken fighting on the wrong side during the empire's troubles in the middle of the century. All of them had been badly mutilated by their Persian captors—some had their feet cut off, others their noses, others their ears, and all had had the sign of their slavery branded on them. To quote Curtius: "They seemed to be strange images, not men; there was nothing that could be recognized in them except their voices".[13]

The sight profoundly affected even the hard-bitten Macedonians, whose feelings must have been similar to those of the Allied Forces as they entered the Nazi concentration camps in 1945. The King swore to return them to their homes; but after deliberation amongst themselves the Greeks decided to remain together rather than be scattered about over Greece separately, objects of pity to their fellow-countrymen. They begged the King to assign them land where they could settle freely and live a life apart. Alexander applauded their decision and gladly granted it, making in addition gifts of money, clothing, sheep and cattle and grain with which to sow their lands.

Indignation aroused by these mutilated prisoners provided an excuse for the barbarous act that followed. For the King gave over Persepolis to be sacked and plundered by his soldiers. Only the citadel and the palace-area were excepted; for here were located the treasuries, from which the enormous sum of 120,000 talents of gold and silver were removed. So vast was the quantity of the treasure, which represented the accumulated surplus from the annual tribute of nearly 200 years, that mules and pack-horses and 3,000 camels had to be requisitioned from all over Susiana and Babylonia to move it from Persepolis.

From Babylon, Susa and Persepolis, the Macedonians had seized a sum of money totalling nearly 180,000 talents, which has been estimated at £44,000,000 (sterling) at the 1913 value of the pound. It will not be inappropriate here to repeat what was said earlier, in order to demonstrate the immensity of this amount by Greek standards: Athens, the wealthiest Greek city-state, had an annual revenue of 400 talents; Macedonia was considered rich with an income of 1,000 talents a year from her gold-mines. Little wonder, then, that his native-land receded further and further from Alexander's vision before such immense wealth and luxury. So too was the Roman peasantry overcome by the riches of the kingdoms of Alexander's successors; so too the Mongul Khublai Khan succumbed to Chinese sophistication and luxury.

To give over to the horrors of a sack a city which had surrendered itself was an act of barbarism, but one based on cold calculation. For the soldiers had in the last few months been engaged in three major struggles—at Gaugamela, against the Uxians and at the Persian Gates; they had also passed through the wealthy cities of Babylon and Susa, in neither of which had they been allowed to exercise the victor's privileges. Soon they were going to be asked to follow their King into the wilds of the eastern half of the empire, to lands hardly heard of, let alone known, by the people of Europe. They could hardly be expected to sympathize with Alexander's growing admiration for the way of life of the people they had conquered, or to understand the political urgency of keeping the population down by peaceful means. They wanted one thing in return for their labours—loot and beautiful Persian women. Hence Persepolis, which in the last hundred years had lost its importance before Susa and Babylon, was deliberately sacrificed as a bribe to the soldiers.

Equally vandalous is Alexander's own act in burning the royal palaces in the city. For this he has deservedly received the almost universal condemnation of writers, ancient and modern. Various reasons for the act have been offered. Some say that Alexander was taking vengeance on Xerxes for his razing of the temple of Bel at Babylon by destroying the palace which that monarch had built. Others connect it with the panhellenic "Crusade": the burning of the palaces signified both the end and fulfilment of the Crusade and the exaction of vengeance for Xerxes' razing of Athens and firing of Greek temples. Arrian laconically remarks that "I myself cannot see that *this* was any retribution upon the Persians of earlier days".[14] Others, again, see the act as symbolizing the end of Achaemenid rule in Asia.

But the incident was perhaps quite unpremeditated and there is not a little truth in the story, usually rejected as a popular myth, that the idea first was mooted during a wild drinking-party by an Athenian courtesan, named Thais, the mistress of Ptolemy. Thais suddenly called out that it would be a fine and glorious gesture to go in triumphal procession and burn down the palace of Xerxes, who had committed so many wrongs against Greece. Tumultuous applause greeted her words. Someone shouted for torches to be lit; others took up the cry and said that this was a deed worthy of Alexander alone. The King, far gone in drink, was inflamed by their cries; and kindling a torch and brushing aside the protests of Parmenion, led the rest of the company to the palace of Xerxes. He himself threw his torch the first of all. The palace which was built mainly of cedar wood, rapidly caught fire and was soon engulfed in an inextinguishable conflagration. Soldiers came rushing up with water to put out the blaze, but when they saw the King and his companions there stayed to join in the sport.

This account does offer the most satisfying psychological explanation to this otherwise inexplicable act of vandalism. For though Alexander was more and more seeing himself as the new Great King of Asia and acting accordingly in his administrative and religious actions, he was still King of Macedonia, and Hegemon of an Hellenic alliance formed for the purpose of punishing the traditional enemy of Hellas. However little this meant to him in his sober moments, it was the sort of ideal which, if put over with skilful flattery to him when he was flushed with drink, would appeal to his romantic mind, which was always focused on the King's own glory. In the excitement of the party the desire to perform so obviously popular a deed, and the fear that he seem too faint-hearted for it, must have urged the drunken monarch on irresistibly.

The looting of the Persian capital and the burning of its palaces were barbaric acts; yet in a way Alexander performed an act of great benefit to future generations. For Persepolis never recovered from its violation and became a ghost-town, which has proved a blessing to the labours of archaeologists excavating its ruins. The fire in the palaces preserved the magnificent stone reliefs, among the finest examples of Persian art, and baked hard palace documents inscribed in clay that otherwise would have crumbled away. These documents can now be deciphered and afford one of the few non-Greek sources of information for Persian history. There remain too the impressive ruins of the palace-area—the staircases, the friezes and the imposing columns. "Persepolis stands to this day, preserved by its very burning. The palaces of Darius and Xerxes still tower above the plain, a marvel to the passing way-farer".[15]

NOTES

1 Curtius V 1.12
2 Plutarch, *Alexander 35* (Loeb translation)
3 Curtius V 1.31ff.; cf. Diodorus II 8.6
4 Curtius V 1.38
5 Curtius V 1.36
6 Curtius V 1.44
7 Diodorus XVII 66.1
8 Curtius V 2.12 (Loeb translation)
9 A. R. Burn, *Journal of Hellenic Studies* LXXII 1952, p.91
10 Arrian III 17.6
11 Arrian III 18.9
12 J. F. C. Fuller, *Generalship* 234
13 Curtius V 5.7. (Loeb translation)
14 Arrian III 18.12
15 A. T. Olmstead, *History of Persia* p.523

10

The Death of the Great King

The army stayed at Persepolis for nearly two months after the city's looting and destruction. In this time Alexander made yet another of his now-familiar winter campaigns against the hill-tribes, on this occasion those of the remote, snow-covered mountains of southern Persia—a successful operation of thirty days, though the troops suffered severely from winter rains and frosts. Among the tribes subdued was a people called the Mardi, described as troglodites, who fed on the flesh of their flocks of sheep and wild animals. "Not even the women have gentler dispositions, as is Nature's way; they have overhanging bushy hair, their garments do not reach their knees, they bind their brows with a sling; this is both an ornament and a weapon".[1]

The oldest of the Persian cities, and former capital, was Pasargadae, situated on the River Kur in a plain surrounded by high mountains about fifty miles north of Persepolis. It had been founded by the great monarch Cyrus in the sixth century; and though long since displaced as an administrative centre, was still held in deep veneration by the Persians because of its high antiquity. This too was taken over by the Macedonians, its governor, Gobares, surrendering to Alexander without resistance, and provided the treasury with yet another 6,000 talents to add to its loot.

Returning to Persepolis the King busied himself with administrative matters. A "Quisling" civilian government was again installed, the loyalist satrap Ariobarzanes, who had escaped from the battle at the Persian Gates, being replaced by Phrasaortes. This latter's father, Rheomithres, truer to his principles than his son, had fought the Macedonians both at the Granicus and at Issus, where he had lost his life.

However, in view of the hostility and fierce resistance encountered from the native Persians, it was felt necessary to leave a somewhat stronger police-force than usual; thus 3,000 Macedonians were left as a garrison for the province with their headquarters at Persepolis.

After this, probably towards the end of March 330, Alexander led his army northwards out of Persis towards Ecbatana, the capital of the Province of Media (roughly modern north-west Iran). The Medes and Persians racially were kinsfolk; and together they formed the dominant aristocracy of the Persian empire. Ecbatana (modern Hamadan) was, besides the satrapal seat of Media, the Royal Residence for two months of the year and the meeting place of the joint council of the Medes and the Persians. It had an immensely strong citadel and was situated strategically on the main road to the eastern and northern satrapies. From Persepolis to the city the distance is roughly 500 miles.

It was hither that Darius had fled after Gaugamela. As stated above, he reckoned on Alexander's heading southwards to the wealthy cities of the centre, whereby Darius would gain for himself a breathing-space to reorganize his forces. For he had not given up the struggle, and with good reason: the satrapies to the north and to the east had not yet been overrun by the Macedonians, and—in the east especially—were passionately hostile to the foreign invader. In the north, moreover, Darius was well-known personally as the result of his governorship of Armenia before his accession.

Darius' intentions seem to have been as follows: to use Ecbatana as a rallying-point of his supporters, and to wait on events. Should Alexander decide to remain a long time at Susa or Babylon, so much the better, since every day Darius was acquiring new strength; should Alexander decide to move against Darius at Ecbatana before Darius was strong enough to fight another pitched battle, the Persian would then withdraw eastwards through Hyrcania and Parthyaea towards Bactria and Sogdiana, devastating the country as he went and luring Alexander even further into the vast desert tracts of north-east Iran.

Already Darius' forces had swollen to 30,000 infantry and more than 3,000 cavalry, though most of the infantry were of poor, untrained quality. Rapid action was thus essential for Alexander both to prevent any further build-up of men by Darius and to hound him down before he could reach the Far East and the safety of the steppes and the mountains. Hence the shortness of the stay in the heart of the empire and the march northwards before spring had begun. Darius was almost caught by the unexpected march, and especially by its rapidity; for when Alexander was only three days from Ecbatana, having covered more than 400 miles, he was met by a Persian of the noblest blood—Bistanes, a son of King Artaxerxes III (Ochus)—and informed that Darius had fled from Ecbatana only five days before, taking with him a select force of 3,000 Bactrian cavalry, 6,000 infantry (among them nearly 2,000 Greeks), and 7,000 talents from the treasury at Ecbatana. He was making for the mountainous area south of the Caspian, in particular the pass known as the Caspian Gates, to which the women and heavier baggage had been sent some time before in anticipation of a hasty flight.

Though Darius had eight days' start, Alexander knew now that he must surely catch up with him long before Bactria was reached. For though the Persian King might keep up a fast rate of march with his cavalry and infantry, once he joined up with the baggage train the rate of progress would be cut to a snail's pace. Accordingly he stayed for some days at Ecbatana, to rest the troops in preparation for the final pursuit of Darius and to make certain military adjustments and plans.

Firstly he discharged all of the troops of the League of Corinth, including the Thessalian cavalry, who were thus treated as members of the League rather than subjects of the Macedonian ruler of Thessaly. Each cavalry trooper was given a bonus of 6,000 drachmae in addition to his total pay for the expedition; to the infantry was given an additional 1,000 drachmae per man. At the rate of pay obtaining in 334 this represented about eight years' pay for each of the cavalry and nearly three years' pay for the infantry. Proclamation was made, however, that any man who wished might re-enlist with the army as a mercenary receiving a bounty of three talents (or 18,000 drachmae) on enrolment. It is recorded that many, both cavalry and infantry, were won over to stay with the army; and little wonder, since a cavalry-man who thus re-enlisted, providing he saved his bounties and escaped death, could look forward to going home some day as a very wealthy man indeed.

It is not recorded whether a similar bounty was given to the Macedonian troops, who were given no choice of going home or staying; but it is highly likely. It is stated that these largesses to the League troops cost the King 12,000 to 13,000 talents; though such generosity, calculated to win him favour back in Greece, was not difficult in view of the loot acquired in the last six months. The troops who elected to go home were given an escort of cavalry and sent across northern Mesopotamia to the Phoenician coast, there to sail for Greece.

The dismissal of the League troops signified that the Great Crusade was now over, that vengeance had been fully exacted. But more than this, it showed that Alexander, who had received the news of the crushing of a great revolt in Greece by Antipater,★ felt secure enough to send these able-bodied men back to their native-cities, where, it is hoped, thanks to the lavish donations they had received, they would form a solid block of support for the Macedonian hegemony. Any man who re-enlisted would now be serving as a soldier in the personal army of the Macedonian King, to whom alone he would look for orders and pay; he was no longer one of a contingent of free and equal allies. Above all, a big blow was struck at the power and influence of Parmenion; for it has already been noted how the Thessalian cavalry were closely attached to the old general and formed almost his personal troop, the equivalent of the King's Companions. Now at one stroke Parmenion was deprived of these forces; and any of them that re-enlisted would feel their obligation lay with their bountiful paymaster, Alexander.

Parmenion, in fact, deprived of his supporters, was now removed from his position of Chief of Staff and put in charge of the treasury-guard at Ecbatana, together with the supervision of the section of the line of communication that would now extend eastwards from Ecbatana. For this purpose he was given a force of mercenary infantry and cavalry, Thracian foot, totalling perhaps 6,000 men altogether. As second-in-command there was appointed a man whom the King could trust to keep watch on Parmenion's activities—Cleander, the brother of Coenus.

A sedulously fostered campaign to discredit the abilities of Parmenion had been in progress from the beginning of the expedition, reaching its climax with the battle of Gaugamela, where the general's appeal for aid to withstand Mazaeus was interpreted as a sign of incompetence and growing debility—or, on a more sinister level, a deliberate attempt to sabotage Alexander's chance of capturing Darius alive, induced by jealousy of the young King's career of uninterrupted success. Plutarch quotes the words of Callisthenes, the official historian: "There is general complaint that in that battle Parmenion was sluggish and inefficient, either because old age was now impairing somewhat his courage, or because he was made envious and resentful by the arrogance

★The revolt was led by Agis of Sparta (cf. p. 83). Antipater defeated him at Megalopolis in Arcadia (cf. C.A.H. VI.443), perhaps August 331. Alexander's sneer that Megalopolis was a "battle of mice" compared with Gaugamela would indicate jealousy and fear of Antipater even at this stage.

and pomp of Alexander's power". [2] For the moment it was assumed that Parmenion's "inefficiency" was the result of old age; and he was thus removed from front-line service by means of this new command.

The post was both honourable and responsible; but it was nonetheless a serious diminution of power and influence. For, with the sole exception of Antipater back in Macedonia, to be removed from the court was to be removed from the centre of power. The star of the house of Parmenion was definitely on the wane, with only Philotas and Nicanor left holding key positions. Coenus, Parmenion's son-in-law, was unlikely to let family ties stand in the way of his own advancement; in the event of a crisis, Coenus' loyalty was a commodity that could easily be purchased, if the price was high enough.

Parmenion was immediately given a task in his new capacity. He was to take his troops and advance northwards against the mountain-dwelling Cadusians, who inhabited the south-western shore of the Caspian Sea (roughly modern Gilan) and were still loyal to Darius. He was to move eastwards along the length of the territory, subduing the settlements as he came to them, and then continue his advance through the mountains into the territory of the Mardians (not the same as those of Persis), who dwelt in the ranges along the southern shore of the Caspian. From here he was to return to Ecbatana. Alexander himself would take care of the reduction of the areas east of this after he had captured or killed Darius. Whilst Parmenion was away on this mission, whose purpose was to prevent the communications-line being severed from the north, the treasure at Ecbatana (for it was to here that all the loot acquired in the southern satrapies had been transported) was to be guarded by four battalions of the phalanx, together with a few cavalry, who would thus be given a period of rest. Cleitus "the Black" had been left behind at Susa suffering from some illness. He was sent orders by letter that he was to pick up the battalions from Ecbatana, when he had recovered and when Parmenion had returned, and march them eastwards to rejoin Alexander.

Parmenion's immediate superior at Ecbatana was Harpalus, the "Chancellor of the Exchequer". Harpalus' official position was that of finance-officer of the four central satrapies—Babylonia, Susiana, Persis and Media—but in view of the location of the central treasuries in these areas, he was given authority over the other area finance-officers who submitted to him their surplus revenues. And just as these men—Philoxenus and Menes—were in control of matters dealing with the army's supply and communications in their own provinces, so

Harpalus co-ordinated all their activities and acted as a kind of imperial Quartermaster-General. He was perhaps the most important and powerful man in the empire after the King himself, and this power was made all the greater by his general control of the minting of all coinage. At first he had his headquarters at Ecbatana; but he soon transferred to Babylon, where he took up residence in the royal palace, and quickly succumbed to the delights of the life of an Oriental Sultan.

After making these dispositions at Ecbatana Alexander, taking the Macedonian cavalry, a company of mercenary horse, the Macedonian infantry (except the 6,000 left to guard the treasuries), the archers and Agrianians—in fact, all the most seasoned and mobile troops—set out eastwards in pursuit of Darius, whose start must now have been at least a fortnight.

Alexander knew that Darius had stationed his baggage and women-folk at the Caspian Gates (the modern Kotal-e-Dochtar) and hoped that a rapid and unexpected pursuit would find the Persian still there. In eleven days of forced marching the army covered about 200 miles to reach Rhagae (modern Tehran), at a distance of fifty miles from the Caspian Gates. So great was the speed of these forced marches that according to Arrian,[3] many men were left behind and many horses died of fatigue. At Rhagae, however, it was learned that Darius had already passed through the Gates and taken to flight. The sources of information were deserters from the Persian camp. Since his men were worn out and it was no longer possible to catch Darius immediately by means of a forced march, and in view of the desert that lay ahead, Alexander rested his men at Rhagae for five days, before continuing the pursuit.

Beyond the Caspian Gates, extending north as far as the Elburz Mountains, lay the desert tract of Dasht-e-Kavir, known to the ancients as the Parthian desert. In preparation for crossing the northern fringe of this waste, Alexander sent out a detachment under Coenus to forage for provisions. Whilst he was awaiting the return of Coenus, there arrived at the camp to surrender themselves two of Darius' most distinguished followers—the Babylonian nobleman, Bagistanes, together with one of the sons of Mazaeus. As it turned out, they were not deserting their King, and the news they brought was so startling that Alexander was roused to immediate action.

For Darius had been deposed by his own followers as the result of a conspiracy and cast into chains. The chief conspirators were Nabarzanes, the Grand Vizier, and Bessus, the satrap of Bactria and Sogdiana, who was related to the royal house of the Achaemenids and had now assumed the title of Great King. With them were Satibarzanes the satrap of Aria, and Barsaëntes, satrap of Drangiana. Darius himself, it will be remembered, was only a member of a collateral branch of the royal house who had been raised to power by a previous Grand Vizier. From the start of his reign he had had many enemies—men who considered their claims to the throne to be every bit as good as his. Now, after four years of continual disaster, Darius' position was very weak. On the one hand, he was being harried in hot pursuit by the Macedonian conqueror, on the other hand, he was totally dependent on the goodwill of the governors of the eastern provinces who had remained with him.

The Vizier and the satrap, whose 3,000 Bactrian cavalry were the strongest part of the troops left to Darius, saw, now that the King was forced to flee to the eastern satrapies, that the time was ideal to carry out a *coup d'état*. Nor was the plan entirely without merit, for Bessus was well-known and popular within his satrapal area and the people would give him their whole-hearted support against the Macedonians. If a war of national resistance was to be kindled in the east, it could be done better and with more chance of success by Bessus than by Darius, who was little known there and had, moreover, suffered two crushing defeats at Alexander's hands. For Bessus and Nabarzanes personal expediency and gain could be combined with the national interests; and they could rely on the support of the Bactrian cavalry to back up their schemes.

Accordingly, at a conference held soon after Darius had left the Caspian Gates, Nabarzanes came up with a pre-arranged piece of advice to his King: "Let Darius", he said, "abdicate from the throne temporarily in favour of Bessus. When the troubled times are settled, then Bessus will once more restore Darius to his rightful position as Great King". Darius, who saw the guile behind the Vizier's words, flew into a rage and made as though to attack him with his sword.

The conference broke up in confusion and Nabarzanes, together with Bessus and his Bactrians, withdrew from the Persian camp and took up quarters some distance away. There was now an open split among Darius' followers, the Bactrian cavalry obviously looking to Bessus as the source of authority, the Persian troops and the Greek mercenaries looking to Darius.

Any attempt to depose Darius by force was now out of the question, and so Nabarzanes and Bessus decided to feign submission, rejoin the main force and seize Darius at the first opportunity. They would then use the captured King as a lever with which to bargain with Alexander. Should the Macedonian refuse to treat with them, they would kill Darius and make for Bactria, there to continue the war. They were helped unwittingly in this plan by the loyal Artabazus, who continually urged Darius that in their present plight unity was vital.

Accordingly a meeting was held one night with Artabazus at which a reconciliation was arranged; and the following morning, when Darius was breaking camp, he was rejoined by the Bactrians and their leaders. These, says Curtius indignantly,[4] prostrated themselves on the ground and had the impudence to feign veneration of the man whom they intended to put in chains shortly afterwards. Darius, he continues, who was by nature a trusting man, was completely taken in by all this play-acting.

Not so, however, the Greek mercenaries, under their leader Patron. When the army set out on its march Patron ordered his men to keep their arms and armour about their persons and not to put them in the baggage-wagons. He himself stayed close to Darius' chariot, waiting for an opportunity to speak with the King. When his chance came, he addressed Darius in Greek, since Bessus who was in the chariot with Darius, was unversed in that language, while Darius was quite a fluent Greek speaker. He warned Darius that Bessus and Nabarzanes were plotting against his person and advised him to pitch his tent that night in the Greek camp.

Bessus suspected that Patron was disclosing his plot. Darius, however, kept his face calm and betrayed no surprise or alarm. But his answer to the Greek sealed his fate. The loyalty of the Greeks, he said, was beyond question. Yet he could not desert his fellow-countrymen. It was more difficult for him to condemn than to be deceived; and if his own soldiers did not wish him to be saved, then his death was long overdue anyway. Moreover, such an action on the Great King's part would give Bessus and Nabarzanes just the excuse they wanted to declare him a traitor to his own cause and depose him.

That night, when the army encamped, the Bactrians, on Bessus' orders, remained under arms. Darius, not wishing to appear suspicious, had ordered the Persians to bivouac as usual. Then summoning Artabazus to his tent, he informed him of the situation and of his decision, and bade him make his escape whilst he still could. As Artabazus left the King's presence a loud lamentation for Darius' plight arose from the eunuchs and women who were in attendance. This spread fear and tension through the whole camp, nobody knowing what was happening or daring to go and find out because of the armed Bactrians. Eventually word reached the conspirators that Darius had killed himself; this was the cause of the wailing from the royal tent. Bessus, Nabarzanes and their followers hastened to the tent where they found Darius alive but unprotected. This was their chance; Darius was seized, bound in chains and taken off to the quarters of the conspirators.

Artabazus, the Greeks and other loyal followers of Darius, seeing that nothing could be done against the supporters of the conspirators, slipped away from the camp and headed eastwards towards Parthyaea. Two days later the remnants of Darius' followers joined up with Bessus and Nabarzanes "because there was no one else for them to follow".[5] Darius, the Great King of Persia, was kept in chains and, when the camp was broken the next day, placed in an old wagon, so as not to draw too much attention to his person as the army moved along towards Bactria.

Alexander, on receiving this news, decided to press on with the pursuit as rapidly as possible. Coenus and his detachment were out foraging. Alexander could not wait for them. Taking the Companions, the Lancers and the most mobile of the infantry (including the Hypaspists), he set out, leaving Craterus in command of the rest of the army, with orders to wait for Coenus to return, then to follow on by easy stages. His own men carried nothing but their arms and two days' rations.

The pursuers travelled all that night and the following day till noon. They then rested during the hot part of the day, and pressed on again at evening, once more pursuing all through the night. At dawn they reached the camp where Darius had been captured. Here they fell in with Darius' interpreter, an old and infirm man who had been unable to keep up with the army and had been left behind. Darius, for fear of giving offence to his own countrymen, always addressed his Greeks through an interpreter, even though he spoke fluent Greek.

From the interpreter Alexander gained further details about the plans of Bessus and Nabarzanes. He decided to push on with the utmost vigour in the hope of falling upon the Persian column by surprise. Once more travelling through the night and the following morning, he came at midday to the village where only the previous day Darius and his captors had encamped. Here he learned from two Persians— rivals of Bessus who had deserted from his camp—that the enemy were not far away. They told him that they knew of a shorter road through the desert and would act as guides towards Bessus.

Alexander resolved to press on in pursuit. Realizing that the weary infantry would be unable to keep pace with the cavalry—a force that could fight as well on foot as on horseback—he dismounted 500 of his cavalry-men and gave their horses to picked infantry soldiers, no doubt chosen from the Hypaspists. They were to carry with them their usual weapons. With this mixed force the King set out again at dusk, leaving Nicanor to lead the rest of the troops in his rear.

Travelling at full speed, the party is said to have covered fifty miles during the night. As dawn broke they were able to see the enemy ahead of them in the distance, marching without their arms and with no suspicion that their pursuers were anywhere near. Such was the surprise created by their appearance that the majority of the Persians immediately took to flight and it rapidly became a question of *sauve qui peut*.

Bessus and Nabarzanes, with their immediate entourage, and the captive Darius in his wagon, tried to put on speed to outdistance their pursuers. The lumbering wagon slowed them down, and so they urged Darius to mount a horse and escape with them rather than fall into the enemy's hands. Darius refused, exclaiming that vengeance was now close at hand for the traitors.

Alexander was getting closer every minute. Any more delay and the conspirators would be cut off from escape. Darius was obdurate; it was useless to plead further with him to trust themselves rather than the foreign conqueror. In exasperation and perhaps in order to delay the pursuers, they ran Darius through with their javelins and left him in his wagon, dying from several wounds. The regicides then made off with 600 horsemen, scattering in different directions as they went—Nabarzanes to Hyrcania, Bessus to Bactria, Satibarzanes to Aria and Barsaëntes to Drangiana.

The oxen pulling Darius' wagon, now without a driver, wandered off the road and strayed on for about half a mile till they came to a valley with a spring of water in it. Here they came to rest, worn out by the heat and weak from the hastily inflicted wounds they had received from the conspirators. Meanwhile some of the Macedonians were hotly pursuing the fleeing regicides, others were searching through the deserted baggage-train for Darius.

One of these latter, a Macedonian named Polystratus, parched with thirst after the hot and dusty chase, was directed to the spring by one of the locals. As he was quenching his thirst with water from his helmet, he noticed the wagon nearby and the dying oxen with javelins still sticking in their bodies. As he looked he heard from the wagon the tortured groans of a dying man. Overcome with curiosity, he went and drew back the coverings of the wagon and saw Darius there, still in his regal attire and close to death.

The King asked in Greek for water. When Polystratus had brought some and Darius had drunk, he is said to have thanked heaven that he at least would not now have the misery of breathing his last in complete solitude. Commanding Polystratus to pass on his dying message to Alexander, he solemnly enjoined the King to take vengeance on the traitors; to continue to protect and honour his mother and children; and finally to requite the kindness of Polystratus in due measure. Then, grasping the soldier's hand, the Great King of Persia breathed his last.

When Alexander eventually came upon them, he was visibly affected by the sight of his opponent whom he had hounded to such a lonely and wretched death, and removing his cloak, he covered the body and gave orders that it be transported with full honours to be buried in the royal burial ground at Persepolis, alongside the other Kings of Persia. Romantic legend, trying to heighten the drama of the Persian's death, makes out that Alexander came upon Darius still alive and breathing, and held converse with him before his death, promising to pursue and punish the regicides. Certainly Alexander could afford now to be generous to his opponent. For Darius' murder by his own countrymen relieved the Macedonian of a great potential source of embarrassment if the Persian had been taken alive: if Alexander had granted his life, Darius would have remained the focal point for any resistance against the new ruler; and to have executed Darius would have earned Alexander the universal execration of the Iranian peoples and the title of regicide.

Darius died early in May 330 B.C., near Damghan, at the age of fifty. A man of mild, generous and even noble temperament, his reign would have been a time of peace, prosperity and justice for his subjects, had not the aggression of the western power involved him in a long war with a military genius. Despite adverse modern judgements,[6] Darius was a brave and capable opponent for Alexander, showing considerable strategical and tactical powers, as can be seen in his handling of the Gaugamela campaign. His reign was one long tragedy, both for himself and for his country. In the words of Arrian: "His life was one series of disasters, nor, from his accession had he any respite; at once there befell the cavalry disaster of his satraps on the Granicus, and then at once Ionia and Aeolis were in the enemy's hands, with Greater and Lesser Phrygia, Lydia and Caria save Halicarnassus; soon followed the capture of Halicarnassus, and over and above all the coast-line as far as Cilicia. Next came his defeat at Issus, where he beheld his mother made captive with his wife and children; then at Phoenicia and all Egypt was lost; and then again followed his own flight at Arbela, a shameful flight among the foremost, and his loss of the greatest host of all the Persian empire; and now a fugitive from his own kingdom, and a vagabond, at last he was betrayed by his own guards to the worst of fates, both King and prisoner, hurried off with every mark of shame and finally perishing by conspiracy of those who were most bound in duty to him. These were the tragedies of Darius' life. His lot in death was the royal tomb, his children nurtured and educated by Alexander as if he were still on the throne, and Alexander for his daughter's bridegroom".[7]

NOTES

1 Curtius V 6.18 (Loeb translation)
2 Plutarch, *Alexander 33* (Loeb translation). The phrase "arrogance and pomp" is probably quoted as being Parmenion's actual words.
3 Arrian III 20.1
4 Curtius V 10.13
5 Curtius V 12.19
6 Cf. W. W. Tarn, *Cambridge Ancient History* VI, p.386: "a poor type of despot, cowardly and inefficient"; *Alexander the Great* I, p.58
7 Arrian III 22.3ff. (Loeb translation). The marriage to Darius' daughter did not take place for another 6 years. See p. 240 for the Susa weddings.

11

Conspiracy and Treason

With the death of Darius Alexander was now the undisputed and rightful ruler of Persia. Since Issus in 333 he had represented himself as Lord of Asia and had received with courtesy and consideration all of Darius' followers who deserted to him. In Egypt he had been crowned Pharaoh, a prerogative of the Great King; and Plutarch[1] says that after the battle of Gaugamela he was proclaimed King of Asia, which implies a formal coronation ceremony in one of the central capitals. But as long as Darius was alive, the legitimacy of Alexander's position was open to dispute. Now, however, Alexander could be regarded as the rightful occupant of the throne and any who opposed him as traitors or rebels.

The question now faced the King whether he should continue his eastwards advance or leave the unconquered satrapies to themselves. There was much to be said in favour of the second alternative; since economically the eastern provinces were unviable. The country was mostly poor—mountains or desert—and civilization such as the Greeks knew was virtually non-existent: the people were nomads or pastoralists, organized in a feudal system under powerful local barons; there was no city-life, only villages or settlements around the satrapal residence; and in some of the more remote areas even coinage was unknown. Moreover it could be expected that resistance to the new monarch would be much stronger among the eastern Iranian peoples, who had only reluctantly acknowledged a ruler of their own race. Consequently large garrisons would be needed to hold down such huge areas as were involved. Indeed, it is above all in the eastern part of the empire that Alexander pursued the policy of founding "cities", populated mainly by Greek mercenaries and veteran soldiers. These "cities" were not intended primarily to spread Greek culture and civilization; such effects would be purely incidental. They were essentially frontier outposts and garrisons, part of a vast military chain linking together the provinces and intended for their policing and protection.

There were, on the other hand, cogent reasons for continuing the advance: the central satrapies were rich and prosperous, but ill-protected against raids by the nomads to the north and the east, so that the Hindu Kush was the only possible strategic frontier in the east. Moreover, Bessus had escaped to Bactria, where he was already engaged in preparations to continue the struggle against Alexander; and Bessus had showed himself to be a dangerous and capable opponent. Arta-bazus, too, related to the Achaemenid house and loyal to Darius to the last, was still at large with a body of Greek mercenaries. Both these men had to be dealt with, as well as Bessus' fellow-regicides and all the other Iranian nobles who had not yet made their submission. Alexander thus decided to continue his advance eastwards.

The Macedonians, however, viewed the situation differently. They were not concerned with considerations of imperial strategy or in the Great King beating his marches. To them the death of Darius meant the end of the war and they wanted to go home to enjoy the rich booty they had accumulated. Their grumblings, when it was announced that they were not turning back, compelled the King to address them and justify his decision. In a carefully prepared speech he argued that the Macedonians could not go home until Bessus had been captured: apart from the guilt the Persian had incurred as a regicide, there was a strong possibility that, if he were not stopped now, in a few years' time Bessus—a strong and capable man, with designs on the throne— would appear on the coast of Asia Minor, destroying the liberated Greek cities and reclaiming the ancestral territory of the empire; and then the trials and dangers the Macedonians had just experienced against Darius would have to begin all over again. These arguments, backed up by a liberal gift of money, won the army over and they bade Alexander lead them wherever he would.

After appointing as satrap of Media yet another Persian noble, Oxydates, who had been a political prisoner under Darius, Alexander left Hecatompylus and marched northwards towards Hyrcania (roughly Astarabad and eastern Mazandaran). To the north the satrapy bordered on the Caspian Sea and was very fertile; the southern part was wild and mountainous, the home of tigers and wild boar, and peopled by predatory and savage tribesmen. For the moment Alexander had decided to drop the pursuit of Bessus in order to deal with Artabazus, who had escaped with the mercenaries into the hills of Tapuria (to the west of Hyrcania), and to carry out his part of the joint plan with Parmenion and reduce the eastern half of the region which lay above the road from Ecbatana to Bactria. The army was divided into three columns: Craterus was sent westwards into Tapuria, with orders to reduce the province and bring in the mercenaries; Erigyius, taking the baggage-train along the easy road through Shahrud, was to make his way to the satrapal seat of Hyrcania, Zadracarta (modern Gorgan); Alexander himself led the third division, intending to march straight through the mountains, subduing the tribesmen as he passed through. The three columns were to reunite at Zadracarta.

After much skirmishing with the local tribesmen, Alexander crossed the mountains into the Hyrcanian plain and pitched camp on the edge of a small river. Here there arrived a letter from the Vizier (called Chiliarch by the Greeks) Nabarzanes, who, after Darius' murder, had made his way to Hyrcania and illegally assumed control of the satrapy. In the letter Nabarzanes, after taking great pains to excuse his own part in the assassination, offered to surrender in return for a safe conduct and honourable treatment. The King, wishing to isolate Bessus and judging that clemency towards the other regicides would help to achieve this, sent back his promise that Nabarzanes would be received without harm.

At Zadracarta the King was eventually joined by Erigyius and Craterus, who reported that Tapuria had been brought under control, but no contact had been made with the mercenaries. Accompanying Craterus was Autophradates, the Tapurian satrap, who had come to make his submission. In return he was restored to his office. As a further administrative act the King now appointed as satrap of Hyrcania and Parthyaea a Parthyaean noble, Amminaspes, who had been in Egypt when that satrapy had surrendered and had accompanied the court ever since.

The problem of Artabazus and the mercenaries was now partly solved. For Artabazus in person came to Zadracarta, having resolved on surrender. He was accompanied by representatives from the mercenaries, who had hitherto been following him. Artabazus had become an hereditary guest-friend of the Macedonian royal house during a period he spent in exile at Pella in the 350s, and his prestige among his own people was enormous; the reception he now received thus exceeded in its honour and cordiality any given to any other Persian noble. The envoys from the mercenaries, however, received a demand, in plain terms, for unconditional surrender. By serving with the Persians they had flouted the decrees of the League of Corinth; they must now throw themselves on the mercy of its Hegemon. The envoys could do little other than accept the King's terms, and a Macedonian officer was sent back with them to escort the mercenaries to Alexander.

The King now decided to lead an expedition against the Mardians. This people, who, says Curtius,[2] had neither sent envoys to Alexander nor seemed likely to carry out his orders, lived to the west of Tapuria and their conquest would complete the reduction of the southern shore of the Caspian. Leaving Craterus in charge of the troops at Zadracarta, Alexander advanced through Tapuria and made his base-camp near the Mardian border.

The ensuing campaign was fought amidst precipitous mountains and dense forests, the people being driven and harried by the advancing Macedonians and their village strongholds razed to the ground. Terrified, according to Plutarch,[3] by reports of the King's savage rage and threats after his favourite horse, Bucephalas, had been captured by a marauding band of the tribesmen, the Mardians were allowed to surrender and were placed under the control of Autophradates, the Tapurian satrap.

Back at his base-camp Alexander received the mercenaries, who had been conducted there by the officer he had sent. With them were envoys from several Greek states, including Athens and Sparta, who had been with Darius since Gaugamela. These were arrested as traitors to the League of Corinth and its Hegemon. A delegation from Sinope, on the southern coast of the Black Sea, was allowed to go free, since Sinope was not a member of the League but a part of the Persian domain; "the people thus did not seem to be acting unreasonably in sending envoys to their own King".[4] As for the mercenaries, those who could prove that they had been in service with Persia before the League of Corinth was formed were set free; those who had joined later than its foundation were punished by compulsory enlistment with Alexander at the same rate of pay as they had received from Darius; this was now considerably less than Alexander's mercenaries were receiving.

The King's return to Zadracarta coincided with the arrival of Nabarzanes coming to surrender himself. Despite the pledges he had received, he still had misgivings about the sort of reception he would receive; for he came laden with costly gifts for the King, among them a youth named Bagoas, "a eunuch of outstanding beauty and in the very flower of his boyhood. Darius had been in love with him and Alexander soon fell in love with him too".[5] Bagoas accompanied Alexander for the rest of his eastern campaigns and gradually acquired considerable influence with the King. Nabarzanes received his pardon; but in view of his past record he never again held any high office.

The stay in Hyrcania is particularly significant because it was here that Alexander's adoption of the ways of the complete Oriental despot came into much greater prominence as he strove to become the successor to the Great King of Persia in more than just name. Since his first contact with the splendour of the position of the Persian monarch at Issus, the King had been deeply impressed; and since Gaugamela he had pursued a consistent policy of conciliating the Iranian nobility and appointing them to their traditional posts of privilege and power within the empire. Darius had been treated after his death, not as a vanquished enemy, but as Alexander's legitimate predecessor to the Persian throne; and his brother, Oxathres, was formally enrolled among the King's Companions. Moreover, during the pursuit of Darius at least one company of Iranians is found serving in the army alongside the Macedonians and Greeks; for such were the *hippacontistae* or mounted archers mentioned by Arrian.[6] It is quite likely that the other units of the excellent Iranian cavalry had also been enrolled, perhaps serving alongside the squadrons of the Companions. For there was no better way for Alexander to show himself as the true successor to the Persian throne than by demanding military service from his new subjects.

But now for the first time in Hyrcania the conqueror began to adopt the ways of the conquered and to wear the Persian dress and the upright tiara of the Great King. At first he only wore these garments when giving audience to his Oriental subjects or among his close friends; but later he wore them when riding out or when holding general court. Oriental chamberlains were introduced into the court for ceremonial purposes—though at the present their functions probably only extended to Oriental subjects. Along with Persian court-ceremonial the King took up the Persian custom of the harem, which traditionally contained 365 concubines, one for each day of the year and "outstanding in beauty, since they were selected from all the women of Asia".[7]

It may be argued that the adoption of these Oriental habits was merely a "front", intended to win the loyalty of the Iranian peoples.

Yet the fact that the King wore the Persian dress when in private with his closest friends and the gradual extension of Persian ceremonial to all state-occasions suggest that the change went deeper than this and that Alexander was gradually feeling his way towards a position in which the Macedonian element in his new mixed empire would be subordinate in importance to the Persian.

The Macedonians in general did not favour these innovations. Among the senior officers and nobility three different attitudes can be discerned: from the older men, who had served with Philip there was strong disapproval; a second group—mainly younger men under the leadership of Hephaestion—was willing to pander to Alexander and encourage him in his Persian habits; a third group, including such men as Perdiccas and Craterus, while disapproving of such Orientalism, was willing to close their minds to it, provided they were not expected to participate and provided that their own power and influence were not thereby jeopardized. Craterus had a bitter personal feud with Hephaestion, with whom he vied for the King's favour. Alexander made it his practice to use Hephaestion in his dealings with the Persians and Craterus with the Greeks and Macedonians.

To the rank and file the sight of haughty Persian grandees, surrounded by scores of retainers, daily passing through the camp was a bitter pill to swallow. Nor could they have approved of the new Iranian cavalry units serving alongside them as their comrades-in-arms. But most of all, they were grieved to see their own King and leader wearing the dress of the despised and defeated enemy.[8] It was in Hyrcania in the summer of 330 that the first cracks appear in the relationship between Alexander and his men, cracks which were eventually to develop into a wide rift.

About the middle of June the army left Zadracarta to continue its pursuit of Bessus. Travelling directly eastwards along the Royal Road, it soon came to the largish centre of Susia, just over the border from Parthyaea in Aria. Here another of the assassins of Darius, Satibarzanes, came to give himself up. The mild treatment of Nabarzanes was producing results and of the regicides only two were still at large—Bessus and Barsaëntes. Satibarzanes was not only forgiven; he was actually reinstated as satrap of Aria, to which post Darius had originally appointed him. Alexander must either have been running short of reliable Persians to appoint as governors or have mistakenly believed that the submission of Satibarzanes was genuine. The news brought by the satrap showed how urgent was the speedy capture of Bessus:

having assumed the upright tiara, Bessus had changed his name to Artaxerxes and was claiming to be King of Asia; he was receiving impressive support in Bactria and reinforcements were expected from the nomads across the Oxus. After being rejoined by Cleitus and the phalangites from Ecbatana, Alexander set out again from Susia at top speed towards the eastern satrapies.

About this time the fortunes of the house of Parmenion suffered a grievous blow, when Nicanor, the old general's eldest son and commander of the Hypaspists, fell sick and quickly died. Thus, of the powerful family-group that had left Macedonia four years ago, only Philotas and the untrustworthy Coenus were left on active service. Though Nicanor had been one of the most distinguished officers in the army, the King professed himself unable to delay his march towards Bactria to celebrate the funeral. Philotas, however, was permitted to remain behind to attend to his brother's obsequies, with instructions to catch up with the army afterwards.

The army was halted at the river Murghab in its forward progress by the news that Satibarzanes, on returning to his satrapal residence, had thrown off his allegiance, had massacred the Macedonian troops who were escorting him and was raising Aria in revolt. Taking a strong and mobile detachment and leaving Craterus in charge of the main body of the army with orders to follow him, Alexander swung southwards and made for the Arian satrapal seat of Artacoana (near modern Herat). He is alleged to have covered the journey of more than a hundred miles in two days of forced marching. Satibarzanes, deserted by his supporters, was compelled to take flight with 2,000 loyal horsemen to Bessus. The King treated all who were pointed out as followers of Satibarzanes with great severity; but another Persian, Arsaces, was appointed as satrap of Aria.

The ease with which the revolt had been crushed was deceptive. Later in the year Satibarzanes returned and raised a fresh rebellion which necessitated the despatch of a strong force under Erigyius, helped from Parthyaea by its new satrap Phrataphernes. This time the revolt was not ended until Erigyius had brought Satibarzanes to battle and killed him in single combat.

About the end of August, 330, the King left Artacoana, having founded nearby the garrison-town of Alexandria of the Arians (modern Herat). Troops could be spared for this purpose because of a large batch of reinforcements the army had just received from Antipater, together with 3,000 native soldiers from Lydia. Instead of retracing his steps, Alexander decided to continue southwards into Drangiana (roughly south-western Afghanistan and eastern Iran) and deal with the regicide Barsaëntes, then satrap of both Drangiana and the neighbouring Arachosia, a huge and indeterminate area extending eastwards as far as the River Indus. He would swing northwards from Arachosia towards Bactria, thus reaching the satrapy after a diversion of more than a thousand miles.

The capital of Drangiana—the later Parthian city of Phrada—was about 200 miles south of Artacoana, situated on the eastern shore of the Lake of Seistan. As Alexander drew near, Barsaëntes fled into Arachosia, hoping to find support among the Indian inhabitants of the area. The Indians, however, arrested the satrap and sent him under escort to Alexander, who had him executed for his part in Darius' murder and for rebellion against his sovereign; had he surrendered himself in the first place, he would surely have been spared.

For nine days the army rested at the capital of Drangiana; and then, with terrifying suddenness, occurred the downfall of Philotas, who had by now rejoined the army after the burial of his brother. The background of the affair perhaps requires some comment.

One of the King's main concerns had always been lest he lose the goodwill of the soldiers, the ultimate basis of his power. Hitherto, by his reckless personal courage, by his solicitude for the men's welfare, by large bonuses and, above all, by his uninterrupted course of success, Alexander had succeeded in retaining the loyalty and affection of the troops, while at the same time securing his ascendancy over the army commanders. But in many quarters, both among the rank and file and among the nobility, his assumption of Persian dress and habits was regarded in a most unfavourable light. Moreover, the soldiers had shown, after the death of Darius, their reluctance to continue further into the empire and their eagerness to go home. A dangerous situation might well arise, if a popular noble, who disapproved of the King's policies, should attempt to subvert the allegiance of the troops.

Now, the family of Parmenion had been the most powerful group in the army at the start of the Asiatic expedition. Recently, however, it had suffered a major setback, when Parmenion had been removed from his command and left in a less important position at Ecbatana. The death of Nicanor had further helped the dissolution of the Parmenion faction, leaving only Philotas and his jealous brother-in-law, Coenus, holding high commands in the field-army.

Parmenion, who had immense prestige, was popular with the army and must have felt disgruntled at his relegation, and was an obvious focal point to which discontented elements would look. Alexander realized this, but also saw that to attack the popular Parmenion directly would be a difficult matter. But things were different in the case of his son; for Philotas, an arrogant and boastful man, was not liked either by the soldiers or by his fellow-officers. Alexander had long ago realized that, if ever it became necessary to cross swords with Parmenion, the best way of attacking the general was through the person of his son; and since Egypt he had been receiving from the cavalry-leader's mistress a full record of all Philotas' conversations which contained anything that could be interpreted as treasonable. Now, with the discontent that existed among many of the soldiers and officers, Parmenion had become an even greater potential danger; and Alexander was waiting for some opportunity to present itself whereby he could bring about the downfall of Philotas and implicate the father also.

Such an opportunity occurred soon after Philotas had rejoined the army. Among the lesser courtiers was a certain Dimnus, who was deeply in love with a youth named Nicomachus. Dimnus, disgruntled because of some insult he had received from Alexander, entered into a plot with other discontented persons to assassinate Alexander. He disclosed the plot to Nicomachus and invited him to join the conspiracy.

Nicomachus at first protested that he would never join in regicide. But when Dimnus brought threats and entreaties to bear, he pretended to change his mind and said he would agree if the names of the other conspirators were disclosed to him. Dimnus then gave the names of seven others who were in the plot, amongst them Demetrius, one of the Bodyguards.

Whether this conspiracy was serious or whether it was merely the empty talk of a group of foolish young men, Nicomachus decided to take no chances. He immediately disclosed all he had heard to his brother Cebalinus. The two agreed that Cebalinus should report the plot, lest suspicions be raised among the conspirators if Nicomachus were seen lingering around the royal apartments.

Cebalinus, not having the right of access to the King, accosted Philotas outside the royal tent and told him all that his brother had related, begging Philotas to inform the King. Philotas obviously viewed the whole affair as the rash boasting of a lover to his beloved; however, he promised that the King would be told. When Philotas left the tent late that night, Cebalinus was still waiting outside for him, to

Persepolis. The Propylaea, main entrance hall to the Apadana Palace.

Alexander on Bucephelas. Bronze in the National Museum, Naples.

Persian soldiers, from the frieze at Persepolis. Now in the Louvre.

learn what Alexander had said. Philotas replied that Alexander had been too busy to talk with him, and that the matter would be raised the next day.

When the same thing happened the following day, Cebalinus decided to take his story elsewhere. The next person to whom he told it, a young noble named Metron, immediately took Cebalinus and disclosed everything to the King. Alexander's reaction was sharp: he ordered the arrest of Dimnus and then began to interrogate Cebalinus. When he learned that it was now two days since Cebalinus had heard of the plot from his brother, he became suspicious and ordered the arrest of Cebalinus also on the grounds of complicity in the plot. Cebalinus protested his innocence, crying that he had gone to Philotas as soon as his brother had told him; it was Philotas who was to blame for the delay in the disclosure of the conspiracy.

This piece of information gave Alexander the opportunity he wanted for dealing with Philotas and he gave orders that Philotas should come to the royal tent. Whilst he was waiting, Dimnus was brought in, close to death. He had, it was said, been wounded whilst resisting arrest. The King's words to the dying man were ominous: "What wrong so great have I perpetrated against you, Dimnus, that you thought *Philotas* more worthy of the Kingship of the Macedonians than I myself?" Dimnus, speechless because of his wound, was unable to contradict this amazing piece of deduction by the King; he died a few minutes later.

When Philotas was brought into the tent, he was immediately taxed with concealing the conspiracy. Philotas' reply was quite calm and composed: he had regarded the matter merely as a petty quarrel between Dimnus and his lover; but he agreed that the death of Dimnus made the matter look more serious than he had thought. He begged the King's forgiveness for his offence, which was, after all, one of omission rather than action. Alexander, to gain time to mature his plans and to lull Philotas into a state of false confidence, shook hands with the cavalry-leader as a sign that he was forgiven and restored to favour.

After Philotas had departed, the King called a meeting of his intimate friends and officers, all of whom disliked or were envious of Philotas. After Nicomachus had been made to repeat his story, Craterus, who had a special hatred for Philotas, gave it as his opinion that it was impossible to spare him. For Philotas' pride had been injured and now he and his father would always be seeking an opportunity to take revenge on Alexander; both father and son must be removed. Others added further reasons for such an action; all were in agreement on it.

Alexander now decided to arraign Philotas before the army—the usual Macedonian practice—on a charge of high treason. In view of Philotas' unpopularity, the outcome of the trial could hardly be held in doubt; once he had been condemned, the removal of Parmenion would be made much simpler. Absolute secrecy was necessary now, lest Philotas or any of his friends escape and carry the news to Parmenion at Ecbatana. That night, therefore, all the ways out of the camp were closed by cavalry pickets and a party of reliable men sent to arrest Philotas, who was aroused from sleep and put in irons.

The following morning the Macedonian soldiers were summoned to an assembly. Their mystification at the unusual summons was increased as the corpse of Dimnus was brought in. Then Alexander himself came forward and, after a long silence, addressed the soldiers. He stated that his life had been the object of a plot; that Parmenion was its originator, with Philotas as the agent of its execution. The informers were then brought in and made to repeat their tale, while the soldiers were digesting the amazing revelation.

When none of the conspirators named Philotas as an accomplice or instigator, the King assigned this to their fear of the man: they *dared* not name him, even when confessing their guilt. Several incidents in Philotas' career, innocent enough in themselves, were then raked up and given a sinister interpretation to show that Philotas and his father had long been hostile to Alexander. The King ended with an appeal to the soldiers, couched in such terms that it was obvious that their decision would amount to a vote of confidence in Alexander.

Philotas was then introduced in manacles. Despite the general's unpopularity, the sight of his present distress aroused the pity of the soldiers, both for him and for Parmenion. Perceiving this, Coenus, Philotas' own brother-in-law, jumped up and attacked him in violent language. His speech produced the desired effect among the soldiers; and it was only now that Philotas was given permission to speak in his own defence before the army passed judgement.

The speech of Philotas was distinguished by its dignity and contempt for the charges he was facing. He made it quite plain that he realized that the only conspiracy was against himself; and his logically presented arguments tore to shreds the whole flimsy structure of Alexander's accusations. He emphasized—which was true—that the only real charge that Alexander could lay against him was that he had not reported Cebalinus' story: and why, he asked, should he have taken notice of the tale of a mere boy, who could not even back it up with evidence?

Philotas' clear-headed eloquence was of no avail. An old officer, who had come up through the ranks and was imbued with a deep hatred of the hereditary nobility, whipped up feeling against him. The inflamed soldiers shouted out their condemnation of Philotas and the conspirators.

Philotas' execution—by stoning—was fixed for the next day. By Macedonian law Parmenion too was liable for execution now that his son had been convicted of treason. But such was the fame and popularity of the old general that the King decided to exact from Philotas a "confession" of his father's guilt, thus putting a more judicial face on the murder when it occurred. Thus, during the night before the execution, Philotas was put to the torture, among his chief tormentors being Craterus, Hephaestion and Coenus. He finally broke down and made up the required.confession, of which a written copy was made, implicating his father. The next day he and all the conspirators named by Dimnus were stoned to death. Only Demetrius, the Bodyguard, escaped this fate; and he was arrested soon after and deprived of his rank of Bodyguard. His position was filled by Ptolemy, son of Lagus.

Alexander now took advantage of his victory of the previous day to rid himself of another enemy—Alexander of Lyncestis, who had been dragged around in captivity for three years. He was brought before the army and charged with having designs on the King's life. When given the opportunity to speak, "although", says Curtius, "for three whole years he had practised his defence, yet hesitating and trembling he presented only a few words of what he had composed, and finally not only his memory but his thoughts too failed him".[10] As he stood there, bewildered, dazed and stammering, he was run through by the Bodyguards of the King with their sarissas.

Three close friends of Philotas—the sons of Andromenes, Amyntas, Attalus and Polemon—were also put on trial and narrowly escaped condemnation. Among the main charges against them were their friendship with the dead man and accusations which Olympias had been making for more than two years in her letters to the King. Amyntas was the main target of these accusations; he had earned himself the Queen mother's hatred when, on his recruiting mission to Macedonia in 332, he had exerted his powers and conscripted several of Olympias' favourites into the army. The brothers were saved by a sudden change of heart among the soldiers and perhaps also Alexander's fear of alienating the powerful Perdiccas, of whom Attalus was the brother-in-law. Amyntas, indeed, "gained nothing from his acquittal except to die with his reputation unstained",[11] for he was killed soon after in battle.

It now remained to deal with Parmenion. To anticipate any report of his son's death that might reach the old general, one of his closest friends, Polydamus, was entrusted with the task of hurrying across the Central Iranian desert with Parmenion's death warrant. To make sure of his good behaviour the King seized Polydamus' brothers to be held as hostages until the deed was done. Two sets of letters were given to Polydamus: one, written to Parmenion's deputies, contained instructions for their commander's murder; the other set included a letter from Alexander himself to Parmenion and another written in the name of Philotas to his father and sealed with Philotas' signet-ring. These two letters were intended to forestall any suspicions Parmenion might have about the unusual visit. The King knew he could rely on the obedience of Parmenion's senior officers, of whom Cleander was the brother of Coenus.

Using racing-camels, Polydamus and two native guides reached Ecbatana ten days later. Entering the city at night, Polydamus went first to Cleander and handed him his instructions. At daybreak Parmenion was informed that his old friend had arrived, bringing letters from the King and from his son. In great delight Parmenion, surrounded by his senior officers, all of whom had now received their orders from Cleander, went to meet Polydamus in the gardens of the Royal Residence. Polydamus, after greeting his friend, handed over the letters. As Parmenion broke the seal on the one purporting to be from his son, Cleander gave the signal and himself thrust his sword through the ribs of the unsuspecting old man, withdrew it and stabbed him in the throat. The other officers joined in, raining blow after blow, even after Parmenion was dead.

"Such was the end of Parmenion", says Curtius, "a man illustrious in war and peace . . . He satisfied a King who was most fortunate and who required that all things should match the greatness of his good fortune. At the age of seventy he fulfilled the duties of a leader in the prime of life and often even those of a common soldier; keen in counsel, vigorous in action, he was dear to the leading men and still more so to the common soldiers".[12] The soldiers of Parmenion, because of this affection, never forgot or forgave the murder of their general.

The King's associates in the destruction of the house of Parmenion all eventually received their rewards: at Ecbatana, Cleander took over the position of the man he had murdered in the field-army; Alexander decided to divide the Companion Cavalry into two *Hipparchies* (cavalry commands), each under its own Hipparch. Hephaestion received one division; as a concession to the older officers the other was given to Cleitus. Hephaestion, who had hitherto held no military command, thus emerges from this affair as one of the most senior officers in the army. Perdiccas, Craterus and the treacherous Coenus all reached the highest military positions in the next few years.

Alexander had every reason to feel pleased with himself. At one blow he had broken the power of the family of Parmenion for ever; he had secured from his soldiers a vote of confidence and could be sure of their allegiance again; and he had cowed—though, as it turned out, only temporarily—the opposition from certain quarters among the nobility to his assumption of a style appropriate to the Great King of Persia. Fortune had offered him, in the shape of Dimnus' conspiracy, an opening against Parmenion and Philotas. He had seized his chance and struck swiftly, decisively and hard. The execution of Philotas after a farce of a trial was a judicial murder; the killing of Parmenion was a purely political assassination and was carried out in the best traditions of an Oriental despot.

NOTES

1 Plutarch, *Alexander* 35
2 Curtius VI 5.11
3 Plutarch, *Alexander* 45
4 Arrian III 24.4
5 Curtius VI 5.23
6 Arrian III 42.1
7 Diodorus XVII 77.6
8 Cf. Plutarch, *Alexander* 45; Curtius VI 6.11
9 Curtius VI 7.26
10 Curtius VII 1.8
11 Arrian III 27.3
12 Curtius VII 2.33 (Loeb translation)

12

The Conquest of the Far East (1)

After refounding the satrapal seat of Aria as an Alexandria, with the distinguishing title of Prophthasia, or "Anticipation"—an allusion to the detection there and suppression of Philotas' "conspiracy"—the King led his army along the course of the River Helmand into the satrapy of Arachosia (roughly modern Baluchistan). As was stated earlier (see Chapter XI p. 159), though his main objective was the capture of Bessus and the reduction of the eastern satrapies of Bactria and Sogdiana, he wished to avoid having to retrace his steps back to the River Murghab (where he had begun the southward sweep into Drangiana) by approaching the areas from the south. In terms of distance and terrain, the journey would be longer and more difficult; but this would be compensated by the facts that the large south-eastern bastion of Arachosia would meet its new King, and that a drive from the south would mean that Bessus could only retreat northwards or eastwards into the steppes.

Bessus was positioned at Tashkurgan, called Aornus—"the birdless place"—by the Greeks. With him he had 7,000 Bactrians and a force of the nomad Dahae who dwelt south of the River Jaxartes (the Syr Dar'ya). Also under his nominal command were several of the great barons of Bactria and Sogdiana, chief among whom were Spitamenes and Oxyartes. These two were to form the backbone of the war of resistance against the invader—a war which was to occupy him for two campaigning seasons and to cause him some of the most difficult fighting of his career. A brief description of the areas and their peoples will not be out of place, to explain the nature of the fighting of the next two years.

The satrapy of Bactria comprised roughly the rugged mountain-area to the north of the Hindu Kush, bounded by the River Oxus (Amu Dar'ya); its satrapal seat was at Bactria (modern Balkh). Sogdiana comprised the area bounded in the south by the River Oxus, in the north by the great eastern sweep of the Jaxartes. Mountainous in the south, it opens out into the vast level steppes in the north; its satrapal seat was at Samarkand, later to be the capital of Tamerlane and his Mongol empire. The peoples of both satrapies were Iranians, organized in a feudal system. The great nobles or barons prized highly their independence and only grudgingly had acknowledged the over-lordship of the Persian King. This latter had been an Iranian; but Alexander was an absolute foreigner and as such he was met with an opposition similar to that which opposed the French in Spain under Napoleon.

As in the Spanish peninsula, the fragmented state of Bactrian and Sogdianian society determined the character of the resistance to Alexander; in Bactria it took the form of mountain guerilla warfare; in Sogdiana, the "hit and run" warfare of the desert and steppes. In the words of Major-General Fuller: "No great battles awaited Alexander; he was to be faced by a people's war, a war of mounted guerillas who, when he advanced, would suddenly appear in his rear, who entrenched themselves on inaccessible crags, and when pursued vanished into the Turkoman steppes. To overrun such a theatre of war and subdue such an enemy demanded generalship of the highest order, much higher than needed against an organized enemy on the Plains."[1]

Much of the journey through Arachosia was made in deep snow, an indication that the campaigning season was far advanced. It was during this march that news was brought of the revolt of Satibarzanes in Aria, described in the previous chapter, which was only brought to a conclusion after the aged Erigyius had killed Satibarzanes in single combat. That Arachosia was far from subdued seems to be indicated from the appointment of a Macedonian, Menon, as satrap of the country and the foundation of a garrison-city there called Alexandria of the Arachosians, perhaps the modern Kandahar.[2] The time of year was now early November, but wishing to advance as far as possible before taking up winter-quarters, Alexander pushed on up the valley of the Tarnak River, passed the site of the modern Ghazni and then followed the natural road (which is nowadays the main arterial road) up the Kabul valley, where he took up winter-quarters (mid-December) at the southern foot of the Hindu Kush.

Early in the spring, 329, the army began the crossing of the Hindu Kush. Deep snow still lay in the passes, and Curtius gives vivid details of the sufferings of the troops from frostbite, snow-blindness and fatigue.[3] In the district known as the Paropamisadae (roughly the Afghanistan province of Parwan) another Alexandria was founded, with the distinguishing title "of the Caucasus" (this being the ancient name for the Hindu Kush, which was believed to be a continuation of the range in Asia Minor). Its settlers—and garrison—were taken from the Greek mercenaries with the army, and 7,000 of the local inhabitants were permitted to join the foundation. The site of the city was probably at the junction of the Ghorband and Panjshir rivers. A Persian satrap and a Macedonian military officer were left in charge of the district.

It is here that the modern road to Tashkurgan swings westwards at an acute angle to skirt the high mountains, turning northwards again along the valley of the Darri-i-Shikkar River. The ancient route across the Hindu Kush into Bactria seems to have followed the same course. Alexander however struck eastwards along the valley of the Panjshir River and crossed the high mountains by the Khawak Pass, which leads into the fertile Anderab valley. The route taken was a little longer than the regular westward track, but this was compensated for by its lower altitude (11,600 feet). The River Darri-i-Shillar runs through the length of Anderab and Alexander followed its course westwards as far as Doshi, where the modern road meets the river. From here he headed northwards along the Surkhab River and took what is now the eastern fork of the modern road, ending up at Kunduz, about eighty miles east of Tashkurgan in the valley of the Oxus. Bessus, who had ravaged the lowlands on the north side of the Hindu Kush to stop Alexander's advance, thus found his position turned from the east and no longer tenable as a result of the invader's skilful and rapid marching. He therefore decided to evacuate Tashkurgan and accompanied by Spitamenes and Oxyartes, together with a large force of cavalry, crossed the Oxus into Sogdiana, leaving Bactria to Alexander; they hoped that the Macedonian would be tempted by the riches of India to go southwards after occupying Bactria.

Tashkurgan and Bactra, the capital, easily fell into the King's hands. A garrison was left in the former; the aged and devoted Artabazus was made satrap of the whole Bactrian province. From Bactra the army moved northwards towards the River Oxus, in pursuit of Bessus. It was now mid-summer and the desert heat was unbearable. The army suffered greatly from thirst and marched by night. When the Oxus

was reached many men died from immoderate drinking of its water
in the attempt to assuage their thirst. The river is about three quarters
of a mile wide at Kelif, the army's crossing point, and there were in
the region neither boats nor timber with which to build bridges. The
soldiers were ordered to make watertight mattresses from their tent
covers, filled with dry chaff, and using these as coracles the whole
force crossed the river in five days. Before the crossing a large number
of older Macedonian troops, together with the volunteers of the former
Thessalian cavalry, were given their discharge and sent home. The
Cyprian Stasanor was also sent to Aria to replace the Persian Arsames
as satrap.

After crossing the river into Sogdiana, Alexander continued his
pursuit of Bessus, when an astonishing piece of news was brought.
Dissensions between Bessus and his followers, caused perhaps by local
jealousies, perhaps by a desire to put an end to the war, had resulted in a
conspiracy headed by Spitamenes, which had toppled Bessus from
power. Spitamenes now sent a messenger to Alexander saying that he
would surrender Bessus, if a Macedonian officer and a small force were
sent to take him. Spitamenes thus hoped to guard against a surprise
attack by Alexander which might result in the capture of his own
person. The King, delighted at the news but suspecting in turn a trap,
sent Ptolemy (son of Lagus), recently created a Bodyguard, to carry
out the mission with a force that amounted to at least 1,600 cavalry and
4,000 infantry.

Ptolemy himself tells the story of his capture of Bessus.[3] In four days,
he says, he and his force covered a distance equivalent to ten days'
marching in order to reach the place where Spitamenes had Bessus in
custody. On arriving at the place he found that Spitamenes and his
associates, perhaps alarmed at the size of Ptolemy's force and perhaps
made unwilling by their consciences to hand over Bessus to the enemy
themselves, had departed the previous day and at a village a short
distance away had deserted Bessus, leaving him under the protection—
or custody—of a few soldiers. Ptolemy pressed on with his cavalry,
and forming a cordon round the village, issued a proclamation to those
within, offering immunity if they handed over Bessus. The former
Bactrian satrap and self-styled Persian King was surrendered to Ptolemy,
who sent to Alexander for further instructions.

Alexander replied that Bessus was to be brought in to him in fetters,
naked and wearing a wooden collar—the mark of a slave; he was to be
stationed at the side of the road where Alexander and the army would

pass. Alexander, on seeing Bessus, stopped the chariot in which he had taken to riding, and asked the unfortunate man why he had killed Darius. Bessus replied that it had been done to win Alexander's pardon and that he had not been alone in the act. Alexander then gave the order that Bessus be flogged and sent to Bactria, to be dealt with later.

This is Ptolemy's version of the capture; Aristobulus gives a completely different picture, stating that it was Spitamenes and his chief associate, Dataphernes, who brought Bessus in to the King, leading him naked, in fetters and with the wooden collar around his neck. To the collar was attached a chain, by which Spitamenes dragged along his prisoner. Spitamenes was received by Alexander with high praise for his conduct.[4]

During this time, the cavalry horses lost in the crossing of the Hindu Kush were replaced by native Sogdianian mounts, much larger and stronger than the horses of the Greeks and Macedonians. It was also during this pursuit of Bessus that there is said to have occurred the massacre of the Branchidae, a story not found in Arrian and rejected by some writers as an invention of Callisthenes.[5] The Branchidae, a priestly family group from Miletus, are said to have violated the temple of Apollo in that city to win the favour of Xerxes at the beginning of the fifth century. When Xerxes returned from his Hellenic expedition, he took the Branchidae with him and settled them in Bactria, where they had so multiplied that their descendants now formed a small town. When Alexander came to this town, he is said to have asked the Milesians with him what they wished him to do with these Branchidae. They were divided in their opinions, so the King took matters into his own hands and ordered the destruction of the town and the massacre of every one of its inhabitants. "If", says Curtius, "this had been designed against the actual authors of the treason, it would seem to have been a just vengeance, and not cruelty; as it was, their descendants expiated the guilt of their fore-fathers, although they themselves had never seen Miletus, and so could not have betrayed it to Xerxes".[6] It may be observed that the absence of the story in Arrian does not necessarily invalidate it; for it reflects badly on Alexander and for that reason might well have been passed over by Ptolemy and Aristobulus, Arrian's sources.

After the capture of Bessus, Alexander pushed on to the Sogdianian satrapal residence of Samarkand. From here he advanced to the River Jaxartes (Syr Dar'ya), the farthest point northwards in the empire. He was now beating the marches of his realm and inspecting its frontier defences against the Sacae nomads who lived across the river. The main Persian frontier-post in this area was a garrison-town called by the Greeks Cyropolis, the city of Cyrus, by whom it had been founded 300 years before. Cyropolis was situated near where the Jaxartes swings eastwards and connected with that river by a chain of seven fortresses. All these Alexander garrisoned by detachments of mercenaries.

But as soon as the King's back was turned, whilst he was on the Jaxartes planning the building of a new city as a bulwark against the nomadic Sacae across the river, a fierce revolt broke out along the length of Sogdiana. The surrender of Bessus had lulled the King into a false sense of security. He thought that Sogdiana and its leaders were reconciled to the new ruler, when in fact, they were merely weary of the Bactrian Bessus and hoped that by his surrender they would obtain immunity for their country. But Alexander had invaded Sogdiana and had shown that he intended to exert a close control on it; moreover, he had issued instructions for the Sogdianian barons to come to meet him at a convention at which, they believed, hostages would be taken for their good behaviour and new laws of subjection imposed on them. The leading spirit in the revolt was Spitamenes. It was well organized: Cyropolis and the seven outposts rose and massacred their garrisons, while Spitamenes and a large force began the siege of Samarkand.

Alexander knew nothing of the extent of the revolt, only that the frontier-posts were again in enemy hands and that they had to be recaptured quickly, since there were signs of a growing threat from the tribesmen across the river. Craterus, with a large force, was instructed to lay siege to Cyropolis, the centre of the revolt in that area, and so prevent it sending help to, or receiving refugees from, the other fortresses; these the King intended to deal with in person. In three days of savage fighting five of the seven forts were recaptured and their occupants either butchered, in the case of the men, or enslaved, in the case of the women.

Leaving the remaining two forts for the moment, Alexander returned to Cyropolis, which Craterus had now surrounded with a ditch and a stockade. At least 15,000 fighting men were collected in the town, which, being fortified by a high wall, promised to cause the besiegers considerable toil in the recapturing. Luckily it was observed that a stream, which ran through the town in the rainy season but was now only a dried up channel, had left a narrow gap under the walls, large enough to permit the passage into the city of armed men. Accordingly, Craterus was ordered to assault the walls on one side of the town with the siege-engines, and whilst the occupants were engaged in repelling Craterus, Alexander slipped through the channel into the town with a few men, opened the gates on his side of the town and admitted the Hypaspists, archers and Agrianians. The besieged, when they saw this, turned and made a desperate attack on Alexander's force, in which Alexander himself was struck violently on the neck with a boulder. Meanwhile the main force assaulted the wall at the other side and the town was taken. 8,000 of the enemy perished in the assault; the remaining 7,000 took refuge in a citadel at the town's centre, where they were reduced to submission, after a day's blockade, through the torments of thirst. Curtius says that the town was razed to the ground;[7] the fate of the captured men was not recorded, but was doubtless the same as that of the occupants of the two remaining fortresses, which were now easily captured. Aristobulus says that these were all put to death; Ptolemy says that they were all put under guard till Alexander left the area.[8]

The savage brutality of the King in the retaking of these forts may have been due to a situation that was growing increasingly ugly. For the Sacae across the river, learning of the revolt, had gathered in large numbers on the banks of the Jaxartes, ready to cross and attack the Macedonians in the rear. At the same time the news came through that Spitamenes was besieging the garrison of Samarkand. Either the size of Spitamenes' force was minimized in the report, or Alexander himself did not fully appreciate the extent and seriousness of the revolt; at any rate, a totally inadequate force was sent to the relief of Samarkand: 60 Companion Cavalry; 800 mercenary cavalry; and 1,500 mercenary infantry. A further mistake was made in the command of this force; three Macedonian officers were put in command of the detachments and a Lycian interpreter, Pharnuches, who was well-acquainted with the country and its language, was assigned to the party in some vague supervisory capacity—so vague that the three Macedonians refused to acknowledge his superiority. It would seem, in fact, that in giving the Lycian this important post Alexander was hoping that Spitamenes could be brought into line by diplomacy rather than naked force.

Alexander himself spent three weeks on the banks of the Jaxartes in building the wall of the new city he had decided to found there. It was called Alexandria Eschatē (Alexandria the Farthest, now perhaps Leninobad in the Soviet province of Tadzhikistan); its inhabitants were Greek mercenaries, time-expired Macedonians and native volunteers.

The Greeks and Macedonians, it will be seen, in all the settlements in the Far East can rarely be called volunteers.

All the while that the city was being built, the Sacae nomads across the river, which was not broad at that point, kept up a continuous barrage of insults, challenging Alexander to cross over and find out how the "Scythians" differed from the barbarians of Asia. It was against the looting raids of these nomads that the city was being raised up; and now, decided the King, provoked into deep anger by their insults and belief in their impunity, was a good moment to teach them the length and strength of the arm of the new Great King. He was still without boats, and so gave orders for the stuffed hides to be prepared for the crossing of the river; and such was his determination to punish the insults he had received that he continued with the enterprise even after Aristander had given repeated warnings of unfavourable omens.

When all was ready for the crossing and the troops were lined upon the banks, the artillery was trained upon the Sacae and several volleys were fired. The Sacae had never encountered artillery before and were somewhat perturbed, especially when a long dart pierced one of their chieftains through his shield and corselet and struck him dead from his horse. When they retired from the rain of missiles, Alexander sounded the advance. The archers and slingers crossed first and then protected the phalanx as it crossed. Last of all the cavalry passed over the stream.

The ensuing operations are well analysed by Fuller.[9] The usual tactics of the nomads was to ride round the enemy in a circle, shooting from the saddle and retreating when the enemy made a counter-attack. Alexander's problem was to draw the Sacae into a position where he could come to close quarters with his heavy cavalry. He thus threw forward a weak cavalry force (mercenaries and Prodromi) against the Sacae, who at once began to encircle it and shoot their arrows. Alexander then advanced a screen of light missile troops to hem the Sacae in between them and the forward cavalry force. Next three squadrons of Companions and the mounted javelin-men were sent forward to attack the Sacae from the flanks. The result of these manoeuvres was that a large body of Sacae were trapped between the first group of cavalry, the light infantry and the enflanking cavalry. Alexander then brought up his main body of cavalry, passed through the light infantry, charged and cut down the enclosed Sacae to the number of a thousand. The rest of the Sacae turned in flight and were hotly pursued by Alexander. The pursuit must have been extensive, since during the course of it the King contracted violent diarrhoea—perhaps gastro-enteritis—from drinking tainted water.

"The tactics of the battle," says Fuller, "are full of interest, as they show the fertility of Alexander's mind when faced with a new tactical problem".[10] For this was the first time the King had encountered the desert tactics of the nomads, and yet he had immediately recognized the dangers they involved and taken the necessary measures, not only to counter, but also to defeat them. Nearly 300 years later the Roman Licinius Crassus was to show what could happen to a merely competent commander against such tactics, when his army was annihilated by the Parthians at Carrhae. Certainly Alexander made a tremendous impression on the Scythians. For the ruler of the tribe across the river sent a delegation expressing his regret for the actions of his fellow-nomads and dissociating himself and his people from their attack; the men Alexander had fought, he said, were nothing but brigands in search of booty. Alexander, who had not the time to engage in a long drawn-out campaign with the nomads, pretended to believe the Scythian's story and to be mollified by the explanation.

Meanwhile the relief-force under Pharnuches was approaching Samarkand. Spitamenes withdrew from the siege and made a feint towards the second town of Sogdiana, Bukhara, on the River Polytimetus (Zarafshen). This river formed the north-western frontier of the satrapy; beyond it lived the Massagetae, a Saca people. Pharnuches, instead of securing Samarkand, pursued Spitamenes, hoping thus to carry off the glory of putting an end to the war in Sogdiana. The chase carried both Spitamenes and his pursuers across the Polytimetus into Massagetic territory—whither the crafty Sogdianian had intended all the time to lure the Macedonians. Pharnuches foolishly authorized an attack on some of the Massagetae, who promptly lent their weight to Spitamenes.

As Pharnuches and his men pressed on ahead through the desert, Spitamenes, now reinforced by 600 of the Massagetic horsemen, drew up his men on the level ground ahead. As the Macedonians drew near, the Sogdianian and Scythian cavalry began their deadly encirclement, wheeling round and shooting volley after volley of arrows into the defenceless infantry. When the Macedonian cavalry, weary from its long hot journey, charged, Spitamenes escaped with ease and then returned to the attack. "Whether they stood their ground or withdrew", says Arrian, "the Scythians pressed them strongly".[11]

At this juncture the Macedonian commanders decided to retreat to the Polytimetus, near which was a woody glen where the Scythians could no longer ride round them. Forming a hollow square, they began to withdraw; but as they approached the river Caranus, the cavalry commander, pressed on to try to cross. The infantry, fearing that they were being deserted by the protecting cavalry, panicked, broke ranks and fled after them. A general massacre ensued. For Spitamenes' men were now on both sides of the river and shot or cut down the unfortunate Macedonians as they were entering the water, as they were crossing the river, and as they were staggering out on to the Sogdianian bank. Not one man escaped death.

Aristobulus gives a variant to this version, which comes from Ptolemy. He says that Spitamenes and the Massagetae ambushed the relief-force in a park (perhaps some nobleman's residence near Bukhara), when a violent dispute was in progress among the Macedonian commanders—Pharnuches wishing to relinquish the command to the Macedonian officers, they refusing to accept it because all the blame would fall on them in the event of a defeat. Aristobulus maintains, also, that forty cavalry and about 300 infantry made their escape.[12]

Whichever version is correct, the fact still remains that the Macedonians had suffered a severe defeat and set-back at the hands of Spitamenes. It was the first—and the last—major defeat that Alexander ever suffered. The blame must obviously be set immediately on the incompetence of Pharnuches, but ultimately on Alexander himself both for sending an inadequate relief-force and for giving it such an ill-defined command.

Spitamenes immediately returned to the siege of Samarkand, where the garrison still held out in the citadel. When the news reached Alexander he realized fully for the first time how dangerous an enemy Spitamenes was. Taking half the Companions and a picked infantry force he marched at top speed towards Samarkand. It is said that he covered the distance—nearly 150 miles—in three days and nights. On his approach Spitamenes fled, realizing that this time he would be faced with a more able foe. Alexander pressed him hard as far as the desert across the Polytimetus; then, returning to the battle-field he buried the dead soldiers of Pharnuches. To form a *cordon sanitaire* to the west of Samarkand, he ravaged the countryside along the length of the Polytimetus valley. Spitamenes and the Massagetae would thus be unable to obtain fodder for their horses and provisions for themselves, if they were to attack Samarkand during the approaching winter.

Both parties now went into winter-quarters, Spitamenes at Bukhara and Alexander at Bactra. Both had reason to feel some satisfaction with the campaigning of 329; Alexander had rapidly overrun Bactria and held the Sogdianian capital of Samarkand, together with a chain of strongly fortified and defended garrisons in the far north of the satrapy; Spitamenes had harassed Alexander severely during the summer, was still in undisputed possession of the large part of Sogdiana, and had completely destroyed a powerful Macedonian force.

At Bactra, during the winter of 329-8, the Great King held court. Satraps and officials came from as far away as Syria and Asia Minor, among them Nearchus, who now relinquished his satrapy of Lycia. Nearchus was placed in command of one of the battalions of the Hypaspists. Reinforcements of Greek mercenaries were also brought up from the sea-coast; the Macedonian royal army was rapidly becoming a mercenary-force with a small nucleus of native Macedonians.

Bessus was now brought out of captivity. Several of his partisans had already been brought into court and punished. Condemned of treachery towards Darius—and probably too of rebellion against Darius' successor—Bessus was first mutilated by having his nose and ears cut off and then sent to Ecbatana to be executed in the approved manner at a full gathering of the nobility of the Medes and Persians. Alexander's modern biographer attempted to excuse the King's cruelty;[13] but Arrian is less partial and not afraid to speak the truth: "I do not praise this excessive punishment of Bessus; I consider that the mutilation of the extremities was barbaric and I acknowledge that Alexander was seduced to an imitation of the Median and Persian wealth and of the overbearing way that barbarian monarchs have of conducting themselves towards their subjects".[14]

That same winter saw two interesting embassies to Alexander at Bactra. One came from the nomadic Scythians dwelling to the north of the Caspian, to whom Alexander had already sent ambassadors on his first arrival at the Jaxartes. The Scythian ruler gave an offer of friendship and alliance to Alexander and the readiness to acknowledge his suzerainty; to prove his sincerity, he wished Alexander to marry his daughter, or any other noble Scythian lady he might wish. These Scythians were too far away to present any real threat to his domains, and so Alexander courteously refused the offer. Scythian princesses were renowned for their virtue; but, in pastoral simplicity, they ate rancid butter, dried horse flesh, and were little addicted to personal hygiene.

The other embassy came from and included Pharasmenes, the ruler

Alexander (*above*) and Darius (*below*) at the Battle of Issus. Details from a mosaic found at Pompeii and now in the National Museum, Naples.

The "sarcophagus of Alexander", found at Sayda and now in the Archaeological Museum, Istanbul.

The simple tomb of Cyrus at Pasargadae.

of the Chorasmians, a people who dwelt between the Massagetae and the Aral Sea. The purpose of Pharasmenes' visit seems to have been to attempt to win Macedonian military support in crushing the territories bordering on Chorasmia; and the King held out to Alexander lavish baits of territorial gains and strong support for an expeditionary force. He was doomed to failure. Poor interpreting and an even poorer knowledge of the geography of Central Asia gave Alexander the impression that Pharasmenes lived on the coast of the Black Sea and wanted Alexander to lead a military expedition there. Thanking Pharasmenes for his offers and making a formal alliance with him, Alexander courteously dismissed the King, saying the time was not convenient for an expedition to the Black Sea. When he was master of all Asia, he continued, he would return to Greece and from there would make a full-scale expedition to the Black Sea; then would be the time for Pharasmenes to fulfil his promises. But, he said, before he could become truly Lord of all Asia, he must first go to India and subdue that country. Pharasmenes departed, and Alexander prepared for the coming campaigning season and the thorough reduction of Sogdiana. Then and only then would the way be open for the proposed invasion of India.

NOTES

1   J. F. C. Fuller, *Generalship* p.117
2   Curtius VII 3.12ff.
3   At Arrian III 29.7ff.
4   Arrian III 30.5; cf. Curtius VII 5.36ff.
5   W. W. Tarn, *Alexander the Great* vol. II 272–4
6   Curtius VII 5.35 (Loeb translation); for the Branchidae story cf. Strabo XVII 143.
7   Curtius VII 6.23
8   At Arrian IV 3.5
9   Fuller, *Generalship* 238ff.
10 Op. cit. 241
11 Arrian IV 5.5
12 At Arrian IV 6.1ff.
13 Tarn, *Alexander the Great* I 70; *Cambridge Ancient History* VI 394
14 Arrian IV 7.4

13

The Conquest of the Far East (2)

As soon as the campaigning season of 328 began Alexander made his way back towards Sogdiana, where Spitamenes had been engaged during the winter in intensifying the native opposition to the King. As trouble was also feared among the people of Bactria, Craterus was left behind with four battalions of the phalanx. At the crossing of the Oxus Ptolemy relates how a spring of water and another of oil were discovered near the King's tent. When the King reported this portent to Aristander, the seer interpreted the spring of oil as a sign of labours to come, with victory to follow the labours. It is thought that the spring of oil was petroleum.

After crossing the river, the army was divided into five columns, one of which was commanded by Alexander himself. These columns swept the plains to the north of the satrapy, destroying pockets of resistance and local strongholds. These extensive operations are described very summarily by Arrian,[1] but they must have included the establishment at strategic points of fortified posts, which would hamper the mobility of Spitamenes; Strabo mentions eight such military establishments in Bactria and Sogdiana, while Justin gives as many as twelve.[2] It was also perhaps at this time that the six "cities" mentioned by Curtius were founded in the area to the west of Sogdiana and Bactria known as Margiana. Curtius' description indicates that they were military posts: "they were distant from one another only a moderate space, so that they might be able to aid one another without seeking help from a distance. All these were situated upon high hills. At that time they served as curbs upon the conquered nations; today, forgetful of their origin, they serve those over whom they once ruled".³ Curtius' reference here is to Rome's great enemy, the Parthian empire.

The columns reunited about mid-summer at Samarkand. From here Hephaestion, according to Arrian, was sent to plant settlements in the "cities" of Sogdiana;⁴ perhaps he was to make a tour of the military posts with a view to inviting local co-operation in joining the settlement. Coenus, together with Artabazus, was despatched northwards. Spitamenes had avoided contact with the Macedonians up to this time; now the report came in that he had taken refuge with the Massagetae and Coenus was sent to deal with him. It was during the period when the army was reunited at Samarkand that Alexander's quarrel with and murder of Cleitus, the Hipparch, occurred; the incident which led to the quarrel shows that the recent operations in Sogdiana had not been uniformly successful (see next chapter).

The report that Spitamenes had taken refuge with the Massagetae was correct, but out of date when Alexander despatched Coenus against him. For Spitamenes, having raised a force of 600 cavalry among the nomads, had made a flying descent southwards, avoiding Alexander's military posts, and suddenly appeared on the Sogdianian-Bactrian border at the very moment when Coenus was heading in the opposite direction.

The nomads surprised and stormed the garrison of one of the Bactrian border-fortresses, killing all the soldiers and taking the commandant prisoner. Then a few days later they appeared in front of Bactra, where, not feeling strong enough to assault the city, they contented themselves with plundering the neighbouring countryside.

Bactra, at this time, was very weakly garrisoned, Craterus and his four battalions of the phalanx being on patrol elsewhere. There were in the town only a few troopers of the Companion Cavalry, left behind on account of ill-health but now recovered, some Royal Pages, and a detachment of mercenary cavalry. The senior officer present, a Macedonian named Peithon, assembled this force and made a surprise attack on the Massagetae as they were driving off their booty. Falling upon the unsuspecting nomads, they put them to flight and recovered the booty. But on the way back a spirit of indiscipline set in among the triumphant cavalry and Spitamenes and his Massagetae, determined not to lose their booty, caught them in an ambush, in which nearly seventy troopers were killed and Peithon taken alive. This was the second time that Spitamenes had cut to pieces an undisciplined Macedonian force.

When this disaster was reported to Craterus, he hastened towards Bactra. The Massagetae retreated towards the desert on his approach, but Craterus, who must have had a considerable detachment of cavalry in addition to his phalanx battalions, pressed them hard. The Massagetae, reinforced by their fellow-countrymen to over a thousand in number, were forced to join battle with the Macedonians. Arrian says that the Macedonians were victorious, but only 150 of the nomads were killed, the rest escaping into the desert.[5]

The campaigning season was now drawing to a close, and Spitamenes was still at large. Alexander decided to rest the main body of the army at Nautaca in Sogdiana during the cold weather, with the intention of making a winter-campaign to complete the reduction of the satrapy before the next campaigning season got under way. He had now been in the north-eastern satrapies for two campaigning seasons—much longer than he had anticipated—and was impatient of spending a third season there before he could begin the next adventure, the invasion of India. The recent disaster at Bactra and the unsettled state of the satrapy produced a change in policy; Artabazus was relieved of his office—officially on the grounds of old age—and replaced by a Macedonian, Amyntas, son of Nicolaus. Military operations against the marauding Spitamenes were to be kept up whilst the army rested. Coenus was given the unenviable task of supervising operations against the Sogdianian noble and his nomad followers. For this he was given two battalions of the phalanx and a large force of cavalry, of whom, significantly, the majority were Iranians, including Bactrians and Sogdianians who had given their allegiance to the new Great King; these were now to be used against the man who was fighting to keep their country free from the foreign invader.

As for Spitamenes and his supporters, they were increasingly being harried by a network of fortified posts established throughout Sogdiana and by the presence of Coenus' force. Deprived of bases and means of provisioning and replacing their horses, they decided on a desperate attempt to break the stranglehold. Holding out the attractive prospect of plunder, they persuaded nearly 3,000 of the Massagetae to join them in an invasion of Sogdiana from the north-western corner of the satrapy.

The news of Spitamenes' approach was just what Coenus had been hoping for and he advanced to meet the rebel leader. In a fierce battle Coenus showed that he had learned well from his own experiences and those of his King how to counter the nomads' method of fighting. The

tribesmen were routed, with losses of over 800. The Sogdianian supporters of Spitamenes deserted him during the engagement and went
over to join Coenus and their fellow-countrymen. Their personal
effects, which they had been forced to leave behind, were seized as
plunder by the Massagetae, who fled, accompanied by Spitamenes, into
the desert. The defeat shattered the influence that Spitamenes had
gained among his people. Now deserted by his own countrymen, he
was seized by his former allies when it was reported that Coenus was
intending to press on in pursuit. He was treacherously killed and his
head cut off and sent by the Massagetae to Alexander as a conciliatory
offering.

Curtius gives an alternative version of the death of Spitamenes,
though he too places it among the nomads. According to this version
the murderer was Spitamenes' own wife, who, weary of the continual
flight and danger, tried to persuade her husband to throw himself on
Alexander's mercy. Spitamenes, a jealous man, suspected that his own
wife, who was very beautiful, had formed the design of winning the
King's goodwill towards herself by bestowing her favours on him. In
a rage, he banished her from his sight and began to sleep with concubines. Soon, however, he returned to his wife, with whom he was
deeply in love, though refusing to entertain thoughts of surrender.
The cunning woman pretended compliance; but one evening after
Spitamenes had drunk too heavily at dinner and was lying asleep in
their bedroom, she cut off his head with a sword. Accompanied by a
slave, who was carrying this grisly trophy, she came to Alexander.
Thereupon, the King, reflecting that the woman had rid him of a great
enemy, but repelled by the crime, ordered her to leave the camp,
"lest she might bring this example of barbarian lawlessness into the
ways and gentle dispositions of the Greeks".[6] Curtius adds the detail
that the nomads, on learning of the death of Spitamenes, surrendered to
Alexander his chief lieutenant, Dataphernes, and thus won pardon for
themselves.

Spitamenes has perhaps correctly been described as "the best
opponent Alexander met";[7] he was certainly the most successful. He
was the only man to inflict a major defeat on the Macedonian forces
and for two whole years he tied up in Bactria and Sogdiana an army
many times the size of his own irregular forces. In this respect his
career may be compared with those of the Spanish guerilla leaders in
the war against the armies of Napoleon. But whereas these latter had
the backing of a well supplied and well disciplined British army to take

advantage of the demoralization and confusion caused by their activities, Spitamenes, though fighting to free his country from a foreign ruler, could only find support in large numbers among the nomad tribesmen across the Oxus and Jaxartes—men whose only motive for lending their support was a desire for plunder. Whether Alexander would have granted him his life, if he had surrendered, is doubtful; for the man was too competent and too dangerous. But with the convenient death of Spitamenes Alexander could afford to be magnanimous towards his relatives, of whom his daughter, Apama, four years later was married to Seleucus, one of the most senior Macedonian officers.

With the death of Spitamenes all resistance in the plain-land of Sogdiana died out. The mountainous region in the south of the satrapy, known as Paraetacene, still required reduction, since there were four of the most powerful of the local barons—Oxyartes, Chorienes, Catanes and Austanes—still in arms. After making several administrative arrangements, including the replacement of the Median satrap for alleged ill-will towards the King, the appointment of another Persian to Babylonia to take the place of Mazaeus, whose death was now reported, and the despatch of three officers to Macedonia for reinforcements, Alexander, early in 327 B.C., led out the army from its winter-quarters at Nautaca against these four rebels.

Oxyartes was the first to face the army's advance. On top of a precipitous mountain he had a fortified stronghold to which he had conveyed his family and many of his retainers; Oxyartes himself was not in the "Sogdianian Rock" (as the stronghold was known) at this time. The fortress was surrounded on all sides by sheer cliffs and was well stocked with provisions to face a long siege. Moreover, heavy snow fell at this time, which was a great hindrance to the Macedonians, but a source of abundant water to the rebels. There can be little wonder that the rebels had such faith in their position that, when Alexander offered them a free pardon if they submitted, they laughed and bade him find himself winged soldiers, since these alone would trouble them.

Alexander had learned much from his two years of fighting in the mountains of Bactria and Sogdiana, and there were in the army a large number of men skilled in rock-climbing. Selecting 300 of these, and stimulating them with the promise of liberal rewards, the King ordered them to be issued with metal tent-pegs and strong ropes. The party set out at the dead of night and began their perilous climb in pitch darkness up the sheerest—and hence least guarded—face of the rock. The tent-pegs were used as crampons, being driven into the rock-face and the frozen snow, and the men pulled themselves up with the ropes. About thirty men perished in the ascent, losing their hold and crashing to a horrible death on the rocks below. But the remaining 270 gained the summit, which overlooked the Sogdianian stronghold, and at dawn signalled to the Macedonian camp. Alexander then sent an envoy to the Rock, bidding the tribesmen to turn and look at his "Flying Soldiers" and to surrender themselves.

Oxyartes' followers were deeply impressed by this superb piece of "commando" warfare and thought in their amazement that the "Flying Soldiers" were far more numerous than 270. Therefore they agreed to Alexander's demand for their surrender. Among the family of Oxyartes captured there was Roxane, one of his daughters—"a maiden of remarkable beauty of person and of a dignity of bearing uncommon among barbarians",[8] and generally agreed by those who served with Alexander to be the most beautiful woman in Asia, now that Darius' wife was dead. Romantic tradition makes the King fall so deeply in love with the girl that he asked for her hand in marriage. He certainly did marry her, but equally certainly not from love. As one writer says, "it is doubtful if he ever cared for any woman except his terrible mother",[9] and Roxane only became pregnant in the last year of Alexander's life. It was a marriage of policy, intended as a gesture of goodwill towards the great barons of the Far Eastern satrapies, with the object of bringing a rapid end to the warfare of the last two years. Much secret resentment was provoked among the Macedonian nobility; but the policy paid off, since Oxyartes, on hearing of the King's intentions towards his daughter, came of his own free will to Alexander and surrendered himself. His son-in-law accorded to him every mark of honour and friendship.

Alexander now moved on against Chorienes, who also had a fortified mountain stronghold, perhaps in the neighbourhood of Faizabad in the Afghan province of Badakhshan. The mountain itself was said to be at least 12,000 feet high and almost seven miles in circumference. The stronghold, perched on top of the mountain, was approachable only by a narrow track and almost completely surrounded by a deep ravine. The narrowness of the path was such that the only way an assault could be made on the fortress was by filling in a section of the ravine, or bridging it.

"But even so", says Arrian, "Alexander set about the work. He so thought that everything should be accessible and available to him, and he had reached such a pitch of audacity and good fortune".[10] The following method of bridging the gap seems to have been employed: the sides of the ravine reached their narrowest point some way before the bottom and then widened out again. Men were sent down the sides of the ravine to fix firmly in place across the gap (at its narrowest point) stout pine trunks felled on the mountain. These, placed across the gap a short distance from each other, formed a sort of substructure. Hurdles of willow were then placed crosswise on these trunks, after which the army began to heap earth and rubble on the substructure to form both a bridge and a causeway. The army was divided into six shifts, working throughout the day and night.

The work advanced slowly, and the followers of Chorienes at first laughed and mocked the enterprise as being quite hopeless. But as the causeway approached the opposite side of the ravine and the Macedonian missiles began to get their range, they became alarmed, especially since they themselves were unable to harm the besiegers, who were protected by screens. Chorienes, therefore, sent a herald to Alexander, requesting that Oxyartes, who had accompanied the army, be sent to him. A conference took place, at which Oxyartes tried to persuade Chorienes to surrender to Alexander. He argued that there was no place which Alexander and his army could not take; and that Alexander would meet him with fairness and honour, giving as proof his own treatment by the King.

Chorienes, after weighing up the situation, saw the wisdom of Oxyartes' arguments, and went with his family and closest friends to Alexander, surrendering himself and his stronghold. The King received him with friendship and, at his request, Chorienes sent instructions to his followers to depart from the stronghold. Alexander himself, with 500 of the Hypaspists, went up to make an inspection of the fortress. Chorienes was reinstated as governor of the district and the fortress returned to him. The King, in a hurry to finish off the war, had decided that kindness was the best policy; besides, he had made an adequate demonstration of his abilities in siege techniques. It is said that, as a result of a spell of very bad weather during the siege, the army was suffering from shortage of provisions; and that Chorienes supplied the soldiers with two months' supply of corn and wine from the stores in the stronghold, as well as distributing meat to each mess-unit. Even so, he said, he had not used up a tenth of the provisions from the stronghold.

After this success Alexander made his way to Bactra, leaving Craterus, with 600 Companion Cavalry and four battalions of the phalanx to finish off the war by reducing the last two rebellious barons in Paraetacene, Catanes and Austanes. These two, perhaps realizing the hopelessness of a siege after the experiences of Oxyartes and Chorienes, decided to take on Craterus in the open field. After a sharp struggle their forces were defeated with heavy losses; Catanes died fighting, Austanes was captured and taken to Alexander. Craterus then rejoined the main body of the army.

The late winter and spring of 327 at Bactra, where the affair of Callisthenes and the Page Boys took place (see next chapter), was filled with activity as Alexander made his preparations to invade India. To maintain the security of the hardly won areas of the north new cities were founded in the region, in addition to the military garrisons. Bactra was refounded as an Alexandria, and Alexandrias were also founded where now stand the modern cities of Termez (on the Oxus, south-west of Stalinabad) and Marv (on the Murghab, where the river is intersected by the Karakumski canal). Thus, with the addition of the already founded Alexandrias—Eschate on the Jaxartes, "the Caucasian" by the Hindu Kush and Nicaea (Victory) south of this latter—there were at least six major city settlements in this part of the world.

The functions of these cities was primarily that of policing and defending the frontier provinces, though in some cases economic factors must have played a part. Thus it is possible that Termez was established because of the trade-route from the north which crossed the Oxus at this point; while Arrian hints that the region's potential fertility influenced the King in his decision to establish Eschate.[11] The settlers in these cities were mainly Greek mercenaries; natives of the surrounding country might be invited to join in the foundation, but it was the presence of the Greeks which made the place a city, and they probably had more extensive privileges than the native settlers. Each city apparently had a Macedonian governor who exercised a general supervision over the political side of the community—an aspect which perhaps would not go down well with the Greeks. The course of events in these most easterly areas just before and just after Alexander's death show both that the number of Greeks settled was large and that often the settlement was of a compulsory nature. For in two separate revolts more than 26,000 Greeks were involved, and in the second revolt the complaint of the Greeks was that they missed their Greek way of life. Isocrates had advised Philip to ease the problem of the wandering exiles and mercenaries by settling them on land taken from Persia; here Alexander appears to be following the Athenian's advice.

But whereas Isocrates had in mind the colonization of Asia Minor, Alexander was settling these Greeks at the ends of the known world, thousands of miles from the Greek homeland, in a savage land surrounded by enemies—and against their free will. There is little wonder that they hated it and seized the first opportunity to try to return to Greece.*

It was about this time[12] that Alexander gave orders for 30,000 Iranian youths to be chosen and taken away for instruction in the Greek language and the Macedonian methods of warfare. The removal of these youths would, for the present, ensure the good behaviour of the provinces from which they were taken. Later, when the King returned from India, they would have a more positive function—they would enable Alexander to dispense to a large extent with the Macedonians in his army. The Great King of Persia would have his own native troops, but by their training made considerably more efficient than the army of the last Darius. Alexander referred to them as the "Successors"—successors, that is, to his Macedonians. The scheme was not noised abroad at the time to the soldiers—for obvious reasons; but in court-circles it raised considerable discontent among the Macedonian nobles.

As a final security measure for the north-eastern frontier, there was left with the Bactrian satrap, Amyntas, a very strong army of occupation, consisting of 10,000 infantry and 3,500 cavalry. These would be almost all mercenaries, the army having received in 328 reinforcements of 16,000 Greek infantry and over 2,000 cavalry. Amyntas was probably intended to exercise a military supervision over Sogdiana as well as Bactria.

It was now, perhaps, in preparation for the invasion of India, that a drastic reorganization was made in the cavalry. The death of Philotas had resulted in the Companions being divided into two Hipparchies. Since the murder of Cleitus in 328 Alexander himself seems to have taken over temporarily command of one of the Hipparchies. The Cleitus affair had made evident the feelings of a large number of the senior officers, and it was now decided to divide the command of the Companions still further in the hope that the mutual animosities of the officers might restrain them from possible treasonable combinations. Moreover, for some time the King had been drawing on an almost

*It may have been now that Aristotle composed his treatise "Alexander, or On Colonies" (see p. 25)—but as an open pamphlet *criticising* Alexander's Far Eastern colonies (especially their situation and system of government).

inexhaustible supply of native Iranian cavalry. The excellent quality of this cavalry, especially as mounted missile—and light—horsemen, had already enabled the King to dispense with the services of his Balkan horse and, at some unspecified date between 329 and 327, to incorporate the Macedonian Prodromi with the Companions (and so make up for the lack of reinforcements from Macedonia). In the campaigns in Bactria and Sogdiana we meet units of Iranian horse-archers and horse-javelineers; while Sogdianians were found serving with Alexander against their fellow-countryman, Spitamenes. In India there are to be found, in addition to Bactrian and Sogdianian horse, cavalry from Arachosia, Scythia across the Jaxartes and from the Hindu Kush region of Paropamisus. All these units are mentioned as additional to the Companions; but one must infer from the inclusion of these units in the army that there were even more considerable numbers of Iranians from the central satrapies—Persis, Media, Aria and Babylonia—with Alexander. For military service was the most obvious way that Alexander could emphasize his legitimate succession to the Achaemenids as Great King of Persia.

The reorganization of the cavalry probably took the following form: the eight squadrons of the Companions, implemented by the inclusion of the Prodromi, were enlarged by the addition (though not as yet incorporation) of squadrons of Iranians from the central satrapies. The whole number was now split into eight independent commands— or Hipparchies—of which the nucleus was a squadron of the Companion Cavalry. Outside of this organization (probably because of their more recent conquest) were the cavalry units of the eastern satrapies. The number of cavalry available for the Indian expedition cannot be even guessed with any certainty and estimates vary between about 6,500 and 15,000; it can be said that there were at least 2,000 Macedonians with the King, the rest being Iranians. Similarly with the infantry, estimates vary tremendously for the army of invasion—between 20,000 and 120,000; again, we can say with some certainty that not more than 13,000 of these could have been Macedonians.

It is possible that the figure of 120,000 represents the total number of people—combatants and non-combatants—who followed Alexander to India. For the army, which had always contained the royal court, was now also becoming like a moving city, accompanied by the mistresses of the soldiers, their illegitimate children, butlers, grooms, traders and other camp-followers.

In the early summer of 327 the huge throng passed southwards over the Hindu Kush to begin the invasion of the almost legendary land of India. Very few of the 120,000 were to return home again.

NOTES

1 Arrian IV 1613
2 Strabo XI 9.4; Justin XII 5.73
3 Curtius VII 10.15
4 Arrian IV 16.3
5 Arrian IV 17.2
6 Curtius VIII iii 1-15
7 Tarn, *Alexander the Great* I, p.73; *Cambridge Ancient History* VI, p.395
8 Curtius VIII 4.23 (Loeb translation)
9 Tarn, *Alexander the Great* I 76; *C.A.H.* VI, p.397
10 Arrian IV 20.3
11 Arrian IV 1.3
12 Curtius VIII 5.1ff.; cf. Plutarch, *Alexander 47*, who dates the measure to the King's stay in Hyrcania, Curtius' date is preferable in view of the "hostage" aspect of the youths.

14

The Affairs of Cleitus and Callisthenes

The Cleitus affair took place sometime during the summer of 328 B.C., when the army was at Maracanda (Samarkand) in Sogdiana. The actual details are difficult to sort out of the differing accounts of the sources, though the basic impulses that led to Cleitus' death are clear enough—the long-standing opposition of the older officers to the King's penchant and practice of the Persian way of life and his adoption of Persian court-ceremonial. They hated to see a Macedonian King deserting—even despising—the simple and nationalistic ideals that they imagined to be typified in the reign of Philip; and they objected to Alexander's increasing belief in his own greatness and its alarming manifestation in a growing conviction that he was something more than a mere mortal being, a conviction constantly being stimulated by the flattery of the Greek courtiers. The deaths of Philotas and Parmenion had temporarily cowed the opposition among the older nobility; but it was still there, under the surface, and among its foremost representatives was Cleitus, son of Dropides, Hipparch of half the Companion Cavalry.

Plutarch is the most circumstantial account of the affair, and perhaps the best, since he probably draws his description ultimately from the work of Chares, the Court Chamberlain, who was present at the affair.[1] His version of the story will be followed in the main. Every year the Macedonians performed a sacrifice to the god Heracles, which was followed by a banquet. Macedonian banquets tended to turn into immense drinking-orgies at which the barbarism that lurked in every Macedonian noble often manifested itself under the influences of strong wine, so that bitter, and sometimes deadly, quarrels came to the surface. This has already been seen at the wedding-banquet of Philip and Cleopatra, where Alexander threw his goblet at Attalus in a drunken rage, and the even more drunken Philip attempted to kill his son.

This particular banquet was no exception. The drinking was heavy and most of the guests were far advanced in intoxication. During a lull in the conversation a Greek courtier, whose name is given as either Pranichus or Pierion, was asked to recite a poem he had written. The subject of the poem was deliberately provocative: it was a satire on certain—unnamed—commanders who had recently suffered a reverse. The older guests were annoyed, both at the verses and at the fact that a Greek had the insolence so to write about Macedonians; and they expressed their resentment in abuse of the poet. Alexander, however, and the close friends who were sitting around him, were delighted with what they heard and bade the man who was reciting the poem to go on. The King must have realized that his malicious approbation could only infuriate the elder officers all the more, and his instructions to proceed may well have been given with the intention of provoking some outburst from that quarter.

If this is so, the King was not disappointed. Cleitus "who was already drunk and naturally of a harsh temper and wilful, was more than ever vexed, and insisted that it was not well done, when among barbarians and enemies, to insult Macedonians who were far better men than those who had laughed at them, even though they had met with misfortune".[2] In Cleitus' outburst we can see clearly expressed the attitude of the older, more conservative Macedonians both towards the conquered race and towards the attitude the King had adopted towards them.

Alexander himself replied to Cleitus' remarks in a most unpleasant manner. The reverse that the Macedonian generals had suffered is not described in our sources,* but it is obvious from Alexander's jibe that Cleitus was present there. "Cleitus", he said sneeringly, "is obviously pleading his own cause, when he gives the name of misfortune to cowardice". The remark was meant to hurt; Cleitus sprang to his feet in a blind fury and, forgetting where he was and that it was the Lord of all Asia he was addressing, roared out, "It was this same cowardice that saved you—the offspring of a god!—when you were turning your back on the sword of Spithridates,† and it is by the blood of the Mace-

---

* It cannot have been the Pharnuches episode since Cleitus was not present.
† I.e. at the Granicus.

donians and by these wounds of ours that you have become so great as to renounce Philip and take up Ammon as your father".

Cleitus spoke from the heart and every word he spoke was true. But no autocrat likes to be reminded of his debts to others, especially in front of an audience; and Alexander was very touchy on the subject of the alleged paternity of Ammon and could brook no criticism or mocking on this score. Besides, Cleitus had made it all too plain how much he and the others like him loathed and despised the King's new way of life. Inflamed by the drink, the King's violent and uncontrollable temper, seen already at his father's wedding and now made far worse by the exercise of unrestrained power, burst forth. "You scoundrel", he raved, "this is how you talk about me all the time; this is how you split the Macedonians up into factions. Do you think you'll get away with it now?"[4]

Straightway came back the reply of Cleitus: "But we don't get away with it, Alexander," he said—and the simple "Alexander" without the title of "King" was a deliberate insult—"For such are the rewards that we receive for our labours. We consider blessed those who have already died before seeing Macedonians thrashed with Median rods and grovelling before Persians to gain access to their King." As he finished speaking, a riot nearly broke out in the room. Alexander's friends and flatterers sprang up and began abusing Cleitus, whilst the elder men, seeing what was likely to happen, tried to quell the uproar. As the noise died down, Alexander, restraining his fury for the moment —and thereby all the more deadly—turned to two of his Greek friends and said mockingly, "Don't you think that the Greeks walk about among Macedonians like demi-gods among wild beasts?".[5]

It was a brutal remark, and one which would have revolted and infuriated any Macedonian of the generation of Philip. Cleitus, because of his own anger and the dying remnants of the uproar, seems to have caught only the tail-end of the remark, but he realized that it was something very insulting, either to himself or to the Macedonians as a whole, and he shouted out to Alexander to speak out openly what he wished to say or else not to invite to dinner men who were free and had the right of free speech; otherwise let him rather go and live with barbarians and slaves, who would grovel before his Persian girdle and lily-white tunic.

Alexander could no longer restrain his anger at this. He hurled at Cleitus the first thing that came to hand, which happened to be a pomegranate, and then fumbled for his sword. One of his Bodyguards,

Aristophanes, anxious to prevent bloodshed, hid the weapon before the King could find it. This enraged Alexander even more, and lurching to his feet, he called out in the Macedonian dialect, just as an Englishman from the "provinces" will often betray his origin in times of great emotional strain, for the trumpeters to sound the alarm and arouse the Hypaspists of the guard. The trumpeter, bewildered by the rapid sequence of events and reluctant to take a step that would throw the whole camp into confusion, hesitated and received a stinging blow from the King's fist for his disobedience.

In the meantime, Ptolemy, son of Lagus, and certain other men, who were alarmed at the violence of Alexander's wrath, unceremoniously bundled the still seething Cleitus out of the banqueting-hall. Cleitus, however, was not through yet. Breaking loose from his friends he staggered back into the room and declaimed at Alexander a verse of Euripides: "Alas what evil custom there prevails in Greece!"[6] It is indicative of the degree to which Greek culture had penetrated the Macedonian court both that Cleitus could, in the spur of the moment, quote this verse, and that Alexander could immediately recognize its appropriateness to what Cleitus had been saying. For the passage continues:

> When with the spoils of vanquished foes, the host
> A trophy rear, they think not how 'twas gained
> By those brave soldiers who endure the toil
> Of battle, while their general bears away
> All the renown: though he was only one
> Who stood 'midst thousands brandishing his spear,
> Nor any single combatant surpassed,
> He gains a larger portion of applause.*

Alexander, insane with rage, seized a pike from one of the guards and ran it through the body of Cleitus as he was turning to leave the room after delivering his Parthian shot. Cleitus gave a great bellowing cry of agony and fell dead on the spot. At the same time, the King's fury left him, as he realized, with horror, what he had done. He had intended to provoke a quarrel, perhaps with Cleitus personally, certainly with the other officers in general, that would make them disclose any treasonable thoughts towards himself. His provocation had been brilliantly successful; but his scheme had been brought to ruins by his own inability to master his emotions. Now it was he himself who was guilty of murder.

* Translated by A. Morley.

Nor was he unaffected by the horrible nature of the deed. Though an ideological rift had been growing between the two men for some time, Cleitus had been an old friend and faithful servant; moreover, Cleitus' sister, Lanice, had been Alexander's nurse, when the King was an infant. We need not assign merely to theatrical motives his attempt to run himself through with the pike, an act from which he was prevented by his Bodyguards, who then forcibly carried him to his bedchamber.

For three days, it is said, the King lay on his bed, without food or drink and paying no attention to all the other bodily needs. Again and again he kept calling himself the murderer of his friends and crying out that it was indeed a fine reward that he had paid to Lanice for her nursing. "She had seen her children die fighting on his behalf, now he himself with his own hand had killed her brother".[7] At length he was induced to eat and to give some care to his person, after the faithful Aristander had informed him that Cleitus' death had been predestined by fate and that it was therefore inevitable. This, he said, was apparent from adverse omens concerning Cleitus which Alexander had reported to him before the fateful banquet.

Some authorities add the detail that the court-philosophers, Callisthenes and Anaxarchus, were brought to try to calm the King; and that Callisthenes attempted gentle persuasion, but Anaxarchus, one of the type of courtier whose flattery takes the more subtle form of abusive liberty of speech, finding Alexander lying there moaning, laughed at him and said that Alexander had not yet learned that, just as whatsoever is done by Zeus is done with Justice, so it is right that all things done by a Great King should be considered just. Anaxarchus deservedly incurs the censure of Plutarch and Arrian for this advice, in that it made Alexander even more arrogant and lawless; though the sophist did win for himself great popularity with Alexander, which was detrimental to the favour enjoyed by his rival, Callisthenes, who was of a much more austere outlook than Anaxarchus.

It was officially announced that Cleitus' death was due to the anger of the god Dionysus, because the regular sacrifice had been overlooked. The soldiers, simple and superstitious peasants, may have been satisfied with this explanation; the same can hardly be said for the great nobles and senior officers at the court. All who had been present at the banquet knew that Cleitus had been murdered because he had opposed the ideas of the monarch and had dared speak his mind; and, except for three days of hunger, the murderer had gone scot-free. It is difficult to believe, with one eminent historian, that "it [the killing] probably affected the generals very little; life was cheap and you took your chances";[8] the deaths of Parmenion and Philotas are said to have made Alexander an object of terror to many of his colleagues and even Antipater in Europe began to have his doubts about the ruler he had created. Parmenion and Philotas were killed with an appearance, at least, of legality. The effect on Cleitus' contemporaries of his death can well be imagined. Again, a leading member of the "old school" had been removed; but the opposition remained and spread to other quarters, as was seen a year or two later with the affair of Callisthenes.

This affair falls into two parts, the first of which took place in the spring of 327 at the Bactrian Royal Residence, Bactra. Between the death of Cleitus and this time the King's policy of winning the favour of the Iranian aristocracy had made considerable progress. Late in 328 he had taken as his wife, Roxane; and in the same year he had made arrangements for the training of 30,000 native youths in Macedonian military techniques. These he called his Epigoni—his "successors" (see Chapter 13).

Encouraged by the apparent lack of opposition to these two steps, and urged on by the flattery of his Greek courtiers and the advice of his Iranian intimates, the King now determined to emphasize that he was Lord of Asia and that Macedonia was but part of his realm. To do this it was decided that a piece of court-ceremonial, which was regular and normal practice for all Iranians, should be introduced for the Greeks and Macedonians as well. This was the institution called *proskynesis*, the Greek word meaning "prostration" or "obeisance", whereby the subject prostrated himself before the feet of the monarch. Its introduction, as Alexander recognized, would be a highly delicate matter. For though to Iranians it was nothing more than a sign of respect from an inferior to a superior (and as such was probably practised by the retainers of the Iranian barons to their masters), to Greeks and Macedonians prostration was a thing done only before cult-statues of the gods—or by a slave to his owner. Under the Achaemenids, Greek envoys to the Great King performed the ceremony only under strong protest; the story is told that one such envoy, to salve his conscience and the proprieties of Persian etiquette, deliberately dropped his seal before the King and went down on hands and knees to retrieve it. The ceremony, then, was not likely to be universally popular with the Greeks and Macedonians. But an attempt to introduce it was politically necessary. For apart from considerations of Alexander's vanity, it must have been embarrassing to the King to have half of his court prostrating themselves before him, while the other half stood upright and silently sneered at the spectacle; while the Iranians must have felt no small surprise that the Great King could allow such a situation.

Accordingly it was arranged by Alexander, the leading nobles of Persia and Media and certain close Macedonian friends—among them Hephaestion, Lysimachus, the future King, and the Bodyguard Demetrius—who saw in the promotion of the King's schemes the promotion of their own power, that during a forthcoming banquet, when the loving cup was handed round, each one should rise, do obeisance to the King and then kiss him (the royal kiss being a token of kinship with the monarch). It was hoped that the other guests would feel themselves morally obliged to follow suit, and thus the practice could be introduced gradually.

The scene at the banquet was described in his book by the Chamberlain, Chares.[9] He says that at the appropriate time Alexander sent round a golden loving-cup firstly to those who were in the plan; then the first to receive it rose up, drank, prostrated himself and received the King's kiss; and so it went on until the cup reached Callisthenes. He, says Chares, rose up, drank, and then, without prostrating himself, approached the King for the kiss. Alexander at the time was conversing with Hephaestion—perhaps engaging in mutual congratulations on the success of the venture—and hence did not see Callisthenes' omission. Demetrius, however, had seen, and called out to Alexander "Don't give him a kiss, Sire. He's the only one so far who hasn't prostrated himself before you". Alexander therefore refused to kiss the philosopher; to which Callisthenes remarked in a loud voice as he turned away, "Well then, I'll depart the poorer by a kiss".[10]

The murmurs of applause that greeted Callisthenes' act showed the King quite plainly what the general attitude was to *proskynesis*. It is even recorded that when a Persian noble went up to prostrate himself, one of the Macedonian generals—Leonnatus or Polyperchon—mockingly shouted to the man to *bang* his chin on the ground, not just touch it. Alexander's cherished plan dissolved amidst satirical laughter; but the dislike he already entertained for Callisthenes was turned into resentful hatred, while Hephaestion added the fuel to the flames by telling the King that Callisthenes had previously agreed to prostrate himself, and had then broken his agreement.

It has been suggested that Callisthenes' opposition to *proskynesis* was a remarkable volte-face.[11] For Callisthenes was the official historian of the expedition, whose task was to depict Alexander in the most favourable light to the Greek world and to show that the Crusade and its leader were especially blessed by the favour of heaven. Thus he had written that the long silent oracle of Apollo at Didyma had suddenly broken silence and declared that Alexander was the son of Zeus; that as he passed Mount Climax along the seashore, the waves had retreated and done obeisance to him (again the word is *proskynesis*); and that the priest of Ammon had addressed the King as the son of Zeus. Yet here is the same Callisthenes refusing to prostrate himself before the same Alexander.

However, to accuse Callisthenes of a volte-face is to ignore an important fact: what Callisthenes wrote and what he thought of Alexander need not necessarily be in harmony. In his capacity as "official" historian Callisthenes wrote for the Greek world what Alexander wanted to be written; and if Alexander wished it to be thought that he stood in a special relationship with heaven, Callisthenes would so depict the King—an attitude that was cynical, perhaps, but in perfect harmony both with his openly declared reason for accompanying the expedition, to obtain the refounding of Olynthus, his native city destroyed by Philip, and with his statement that Alexander's fame would rest not on the King's deeds, but on the way he, Callisthenes, described these deeds.

Now, Callisthenes had taken his history down at least to 331 B.C. and the battle of Gaugamela and had sent his work back to Greece for publication. Down to this time the relations between Alexander and the historian, who had once taught him at Mieza, seem to have been at least cordial. But Callisthenes was the nephew of Aristotle, and like his uncle had a deep contempt and dislike for the Persian "barbarians" and their luxurious, unmanly way of life. He was, moreover, naturally of a somewhat austere disposition—perhaps even ostentatiously so—a quality which his enemies described as boorishness. The assumption by Alexander of the title of Great King, his promotion of Iranians to high office, and his increasing taste for oriental luxury will have been most painful to Callisthenes, who shared his uncle's belief in treating the barbarians as slaves. Thus, from the death of Darius onwards, there was a gradual drifting apart between Alexander and the historian. Callisthenes disliked the new form of monarchy and expressed his dislike both verbally and by shunning the extravagant banquets and parties which the King gave; while Alexander for his part resented Callisthenes' freedom of speech and austerity and gave ready ear to the malicious gossip of the latter's enemies, amongst whom was the sophist Anaxarchus. We have already seen how in the Cleitus' affair it was the blustering flattery of Anaxarchus to which the King turned for comfort. Plutarch adds the detail that Callisthenes' attempt at consolation brought him into additional disfavour with Alexander because of its austerity.[12]

An anecdote in Plutarch will further illuminate the hostility that existed between the King and historian. At a dinner-party some time before the *proskynesis* affair, which Callisthenes had deigned to attend, Alexander, whose education under Aristotle had included a course in eristics (see Chapter 2), asked Callisthenes to give a display of his eloquence by declaiming *ex tempore* a speech in praise of the Macedonians. This Callisthenes did with such fluency that the Macedonians rose up at the end and threw their garlands of flowers over him. The King then asked the orator to give a further—and more difficult—display of his eloquence and eristic skill by *denouncing* the Macedonians. Callisthenes spoke long and boldly on the theme (which was perhaps more congenial to him), showing that the cause of the rise of Macedonian power was the faction and disunity of the Greeks. He concluded with a verse quotation, which was meant to refer to Philip, that: "In time of faction, even the utterly bad man obtains honour". His brilliant rhetorical *tour de force* was met with a stony silence from the Macedonians, while the King, whose Greek education had not succeeded in imparting the quality of objectivity to him, observed bitterly that Callisthenes had given a display, not of his eloquence, but of his hostility towards the Macedonians.

On both personal and ideological grounds, then, Alexander and Callisthenes intensely disliked each other by the spring of 327; and it is not surprising to find Callisthenes, the nephew of a philosopher who believed deeply in the liberty and dignity of the Greek people, refusing to indulge in an act of servile obeisance to an oriental despot. It was an act of great personal courage, but it was to be fatal to Callisthenes. For Alexander could never forgive him, and henceforth was constantly on the watch for some means of taking vengeance on the historian.

His opportunity came not long afterwards in the incident of the Royal Pages. These youths were the sons of leading Macedonian nobles, entrusted to the King's care by their fathers, for whose good behaviour they doubtless formed valuable hostages. Among their duties were to keep watch in turn before the King's bed-chamber at night, and to attend the King when he went out to the chase or battle; they were given the special honour of sitting at the King's table, and in his court they learned the arts of war and administration. Curtius calls the institution "a seed-bed of generals and governors".[13] One of these youths, Hermolaus, was a keen disciple of Callisthenes, in whose company he was frequently observed, imbibing the wisdom of the philosopher-historian. This same Hermolaus, when out hunting one day with Alexander, had anticipated his royal master in despatching a wild boar, and for his breach of etiquette had been flogged by the King and deprived of his horse.

Smarting in body and mind, Hermolaus betook himself and his grievances to his lover, another Page called Sostratus, vowing that life would be unbearable unless he avenged himself on Alexander for this injustice. The pair won over three more Pages and a plot was formed to kill the King on a night when all five were on guard together outside the King's door. This plan entailed changing the duty-roster so as to have all five on guard at the same time, and a month was spent in these manipulations.

On the night arranged for the assassination the King was attending a dinner-party which was prolonged until well into the night. When eventually Alexander rose to leave, he was accosted by an old woman, believed to have the gift of prophecy, and warned to return to the party for the rest of the night; for, she said, evil awaited the King if he left the banquet. Alexander had a superstitious faith in the old woman's predictions, and so he returned to the drinking and stayed there until the morning, when the guard was changed.

The next day, one of the conspirators, whose nerve seems to have broken under the tension of the previous night, disclosed the plot to his lover, who in turn disclosed it to a third person. This latter immediately went to the King's tent and revealed the whole plot to Ptolemy, son of Lagus. Ptolemy woke Alexander from his drunken sleep, informed him of the plot and straightway had the conspirators arrested on the King's orders. Alexander also ordered the arrest of Hermolaus' tutor, Callisthenes.

The following day, when Alexander had slept off his hangover, he summoned his friends and the parents of the Pages to a meeting, and when all were assembled, the King had the Pages—without Callisthenes—brought in. All, without exception, confessed to having plotted against the King; all without exception refused to implicate Callisthenes in the plot. Hermolaus, when given the chance to speak and explain his conduct, delivered a bitter and obviously premeditated speech, cataloguing the by now familiar grievances of the Macedonians: the deaths of Philotas, Parmenion and Cleitus; the adoption by the King of Persian dress and habits; and the attempts to introduce Persian court-ceremonial. A free man, he said, could no longer endure the King's arrogance; hence he had decided to liberate the Macedonians from their tyrant.

The Pages were all condemned to death by stoning. But before the execution was carried out they were put to the torture to try to make them incriminate Callisthenes. Despite the lies of Ptolemy and Aristobulus[14] not one of the Pages would say a word against him. But Alexander was determined that Callisthenes must suffer, and to prove that it was he who had incited Hermolaus to the deed recourse was had to "treasonable conversations" between the two—innocent remarks, which, when taken out of context, could be perverted to suit the King's purpose. Thus it is recorded that when Hermolaus complained to Callisthenes about his flogging, Callisthenes replied that he should remember that he was now a man. Callisthenes meant that Hermolaus should endure in silence; out of context the remark could be interpreted as an incitement to the Page to avenge the insult like a man.

The fate of Callisthenes is variously recorded. Ptolemy says that he was tortured and hanged; Aristobulus and Chares, that he was carried around with the army for seven months, bound hand and foot, and died of a sickness, after growing obese from lack of exercise and verminous from lack of bodily attention.[15] Plutarch preserves a letter of Alexander's to Antipater, in which the King accuses Callisthenes of the crime and adds "The Pages were stoned by the Macedonians but I personally will punish the sophist, as well as those who sent him out and those who are harbouring in the Greek cities men who plot against me".[16] By "those who sent him out" Aristotle, the historian's uncle, is meant; the second clause, "those who harbour etc." may well be a reference—and warning—to Antipater himself. For both Aristotle and Antipater had been in continual correspondence with Callisthenes; both were known to disapprove strongly of Alexander's orientalism; and it was thanks to the protection of Antipater that Aristotle's new school of philosophy at Athens, the Lyceum, was flourishing.

Callisthenes died the victim of a despot's resentment. He was a brave man who, like a true philosopher, did not hesitate to speak out freely against a degrading practice, even though it cost him his life. He was deeply mourned by his friends in the school of Aristotle, and if he quickly became cast as a martyr at the hands of a despot, this picture is not far from the truth. For Alexander's spiteful and ruthless persecution of his former teacher one can feel nothing but abhorrence and contempt; and the King must have received a severe warning of the extent to which opposition to his orientalism was spreading with the affair of the Pages. We may leave the last word on Callisthenes with Plutarch: "In the matter of *proskynesis*, by rejecting it strongly and like a philosopher, and by bringing into the open—alone though he was—and relating in detail the grievances which all the best and oldest of the Macedonians entertained in secret, he delivered the Greeks from a great disgrace and Alexander from a greater, in that he turned the King away from *proskynesis*. But he destroyed himself in so doing; for it seemed that he had *forced* the King to drop it, rather than persuaded him".[17]

NOTES

1 Plutarch, *Alexander* 50ff.
2 Plutarch, *Alexander* 50 (Loeb translation)
3 Plutarch, *Alexander* 50
4 Ibid. 51
5 Plutarch, *Alexander* 51
6 Euripides, *Andromache* 694
7 Arrian IV 9.4
8 W. W. Tarn, *Alexander the Great* I, p.75; *Cambridge Ancient History* VI, p.397
9 At Plutarch, *Alexander* 54; cf. Arrian IV 12.3ff.
10 Plutarch, *Alexander* 54
11 Cf. Tarn op. cit. I, p.80; VI, p. 399
12 Plutarch, *Alexander* 52
13 Curtius VIII 6.6
14 At Arrian III 14.1
15 At Arrian 14.3 (Ptolemy and Aristobulus); Plutarch, *Alexander* 55 (Chares)
16 Plutarch, *Alexander* 55
17 Plutarch, *Alexander* 53

15

India

To the Greek contemporaries of Alexander little was known about India. The most important geographers of the day believed that the continent of Asia was bisected by a continuous mountain chain which began in Asia Minor with the Taurus range and continued, like a backbone, by way of Armenia to Bactria, where it becomes the range known both as Paropamisus or Caucasus. The whole world was surrounded by a great sea, called Ocean, and into this sea, which marked the end of the world, the Caucasus range extended itself in the east. From this great mountain backbone, on either side, there flowed the great rivers of Asia, some emptying themselves into the northern Ocean, others into the southern Ocean. The land of India was conceived as a peninsula south of the Caucasus, at its most easterly point, jutting out in an easterly direction into the Ocean. Cutting across this peninsula and flowing into the southern Ocean was the river Indus, which gave the land its name. When once one had crossed the Indus, it was believed, there was little land left before one came to the eastern Ocean, the boundary of the world. Of the vast mass of the Indian sub-continent to the east and the south; of Kashmir and Nepal; of Malaysia, Indonesia, China and the lands of the Far East, nothing was known. To the Greeks—and to the Persians—India meant the land of the Indus; that is, it did not mean at all what is nowadays understood by India, but merely western Pakistan—the Punjab and Sind.

The Persians had once possessed Indian satrapies and the Punjab and Sind had been quite well known. In the north were the satrapies of Paropamisus (roughly Kabul) and Gandara (very roughly Peshawar and Rawalpindi); of the latter the capital city had been Pukhala, called by the Greeks Peucela. Further south a considerable part of the Punjab—

"the land of the five rivers"—had been conquered by the first Darius and turned into the satrapy of Hindush; its capital was Takshacila, called by the Greeks Taxila. In the middle of the 5th century B.C. this satrapy was assessed for tribute purposes at 360 talents weight of gold dust each year. In the lower reaches of the Indus some Persian control had been exercised over Sind. Darius' admiral, Scylax, had made a voyage down the Indus and then westwards across the Arabian Sea and up the Red Sea as far as Suez; his experiences were described by him in the book he published called *Periplus* or *Voyage round the World*.

In the 4th century, however, Persian influence had waned east of the Hindu Kush and the Indian satrapies had been abandoned. To the western world, India quickly became a "wonderland", as Cathay was to the Middle Ages, a place where ants as big as foxes dug up gold from the ground. Greek legends told how the god Dionysus invaded India, giving the peoples wine, laws, religious rites and a settled way of life; and how Heracles in the course of his labours penetrated as far as India, taking many women to wife and producing a daughter who later ruled over part of the country as queen. The legendary queen Semiramis is also said to have attempted an invasion of India, but to have died before bringing her designs to fulfilment.

To the question "why did Alexander make the expedition to India?" an answer suggests itself straightway: India had once been a part of the Persian realm, and the new Great King was intending to recover his lawful possessions. But there were other reasons, amongst them a desire to emulate—and surpass—the achievements of the divine beings, one of whom was amongst his ancestors, who had previously invaded India. Curiosity about this strange and unknown land certainly played a part. Moreover, the conquest of India was essential if Alexander was to fulfil his ambition to be Lord of all Asia; for India was the farthest limit of Asia, beyond which was nothing but Ocean. It may be that he intended, even before setting out from Bactra, to equip an expedition that would imitate the voyage of Scylax and sail down the Indus and across the southern Ocean. We can certainly say that some detailed information of the political geography of India had been imparted to him by a chieftain from Gandara, Sasigupta, who had previously been a supporter of Bessus, but had deserted him and come over to Alexander.

Early in the summer of 327 the great invasion began. Setting out from Bactra, the army is said to have crossed the Hindu Kush in ten days. At Alexandria of the Causacus, the city-governor was replaced for inefficiency and an Iranian, Tyriaspes, appointed as the satrap of the area known as Paropamisus—a vital appointment, since Paropamisus was the key to India; a hostile satrap could cut off the army from a return by the north and prevent any reinforcements passing through.

Advancing to the River Cophen (the Kabul), he was met by the local chiefs and by the rajah of Taxila, across the Indus. His name was Ambhi, but he is often known by his official title of Taxiles. He had only recently come to the throne, but had immediately renewed the submission to Alexander which his father had previously made. Both father and son wanted the help and protection of the Great King against the ambitions of a powerful neighbouring ruler, Porus, whose kingdom lay across the River Hydaspes (the Jhelum). Ambhi now met Alexander, bringing him gifts and presenting him with a number of elephants.

At the River Cophen, Alexander divided his army. Three battalions of the phalanx, half the Companion Cavalry and the mercenary horse were assigned to Hephaestion and Perdiccas, who were ordered to march along the Cophen to the Indus, reducing *en route* all places that resisted, and to make the preparations necessary for the crossing of the river. Opposition was met at Peucela, where the ruler of the territory had to be put to death and the city taken by a siege; a traitor who had gone over to Ambhi, was appointed in his place, his treachery being considered an adequate guarantee of his goodwill towards Alexander.

Alexander, meanwhile, with the rest of the army, had turned northwards at Jalalabad, following the course of the River Choaspes (Kunar). His intention was to invade and subdue the mountainous areas known today as Bajour and Swat, and at the same time to protect the left flank of Hephaestion's army as it moved towards the Indus.

Between the River Choaspes and the Guraeus (Panjkora) lies Bajour; its natives, called Aspasii by the Greeks, were determined to resist Alexander's passage through their territory. They gathered in several fortified strongholds fiom which they intended to harass the Macedonian column; and Alexander was compelled to reduce these fortresses. At the first of these he was wounded in the shoulder by an arrow, and when the place was stormed, all the Aspasians who did not manage to effect an escape were butchered by the soldiers, "angry that Alexander had been wounded by them".[1] The fugitives from the fortress were pursued by the Macedonians to the hills, and during the pursuit Ptolemy, never backward in recounting his own deeds of valour, narrates how he engaged in single combat their chieftain, slew and despoiled him of his arms. A sharp fight ensued for possession of the body, and the tribesmen were eventually driven off.[2]

Crossing the mountains, Alexander next took over the main town of the Aspasians, Arigaeus (perhaps the modern capital Nawagai), after the inhabitants had set fire to and deserted it. Craterus was given the thankless task of resettling the town with veterans from the army and any volunteers from the native population; if the Jaxartes was bad in Greco-Macedonian eyes as a place to be settled in, this was infinitely worse. Alexander himself pressed on to a range of hills where he had learned that the tribesmen of the area had concentrated. When they came upon the enemy encamped on a mountain, Alexander divided his forces into three groups, led by Ptolemy, Leonnatus and himself. With these three columns he attacked the Indian position and after a hard battle the Macedonians were victorious. Ptolemy says, with obvious exaggeration, that more than 40,000 prisoners were taken, as well as over 230,000 oxen, and that Alexander, impressed by the beauty and size of these oxen, selected the finest in order to send them home to Macedonia. Since the journey was well over 3,000 miles, the idea may be thought laudable but somewhat irrational.[3]

Leaving the territory of the Aspasians, the army crossed the River Guraeus and entered what is now the district of Swat, situated between the Guraeus and the upper reaches of the Indus and bisected by the River Swat. The inhabitants of the Swat were known as Assacenii by the Greeks; the largest town was named Massaga and the tribesmen had concentrated here, their numbers being increased by a force of 7,000 mercenaries from across the Indus.

As Alexander approached Massaga and was in sight of the town, the tribesmen and mercenaries sallied out to attack the Macedonians. Alexander, wishing to draw them away from the refuge of the city-walls, ordered his men to retreat towards a hill about a mile away from the town. The Indians pressed on in pursuit, and at the critical moment Alexander ordered his men to turn about and attack. The suddenness of the attack upset the Indians, who turned and managed, despite Alexander's trick, to regain the walls. In the pursuit Alexander was wounded in the ankle by an arrow. The next day the Macedonians, who were accompanied by their siege-train, began the investment of the town. On the third day a bridge was thrown across from a tower to a breach in the wall, but when the Macedonians began to press over it, the bridge collapsed under their weight, and in the confusion the Indians made a quick and destructive sally.

The next day Alexander met with a piece of good fortune; a bolt from a catapult killed the Indian leader on the walls. The rest were disheartened by this disaster and sent to Alexander seeking pardon. This the King gave to the tribesmen; the mercenaries were allowed to leave the city under a truce, retaining their arms. They made their way to about ten miles from the town and then encamped for the night. Alexander had been much impressed by the valour and discipline of these men and realized that their swords would be a valuable acquisition to another enemy. He therefore quietly surrounded their camp that night and at a given signal the Macedonians burst in on the unsuspecting men, many of whom were accompanied by their wives and children. In the frightful butchery that followed, all the mercenaries and their followers were massacred. Alexander's excuse was that he had agreed to allow them to leave Massaga—but nothing else; Plutarch voices the opinion of the majority on this act: "it sticks like a stain on his military achievements".[4] Romantic tradition says that the ruler of the town was a woman called Cleophis; that she used her good looks to win the King's favour after her surrender; and that a son was born to her whom she called Alexander.

From Massaga, two columns were sent against the towns of Ora and Bazira; Alexander hoped that the fall of Massaga would encourage these two to surrender, but in this he was mistaken and Ora had to be taken by storm, while Bazira, after a struggle, was deserted by the tribesmen during the night. These too took refuge in a mountain stronghold nearby; the Greeks called the mountain Aornos, but this may be their corruption of the Sanskrit "avarana", which means "a fortress, a place of refuge". A local deity, whose characteristics enabled him to be identified with the Greek Heracles, was said to have made an unsuccessful attempt to storm this fortress. The mountain is described by Arrian as being nearly 25 miles in circumference; nearly 7,000 feet high; and with a plateau on top furnished with a copious supply of water, woods and arable land. Aornus has been identified as Pir-sar, "a flat-topped ridge with precipitous cliffs that commands the Indus 5,000 feet below it".[5] It is likely that the actual "rock" of Aornus was, in fact, a steep crag at one end of the plateau, containing a fortress. There was said to be only one way up the mountain, and that a rough one. The difficulties of the place and the alleged failure of Heracles filled Alexander with a burning desire—a *pothos*—to take Aornus. However, before moving against the mountain, Alexander, with his division of the army, passed through the Malakand pass and joined up with Hephaestion and Perdiccas on the Indus, near Attock. The territory which had hitherto been overrun—which included a large part of the old Persian satrapy of Gandara—was placed under a Macedonian satrap, Nicanor; the town of Peucela was given a Macedonian garrison.

Alexander how headed northwards again towards Aornus. Two day's march from the mountain lay the town of Embolina (perhaps Amb). Here Craterus was left with orders to stock the town with provisions in case Aornus should not fall at the first assault and a long blockade be necessary. Alexander himself then moved against the rock with a picked force. The ensuing campaign is analysed with great thoroughness and detail by Fuller,[6] who calls it "one of the most remarkable of mountain warfare exploits". Ptolemy again plays a major role in the enterprise. With the guidance of some local tribesmen, he was sent ahead with a detachment to occupy a strategic position. When Alexander attempted to join Ptolemy the next day he was prevented by the tribesmen and forced to send a message that night, through the enemy lines, ordering Ptolemy to attack the Indians in the rear whilst he himself bore the brunt of a frontal assault. Once the two forces were joined up the advance was continued. To enable his artillery, which had been dragged up the tortuous mountain paths, to reach the defenders of the rock-fortress, Alexander was forced to cut timber and make a structure that was both a causeway and a platform for the archers and catapults to shoot from. In front of the fortress and at the same height was a hillock. When the causeway approached this, it was seized by a party of Macedonians and the construction extended to it. Alexander now had a stable platform for his missiles to sweep the fortress, and the Indians, "dismayed", says Arrian, "at the incredible audacity of the Macedonians who had forced the hillock",[7] sent a herald to say that they would surrender the rock, if a truce were granted them to make a withdrawal. As they began to withdraw, Alexander, with a detachment of Hypaspists, occupied the part of the rock they had left and then suddenly attacked the tribesmen in their retreat, killing many and forcing others to throw themselves down the cliffs. "And the rock which had thwarted Heracles was held by Alexander".[8]

The renegade chieftain Sasigupta was left in Aornus as commander of the garrison. Alexander himself continued to advance for a few days into the hills. He had heard that the brother of the Assacenian chief had taken refuge there along with thirty elephants, which the King was particularly anxious to obtain. The expedition was unsuccessful; but on returning to the Indus, some tribesmen were captured, from whom it was learned that the fugitive Assacenians had taken refuge across the river with the rajah Abisares—the ally of Porus and enemy of Ambhi—but that the elephants had been left to pasture by the river. The Macedonians were then put to work rounding up these elephants, two of which perished in the hunt. The rest were put to use in the army. From here Alexander and his soldiers floated downstream on rafts to Attock, where Hephaestion and Perdiccas had bridged the river.

It was during the campaign in Swat that there took place an incident indicative of the growing home-sickness of the Macedonians. At the unidentified town of Nysa it was discovered that a local deity, equatable and therefore equated with Dionysus, was said to have founded the city, and to have given it its laws and independence; since which time it had always remained an autonomous republic under an aristocratic regime. The identification with the Hellenic Dionysus was made even more certain by the discovery that a nearby mountain had a name which sounded like the Greek word *mēros*, meaning "thigh"; for Greek legend said that Dionysus was concealed till his birth in the thigh of Zeus. Moreover, on this mountain there grew ivy—the plant associated especially with Dionysus and not seen anywhere else in the Far East by the Macedonians and Greeks. The Macedonians, who had a special regard for Dionysus, are said to have been overcome with emotion at the ivy stems and the vines, which reminded them of their homeland, and plucking the ivy and weaving it into wreaths they celebrated a Bacchic★ revel for ten days, with drinking and feasting in the rich countryside. Alexander wisely made no attempt to cut short this unexpected holiday. Nysa was allowed to keep its independence, though its chief citizen, a certain Acuphis, was appointed by Alexander as his regent in the area.

To return to the course of events, when Alexander reached Attock, where a bridge had been thrown over the Indus, he found waiting for him a deputation from Ambhi. They brought large and expensive gifts and their ruler's formal surrender of his capital and domains to Alexander. After performing the customary religious rites and holding games on the river bank, the King crossed over with his army into the territory of Ambhi and marched towards Taxila, the

★ Bacchus is another name for Dionysus.

capital, the time now being perhaps early 326 B.C. The modern road from Attock to Rawalpindi passes by the ruins of Taxila, whose twelve square miles of extent testify to the size and populousness of the city in the time of Alexander. It had formerly been the capital city of the Persian province of Hindush, and was a great centre of commerce and learning.

As he approached the city, Ambhi came out to meet him, accompanied by his army in full equipment and drawn up in battle-order. This may have been intended as a Royal welcome; it may also have had the purpose of letting Alexander know that Ambhi was no weakling; but it nearly touched off a catastrophe. For Alexander, on seeing this large army approaching, suspected a trap and immediately ordered his men to advance in battle-order. The Indian realized his mistake and galloped forward protesting his good intentions and entrusting his person and kingdom to Alexander. At this Alexander restored his realm to Ambhi and formally conferred the title of Taxiles on him.

For three days Alexander and his retinue were lavishly entertained at the palace, during which time the two rulers vied with each other in generosity. As was befitting, Alexander, the greater of the two potentates, ended by restoring to Taxiles (as he will now be called) all his gifts and adding magnificent presents over and above from the booty the army had acquired. This liberality won him the lasting friendship of Taxiles; but it caused bitter comment among the Macedonian courtiers, one of whom, Meleager, ruined his chances of promotion by sarcastically remarking at dinner one night that he congratulated Alexander in that at least in India he had found a man deserving of 1,000 talents (the main part of Alexander's gifts to Taxiles).

The stay at Taxila, though no indication is given in the sources, must have lasted for two or three months. During this time Alexander gathered all the information he could about the kingdoms and resources of Ambhi's two enemies to the east, Porus and Abisares. From the latter there came an embassy making a formal submission, which Alexander also formally accepted, though he realized that this exchange signified little. Other embassies from the hill-tribes made their submission also. The kingdom of Taxiles suffered a change in status: for Philippus, son of Machatas—brother of Harpalus—was appointed satrap "of the Indians in this area", with his headquarters in Taxila and a force of soldiers under his command. While Taxiles was the formal ruler, he was to be under the general supervision of a representative of the Great King, whose position somewhat resembles that of the British "Resident" when India was part of the British Empire.

About May 326, when his army had been refreshed by its long rest and its losses repaired by the drafting into its ranks of Indians from the realm of Taxiles, Alexander set out from Taxila towards the river Hydaspes (Jhelum) and the kingdom of Porus. Already an envoy had been sent to Porus demanding that he pay tribute and come to meet Alexander at the frontier of his territories. Porus' reply was that he would certainly meet Alexander at the frontier—but he would be in arms to prevent his crossing that frontier. The reply amounted to a declaration of war and Alexander set out to teach the recalcitrant prince a lesson. Porus was reported to have assembled his army on the bank of the Hydaspes; its numbers were put in the region of 4,000 cavalry, 30,000 infantry, 300 war chariots and as many as 200 elephants. He was also hoping for reinforcements from his ally Abisares. The news that his crossing of the river was to be contested made Alexander send back Coenus to the Indus with orders to dismantle the boats which had been used at the crossing of the river and to transport them in carts to the Hydaspes for reassembling.

For Alexander could not afford to waste time improvising a flotilla on which to cross the Hydaspes: not only must Porus be brought to battle before Abisares could join up with him, but the summer rains had also begun to set in, with their attendant steamy humidity and discomfort. Moreover, when the army reached the Hydaspes early in June they found it already dangerously swollen by the rains and running swiftly.

The place where Alexander reached the Hydaspes was probably near the modern town of Haranpur, where the railway line crosses the river; and here he pitched camp opposite the main body of Porus' army. Reconnaissance soon showed that Porus was guarding all the neighbouring fords with pickets and with war-elephants and Alexander knew that his horses would not cross in face of the elephants. Moreover, when Alexander moved his army in any direction—upstream or downstream—Porus followed him on the other side. To keep him in a state of uncertainty, Alexander split his army into several detachments and had them march further afield in different directions; they were not only intended to confuse Porus, but they also surveyed possible crossing-places at a distance from the camp. Porus was kept in further suspense by the activities of the flotilla, which had been reassembled and was now coming up and down the river.

Then, as the river became more swollen by the rains, Alexander had copious provisions brought to his camp and openly gave it out that he intended to camp there till the dry season came on and the river went down, when he would attempt the crossing. This move again was intended solely to throw Porus off guard. For reconnaissance had shown Alexander a place where a crossing of the river by a turning-force might be possible. About 17 miles upstream the town of Jalalpur stands on what is virtually a headland where the river bends. In front of the town, the river is divided into two channels by a large island,

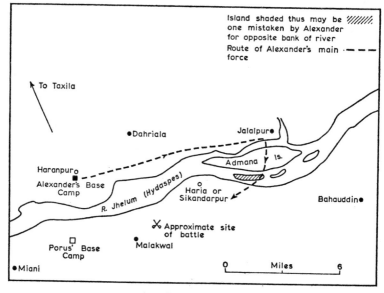

Approach to the Battle of the Hydaspes

Admana, six miles long and about one and a half wide. Alexander believed that, if Porus could be kept in his camp opposite Haranpur, a crossing could be effected here by embarking the turning-force on board the flotilla, and then sailing down the western arm of the Hydaspes, under cover of the island, to land on the eastern bank a few miles before Porus' main force. The embarkation and crossing would, of course, be effected by night.

To keep Porus unaware of the crossing the following strategem was devised: for several nights Alexander sent the cavalry to different points on the bank with orders to make as much noise as possible and to raise their war-cry. Porus, after taking preventive measures for the first few nights, was gradually lulled into a false sense of security and stayed in camp, contenting himself with posting scouts along the bank. He even took no notice when Alexander made open preparations in his camp for crossing, believing it to be yet another of the Macedonian's tricks. But in this he was deceived; for the crossing was to be made that very night.

The final plan was that the army was to be divided into three groups. The largest group (including non-combatants) were to be left in camp under Craterus so as to deceive Porus; the second group was to be posted along the bank—under cover—opposite the main fords further upstream; the third group, under Alexander's personal command, was to be the main turning-force and was to make the crossing from Jalalpur by night and then advance down the eastern bank. As he cleared each ford of its defenders, the second group would cross and join him. When an action began, Craterus was only to attempt to cross if Porus should take all his elephants against Alexander; otherwise he was to stay where he was. The turning-force was to be strong enough to take on Porus by itself if Craterus could not cross; their total strength has been estimated at about 15,000 infantry and 5,500 cavalry.

On the appointed day, Alexander and his forces set out secretly, and marched at some distance from the river to their positions. The ships and rafts had already been transported to and concealed at Jalalpur. As soon as night fell, the embarkation began; a violent storm helped to cover any noise. The flotilla then set sail down the western arm of the river, and as day broke the pickets of Porus on the eastern bank were startled to see the Macedonians passing the southern end of the island with the obvious intention of disembarking on their side; they immediately hurried off to report to their master. A deserved tribute has been paid by Fuller[9] to the superb staff-work involved in the embarking of such a large body of troops in so short a time.

After passing the island, the Macedonians began to disembark unopposed, on what they thought was the eastern bank. This in fact turned out to be nothing more than another small island in the river separated from the eastern bank by a deep channel. Considerable difficulties were encountered in fording this channel because of the swollen state of the river; the water never came below the level of the infantry's chests.

When the cavalry began to land, Alexander sent on ahead as a covering-force his horse-archers, whilst he himself drew up his order of

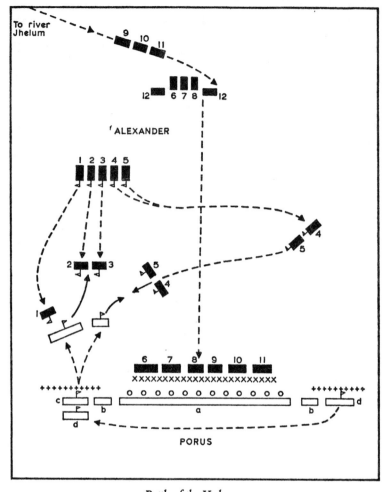

Battle of the Hydaspes

ALEXANDER	PORUS
1 Hippotoxotae (horse archers)	a Infantry
2–5 Four Hipparchies of Companion Cavalry, being, in order, those of Hephaestion, Perdiccas, Coenus and Demetrius. Coenus assumes overall command of his and Demetrius' Hipparchies	b Flanking infantry
	c Left-wing cavalry
	d Right-wing cavalry
	+++ Chariots
	ooo Elephants
6 Hypaspists	
7–11 Five battalions of the phalanx	
12 Agrianians, archers and javelin men (represented by xxx in the final battle positions)	

battle. Then because of his superiority over Porus in cavalry, he led ahead with the Companions, leaving the infantry to complete the crossing and follow on. If Porus should come against him with only his cavalry, he hoped to defeat him without the infantry; but if he encountered the whole of Porus' army, he could, if necessary, fight a holding battle with the cavalry until the infantry arrived.

Porus, in the meantime, had detached a strong force of 2,000 cavalry and 120 chariots under one of his sons, who was instructed to attack Alexander whilst he was crossing and drive him back into the river. When Alexander first made contact with this force, he thought it was the advance-guard of Porus' whole army; when, however, he discovered the truth, he attacked them with all his cavalry. In the fierce skirmish that followed, the Indians were routed, Porus' son killed and all the chariots captured. It was now, probably, that the second group of the turning-force crossed the river.

When Porus received the news of his son's death and the approach of Alexander with a powerful force, he decided to leave a small part of his army and a few elephants to face Craterus and to march against Alexander with the remainder. Advancing upstream he eventually found a place that was firm (for his cavalry and elephants to operate on), level and wide enough for deployment. Here he halted, drew up his line of battle and waited for Alexander. The battle-field chosen by Porus was probably on the plain a few miles south of the village of Sikandarpur—a name that recalls the Macedonian invader. Porus' front line was composed entirely of his elephants, stationed at intervals of about a hundred feet; these were intended to stop the enemy's cavalry making a frontal assault and to trample down his infantry. Behind the elephants, as a second line, were posted the infantry; on each flank of the foot stood the cavalry; and in front of the cavalry on each wing came the remainder of the chariots.

Alexander, meanwhile, after defeating Porus' son, halted out of sight of Porus' army and waited for his infantry to come up. He took especial care to keep the numbers of his cavalry hidden from the view of Porus' scouts, so that the Indian could not properly judge their strength; at the same time, he himself kept Porus' deployment under close observation. Alexander realized, when Porus had finished his deployment, that he could not charge head on because of the elephants; that, therefore, the infantry would have to advance on the elephants without cavalry to support and protect their flanks, which would thus be exposed to attack by Porus' cavalry. It was imperative, therefore, to smash or render inoperative the Indian cavalry before the infantry advanced. To do this Alexander decided to try to induce Porus to concentrate all his cavalry on the one wing and then attack it. To tempt Porus to make this concentration he adopted the following strategem: Coenus, with two Hipparchies of Companions was ordered to advance in the direction of Porus' right wing, carefully keeping out of sight; the horse-archers were then sent forward against Porus' left-wing cavalry to begin the "softening-up" process customary before the charge of the Companions; then Alexander, with his remaining Hipparchies of Companions, began to advance against the left-wing cavalry. He hoped that the forces with which he was advancing would be just sufficiently inferior to the *total* cavalry forces of Porus to induce the Indian to take the opportunity of smashing it by concentrating on the one wing all his cavalry. When this happened, Coenus was to charge across the front of the enemy lines and hit Porus' cavalry in the flank.

This, in fact, is exactly what did happen. On seeing the apparent number of Alexander's cavalry, Porus quickly brought round his right-wing horse and began to advance to meet the impending charge of the Companions. Suddenly there appeared on the right in the distance yet another large detachment of Macedonian horse bearing down on his flank. Porus was now forced to divide his cavalry on two fronts at the same time. Confusion followed and the Indians sensibly did not wait for Alexander's charge, but withdrew to the cover of the elephants —where they were neutralized.

The elephants now moved forward to join the action; as they did so, the Macedonian infantry attacked them and a general frontal engagement ensued. To counter the charge of the elephants, the infantry, in whose ranks were mixed javelin-throwers, adopted the tactic of forming a ring round each elephant and shooting down their drivers. For a while the elephants caused great carnage among the infantry, trampling and tossing them in the air. But discipline told and the Macedonians refused to give ground or break.

The Indian cavalry, now that the elephants were engaged, wheeled about, and in their turn charged the Macedonian cavalry, but were forced a second time to fall back on the elephants. The Macedonian horsemen, now united in one compact body, now seem to have charged and come to grips with both the cavalry and infantry of the enemy, where they began to cause great destruction. At the same time the doggedness of the Macedonian infantry was driving the elephants back into their own ranks. The whole Indian army was gradually being compressed into an ever narrower space and the elephants—especially the wounded or driverless ones—began to inflict more damage on their own men than on the enemy.

At last when the elephants were tired and no longer charging but merely standing still trumpeting or retreating into their own men, Alexander withdrew his cavalry and surrounded the whole Indian line with it. He then gave the order for the infantry to lock shields and advance. This was the beginning of the end for the Indians. Confined in a narrow space, both infantry and cavalry were cut down in great numbers. At last they broke and fled, if they could, through the gaps in the cordon of cavalry. At the same time, Craterus brought his division across the river and in the pursuit of the Indians his fresh men added to the slaughter. Porus himself, mounted on a large elephant, tried for a long time to rally his men, until he was badly wounded in the shoulder by a javelin; then only he wheeled round and began to leave the field. Seeing him escaping, Alexander foolishly sent Porus' old enemy, Taxiles, in pursuit to induce him to surrender; and Porus nearly killed Taxiles for his pains. But at last, worn out by thirst and his wound, Porus was persuaded to surrender and to be brought before Alexander.

The Hydaspes was the last big battle that Alexander fought, and many military historians would say that it was his best. Though not on the same scale as Gaugamela—nor did as much depend on its outcome —it shows throughout that Alexander's tactical genius was of the highest order, from his crossing of the river, to his surprise attack with the cavalry and the method with which he tackled the new and frightening problem of the elephants—the ancient equivalent of the tank. But if it was his best victory, it was perhaps also his hardest won and most costly. Porus is said to have lost at least 12,000 of his army; the Macedonian dead amounted to 280 cavalry and more than 700 infantry, and we are not informed of the hundreds who must have died later of their wounds. But perhaps a more serious wound was inflicted on the Macedonians from a psychological point of view. They had indeed successfully countered the elephants; but the cost had been high and the hideous deaths of their trampled and mangled comrades imprinted itself deeply in their minds. They never wanted to face up to elephants again, and not even Alexander could make them.

NOTES

1 Arrian IV 23.5
2 At Arrian IV 24.3–5

3 At Arrian IV 25.4
4 Plutarch, *Alexander* 59
5 J. F. C. Fuller, *Generalship* p.127
6 Op. cit. p.248ff., drawing mainly on the work of Sir A. Stein.
7 Arrian IV 30.2
8 Arrian IV 30.4
9 Fuller, *Generalship* p.188

16

Mutiny and the Descent of the Indus

The meeting between Alexander and Porus after the battle is described with loving detail by the ancient sources, who saw in it an encounter between two noble and regal spirits. After admiring the proud bearing of Porus, Alexander is said to have asked him how he wished to be treated. "Like a King", replied Porus; and when Alexander pressed him for details, Porus said that everything necessary was contained in the phrase "like a King". At this Alexander restored to Porus his kingdom and even enlarged his domains. Moreover, he was not put under the supervision of a satrap, nor forced to maintain a Macedonian garrison. We may believe that admiration for a defeated foe was not Alexander's only motive in reinstating Porus. The Indian was intended to serve as a counter-balance to the power of Taxiles and his kingdom as the frontier of the empire in the capacity of a buffer-state. For Alexander must have realized by this time the impossibility, with the resources he had, of annexing and garrisoning any further territory. Porus, it was hoped, would have been left, after his heavy defeat, strong enough to maintain his realm against external enemies, but not strong enough to be a serious threat in himself; while Alexander's clement treatment would secure his loyalty. However, a check was imposed on Porus in the form of two cities which Alexander founded on the banks of the Hydaspes, one called Nicaea ("Victory", in remembrance of the battle), the other Bucephela (after his old war-horse who is said to have died there at the age of 30). Craterus was given the task of supervising the building of the cities; he was also ordered to see to the building of additional ships for the King's fleet—an indication that Alexander already had some intention of making a voyage of exploration on the river-system of the Punjab.

After resting the army for 30 days, Alexander continued his journey eastwards, accompanied by both Porus and Taxiles. He was still in search of the elusive eastern Ocean, though it is hard to believe that neither of these two Kings had informed him that there was no great sea for hundreds of miles. Marching northwards through the hills round Naoshera to avoid the heat of the Guirat plain, he passed through the territory of the tribe bordering on Porus' kingdom. Their name was Glausae, and at least 37 of their "cities" surrendered to Alexander; the exaggerated statement of Arrian says that none of these had less than 5,000 inhabitants and many were over 10,000.[1] The Glausae were put under the supervision of Porus.

About mid-summer, 326, the army reached the river Acesines (Chenab). Porus and Taxiles were both sent back to their kingdoms, after being reconciled with each other. At the same time, while the army was encamped on the river-bank, envoys came from the so-called "autonomous" Indians to the south, and from Porus' dilatory ally, Abisares. These latter brought gifts to the King, but were sent back with a threatening message to their master to present himself in person. News also came from Sasigupta, the commandant of the Aornus rock, of a revolt in the north of the Assaceni and the murder of the satrap Nicanor. Philippus, the satrap of the Punjab was despatched to quell the revolt, accompanied by Tyriaspes, the satrap of Paropamisus.

Alexander then crossed the Acesines, leaving Coenus with a detachment on the east bank to supervise the forwarding of supplies from Craterus on the Hydaspes—the first stage in a lengthening line of communications. He himself continued eastwards in pursuit of a rajah whom Arrian calls "the bad Porus",[2] to distinguish from his namesake. This "bad" Porus was an enemy of the "good" Porus, and before the battle on the Hydaspes had made offers of friendship to Alexander. Now, fearing the increase in Porus' power and the possibility of retribution, he had taken to flight and headed eastwards accompanied by a large force of warlike tribesmen. Dropping detachments en route to keep open his communications, Alexander pursued this "bad" Porus as far as the river Hydraotes (Ravi). Here Hephaestion was despatched—probably northwards, towards the mountains—to capture the fugitive and hand over his realm to the "good" Porus. Alexander, with the main body of the army, crossed the Hydraotes, perhaps near Kathna.

Across the Hydraotes, between that river and the Hyphasis (Beas) lived the powerful tribe of the Cathaei (Kathas) and some small states ruled by petty rajahs; these covered an area roughly equivalent to the modern Pakistan province of Amritsar. To the south, between the Acesines and the Hydraotes were the tribesmen called by the Greeks "Malli" (Malavas), who inhabited the western part of the province of Multan; the eastern half of Multan, between the Hydraotes and the Hyphasis, was the territory of the Oxydracae (Kshudraka). These tribes—Cathaei, Malli and Oxydracae—are called "autonomous" by the Greeks, a translation of the Sanskrit "Aratta" or "Kingless people". Their governments were of an oligarchic kind; the people themselves were warlike and considered the best fighters in the Punjab (recently the Malli and Oxydracae had successfully repulsed an invasion by Porus and Abisares). The Cathaei, who were practitioners of suttee,[3] were the first to come into contact with Alexander. It was reported to the King that they were armed and ready to resist any attempt to pass through their country; that they had gathered in force at their main stronghold, Sangala (perhaps near the modern Lahore); and that they were urging the other Aratta tribes to fight Alexander.

Three days after leaving the Hydraotes, Alexander arrived before Sangala. In front of the "city" was a smallish hill and on one side a shallow lake. The Cathaean fighting force had camped on the hill, surrounding it with a triple laager of wagons which served as barricades. After attacking the laager with his cavalry and losing several men from long range fire, Alexander saw that cavalry were of little use in such fighting and led his infantry up the hill against the wagons. The Indians, after bitter hand to hand fighting, were gradually forced from the first two lines of wagons; then abandoning the third line, they took refuge in Sangala.

Alexander now surrounded as much of the town as he could with his infantry; opposite the shallow lake the cavalry were posted. The King believed that the Cathaei, dispirited by their failure at the laager, might try to escape from the town by night. This, in fact, did happen, the attempt being made by way of the lake. When, however, the first of the Cathaei had fallen in with the cavalry pickets and had sounded the alarm, the rest retired again behind the walls. Alexander now decided to lay formal siege to the town and spent the next day in preparations. But before operations had begun some deserters from the town told him that the Indians were going to make yet another attempt that night to escape by the same place.

Forewarned, the King sent Ptolemy with a strong force under cover of night to the lake. He was ordered to let the enemy advance into the trap, then attack them and keep them engaged till the rest of the army arrived. Ptolemy spent the early hours of darkness making barriers and obstacles with the wagons which the Indians had left after the original fight. The tribesmen walked into the trap and about 500 perished; but before the rest of the Macedonians could reach the scene, they again withdrew into Sangala. A few days later, after mining operations caused the collapse of part of the wall, the town was taken by assault. Arrian, drawing on Ptolemy, says that 17,000 Indians were killed and more than 70,000 captured in the assault—a horrible carnage, even allowing for exaggeration. Ptolemy, however, discloses an illuminating fact: though only about a hundred Macedonians are given as having died in the siege, more than 1,200 are said to have been wounded—and these must be the seriously wounded, with little chance of survival.[4] The Cathaei had not, then, belied their warlike reputation. Sangala was razed to the ground and the territory of the Cathaei was divided among the surrounding friendly tribes. An indication is given of how scarce good soldiers were becoming for Alexander, for Porus was instructed to garrison the Cathaean centres of habitation with his own men.

The advance continued through pouring rain and steamy humid heat. Before reaching the Hyphasis the army passed through the territories of two small rajahs, both of whom surrendered themselves. By the first of these two Alexander was presented with a pack of the famous Indian hunting-dogs. To show their resolution and spirit, the rajah had them attack a captured lion. When the dogs had brought the lion to bay and sank their teeth into it, an attendant ran out and cut off the back leg of one of the dogs with his sword. The dog did not let go his hold on the lion till he dropped dead from loss of blood. The second rajah, Phegeus, who lived next to the river gave Alexander detailed information about the country across the Hyphasis: after marching for 12 days one reached the great river Ganges; across this was a populous kingdom (the Nanda empire), with resources amounting to 20,000 cavalry, 200,000 infantry—and 4,000 elephants. The report was confirmed by Porus (now returned to the army); hopeful, however, of further increases to his realm, the Indian tried to belittle the dangers of attacking this empire.

By now, if he had not known of its existence when he invaded India, Alexander must have heard of the Ganges; he must further have realized that the eastern Ocean was nowhere near at hand. But his insatiable thirst for glory and for conquest made him too despise the Nanda power and decide on the crossing of the Hyphasis. But opposition suddenly appeared from an unexpected quarter. For the soldiers, while the King was making ready to cross, refused to go on. Mutinous groups gathered round the camp, grumbling at their lot and declaring that they would go no further, not even if Alexander should drive them on. And indeed the Macedonians had much to grumble about: for eight years now they had been away from their homes; they had marched and fought over 17,000 miles, and still they saw no end in sight to Alexander's burning ambition. India itself had shattered their morale: their losses had been heavy, especially in the battle with Porus, where the elephants had been devastating—and Porus had had only 200 not 4,000, of the beasts. The climate, too, was unbearable to these men from a cooler land, marching and fighting with their heavy equipment. For ten weeks now the summer rains had been lashing down, and the sub-tropical heat made the atmosphere intolerably humid and sticky. It is hardly surprising that the men mutinied; the surprising thing is that they had not done so long before.

As a bribe to the men to continue, Alexander allowed them to occupy themselves for several days in plundering and looting the territory of his unfortunate ally, Phegeus; and during their absence, he distributed gifts to their women and children. But still the soldiers refused to go further and the mutinous murmurs increased. Alexander then summoned a meeting of the divisional commanders of the army and addressed them with a carefully prepared harangue. The substance of the King's speech as given by Arrian[5] is probably correct, stemming from Ptolemy, who was present at the meeting; it was an appeal to their sense of honour and glory, backed up by the prospect of riches and rewards to come: "Glorious deeds belong to those who toil and run risks; and it is a pleasant thing to live with valour and to die, leaving behind an immortal courage".

The King's eloquence was greeted with a silence which continued even after he had invited the officers to speak. For they "neither dared contradict the King on the spur of the moment, nor yet would they agree with him"—so cowed had they become. At length, after Alexander had repeatedly invited comment, one senior officer did rise to speak. This was the Hipparch Coenus—an able, but treacherous man and the last surviving member at court of the old Parmenion faction. He had risen to high office by supporting the King at a dangerous time; now he rose to oppose him. Coenus' speech—which had obviously been thought out beforehand—stressed that Coenus was speaking on behalf, not of himself, but of the army. The men, he said, were worn out and not unnaturally wanted to return to their families; they had served Alexander well and deserved well of him; the King ought not to try to be the leader of unwilling men, but rather he should go home, raise another army and return to India with this, if he wanted to continue his advance.

Coenus' speech was greeted with enthusiastic applause by the other officers—and with strong disapproval by the King, who dismissed the conference. The speech, indeed, had come as something as a shock to him. He always regarded Coenus as one of his most loyal supporters; now Coenus had cut across his deepest ambitions with a speech whose substance would certainly be relayed to the soldiers. Coenus was already popular with the men and his championing of their cause would increase this popularity. As at the time of the Parmenion affair, Alexander was suddenly faced with a frightening possibility—that of a senior officer, backed by the other officers, leading a revolt of the army against his authority, perhaps even to depose him.

Nevertheless, Alexander tried to impose his will on the soldiers. Telling them that he was going on regardless and they could, if they wished, all go home, he shut himself up for three days in his quarters and refused to see anybody at all. He expected that the men would come round to his side if given time to reflect on their duty and loyalty. But he was mistaken; the men were unbending, and instead of undergoing the expected change of heart, actually became resentful of his attitude. Wisely, he saw that he was defeated. But to save his face a little, he made out that he was preparing to cross the river; then, when the sacrifices turned out unfavourable, he announced that he was going to turn back. The announcement was received with great joy by men and officers alike and preparations were made for the retreat, amongst which were the erection of twelve huge altars on the river bank and the construction of a vast camp, in which was to be left equipment made for men and animals of an heroic size—a cheap trick designed to impress the peoples across the river.

The mutiny on the Hyphasis and its consequences was perhaps the biggest defeat Alexander ever suffered in his life, and he never forgave his men and officers for making him turn back from his career of conquest. The loyal Arrian expresses "official" opinion when he writes that "Alexander came and conquered by force of arms all the countries he entered; and would have conquered the whole world, *had his army been willing*".⁶ He was determined that if his men must go home, they would not have an easy journey; to punish them "he went back by the way he had intended to go all along, and gave them some of the hardest fighting and worst marching of their lives".⁷ In Alexander's reaction to the thwarting of his desires by his unhappy soldiers one may see most clearly the despot's spite, egotism and ingratitude. He had no thought for their sufferings and no gratitude for their loyal services; they had crossed him and that was all that counted.

Alexander now began the march back to the Hydaspes, where Craterus was building a large flotilla. For Alexander had intended to make a voyage down the river-system of the Punjab to the southern Ocean after completing his conquests. The mutiny had prevented him from going further and he would now take his men back to the west by way of the Ocean. When the army reached the Acesines, they were met by reinforcements of cavalry from Thrace and of infantry from Harpalus, who had also sent a large number of suits of armour for the ragged troops. They also encountered another embassy from Abisares, who had again disobeyed Alexander's summons to appear in person. The King, who was now rapidly losing interest in affairs of northern India and who realized that his men would refuse to march against Abisares, was forced to leave him as an independent ruler—though the empty title of satrap was conferred on Abisares. All the territory traversed as far as the Hyphasis was added to the realm of Porus, now far more powerful than he had been before he fought Alexander. Arriving back at the Hydaspes, about October, 326, the King was presented with an omen of the future of his Indian empire: both Nicaea and Bucephela had been badly damaged by the flood-rains during his absence.

For the voyage of exploration down the river-system, Craterus—a first-rate executive officer—had assembled a flotilla amounting in all to 1,800 vessels (though most of these would be small, open transports, little bigger than large dinghies). The voyage had two purposes— conquest and exploration. The Aratta peoples further south were to be subdued; and the possibility of navigation between the Punjab and the Ocean, and then along the coast to the central satrapies was to be investigated. Alexander had long since discarded the erroneous belief he had formed when he first invaded India, that he had discovered the sources of the Nile because crocodiles had been seen on the banks of the Indus and this animal had previously only been seen by the Nile. Nearchus, who later wrote a somewhat highly-coloured account of the voyage down the Indus and through the Arabian Sea, was appointed Admiral of the Fleet; Onescritus of Astypalaea, who also wrote his account of the expedition, was captain of the King's flagship. The Macedonian and Greek courtiers made large subscriptions to the fitting out of the expedition.

Before the flotilla set sail, Porus was formally proclaimed "King of all India conquered so far"[8]—excluding, of course, the realm of Taxiles. Porus was, in fact, once more an independent ruler, though technically his power derived from the King, by whom it could be revoked. His position may be compared with the independent satrap-Kings of Caria under the Achaemenids. Also while preparations were in progress, the King was relieved of a possible embarrassment when Coenus was taken ill and died soon afterwards. He was given as impressive a funeral as his rank required; but that Alexander had not forgiven him for his part in the mutiny is seen from the remark made by the King: "Coenus had, for the sake of a few days, begun a long harangue, as though he alone would see Macedonia again".[9]

In November, 326, the expedition got under way. Of the army, 8,000 were on board with Alexander. The rest were divided into three columns under the command of Craterus, Hephaestion and the satrap Philippus. Craterus was ordered to advance along the western bank of the Hydaspes, Hephaestion along the eastern bank, while Philippus was sent east to the Acesines, there to move southwards through the territory not touched upon by the original eastwards march. All three columns were to rendezvous with the fleet near the confluence of the Hydaspes and Acesines. After an impressive amount of religious ritual, the fleet began its journey. Arrian, drawing on the account of Nearchus, has given a vivid description of the scene,[10] telling how the forest on either side of the river re-echoed and resounded with the cries of the boat-swains, calling time to the rowers, and with the splash of the oar-blades; how the Indians flocked to the banks to watch the departure of their conqueror, gazing in amazement at the vast flotilla and astonished at the sight of the horses' heads appearing above the bulwarks of the transport-vessels; and how they followed the fleet for miles down-stream, dancing and singing wild songs.

After three days the fleet put in where Craterus and Hephaestion had been ordered to encamp on opposite sides of the river—a wise pre-caution in view of the animosity felt by these two officers towards each other. Then the King set off again at full speed towards the confluence with the Acesines. For news had arrived that the Malli and Oxydracae, warned by the fate of the Cathaei, were uniting with the intention of stopping his advance, and Alexander wished to crush them before their preparations were completed. The rumour that the confederates could put an army of 100,000 men into the field alarmed the Macedonians so much that Alexander nearly had another mutiny on his hands; morale was cracking badly in the camp.

After encountering considerable danger at the confluence of the two rivers, where the two streams rushing into the one channel created fierce rapids and whirlpools, the whole army reunited at the boundaries of the Malli, a short distance below the confluence. Here, after sending Nearchus and Craterus on ahead to the meeting of the Acesines and Hydraotes, the army was divided into three columns which were to sweep the Mallian territory, with the column of Alexander as the spearhead of the attack.

The ensuing campaign, which covered the southern part of the area between the Acesines and the Hydraotes, had as its objectives the prevention of the Malli joining up with their confederates, the Oxydracae, and the ruthless subjection of the former people; of it one eminent historian has written that "among Alexander's campaigns this is unique in its dreadful record of mere slaughter".[11] Alexander himself was still smarting from his defeat at the Hyphasis; the men were bitter that they were being subjected by the King to still more fighting, instead of being led straight home; and the Malli fought fiercely and desperately. No mercy was shown to anyone who offered resistance. Whole towns were put to the sword and fugitives ruthlessly butchered.

The campaign also showed how rapidly military discipline and courage were degenerating among the Macedonians—a contributing factor, no doubt, to their savage cruelty towards the enemy. At one town, which was controlled by the Brahmins, a caste particularly active in stirring up resistance to the invader, the troops refused to assault the wall when a breach had been made and only advanced after Alexander himself had taken the lead in climbing the breach. More than 5,000 people were slaughtered in the assault of this centre. Worse was to follow: when the army was attacking the centre where the main body of the Malli had concentrated and the Indians had taken refuge in an inner citadel, the soldiers again refused to assault the wall. Alexander furiously seized a scaling-ladder from a soldier, set it against the wall and climbed up in person. He was followed by the Bodyguard Leonnatus, his shield-bearer Peucestas and an officer of the Hypaspists, Abreas. Thrusting the defenders from the battlements, Alexander stood alone on the wall, made conspicuous by the splendour of his armour. Realizing that he was an easy target for the Indians' missiles, he jumped down into the citadel and took up his stand with his back to the wall, keeping all his assailants at bay. He was soon joined by the other three and a fierce fight ensued. A company of Hypaspists tried to follow them up the ladder; but this broke under their weight and precipitated them to the ground. The four men were quite cut off from their fellows outside. Abreas was killed, shot in the face with an arrow; the King himself was shot through the chest, so that blood poured from his mouth and he fell in a faint. Peucestas and Leonnatus fought over the King's body until the men, shamed into action, burst into the citadel, and maddened by the sight of Alexander lying on the ground, murdered and slaughtered every living creature in the town.

The wound was a bad one. The barb of the arrow had to be cut out—some say by Perdiccas, using his sword for the operation, because no surgeon was present—and the King lost a great amount of blood. The rumour went out that Alexander had died from his wound. The soldiers, both those in Alexander's camp and the detachment waiting at the confluence of the Acesines and Hydraotes, were thrown into deep despondency—but not for the King: "they despaired", says Arrian,[12] "how they would reach home safely, with so many warlike nations hemming them in all round". When Alexander had recovered, the men on the Acesines refused to believe the news; it was a story, they thought, put out by the officers. Alexander was forced to sail down the river to their camp, and then, though his wound was not fully healed, ride through the men on horseback before their doubts were dispelled. In Bactria and Sogdiana the report of the King's death induced 3,000 of the Greek colonists, "who had long been dissatisfied with their settlement among the barbarians"[13] to rise in revolt, leave their colonies and begin a long march back towards Greece.

Despite the near-disaster with which it ended, the campaign against the Malli deeply impressed the Indians. From both Malli and Oxy-dracae, who had skilfully been prevented from uniting, came envoys to Alexander. By well-timed flattery of Alexander's divine birth, the Oxydracae avoided the King's displeasure. Both peoples were added to the satrapy of Philippus, the southern boundaries of which were fixed soon after, when the fleet had sailed into the Indus from the Acesines, at the confluence of these two rivers. With Philippus was left a mixed garrison of Thracians and Macedonians. At the junction of the two rivers he was instructed to found a city, called by Arrian[14] "Alexandria

of the Sogdians", and to build dockyards; the possibility of a system of
river-communications obviously fascinated the King. Two administrative arrangements were made at this time: Oxyartes, Alexander's
father-in-law, replaced Tiryaspes as satrap of Paropamisus—an
important post of trust, since the satrapy was the key to the overland
route into India; and Peithon, son of Agenor, a Macedonian, was given
the as yet unconquered area of Sind, to the south of Philippus' satrapy.

Continuing down the Indus, the army approached the kingdom of a
ruler called Musicanus by the Greeks. His realm, which was probably
the area now formed by the province of Khairpur, was said to be the
most prosperous in India. Musicanus, after meeting Alexander with
gifts and apologies for not having already sent envoys, was confirmed
in his kingdom, though the citadel of his capital was fortified and
garrisoned by Craterus. South of Musicanus were two rajahs, Sambus
and Oxycanus. Most of their towns surrendered without trouble,
"so completely had the spirit of all the Indians been broken by Alexander and Alexander's good fortune";[15] but three towns put up
resistance and had to be assaulted. A somewhat different picture is
given by Diodorus and Curtius;[16] in Oxycanus' kingdom the soldiers
were allowed to loot and burn and the rajah himself was killed; in
Sambus' kingdom the towns were sacked and more than 80,000 of the
natives were slaughtered. While Alexander's back was turned, Musicanus revolted, instigated by the Brahmins. The satrap Peithon dealt
with the rebellion; Musicanus was brought to Alexander and hanged
along with the Brahmin leaders.

The fleet was now approaching the head of the Indus delta, and
Craterus was sent with a large force, which included all the less able-
bodied soldiers and the elephants, to march through Arachosia and
Drangiana to police these two satrapies and to suppress disturbances,
reports of which had been reaching the King; he was to join up again
with Alexander in Carmania. The journey, as well as fulfilling a
military purpose, would also be easier for the weaker soldiers than the
desert route which the rest of the army would follow. Hephaestion
took over the position of his detested rival as deputy-commander of
the army. Both in this task and during the descent of the river-system
of Pakistan, it appears that Craterus was being given commissions that
would keep him out of the way of Hephaestion, who was more of a
kindred spirit with the King.

In July, 325, the fleet reached Pattala at the head of the Indus delta.
Identification of this town is difficult because of the tremendous

changes that two and a half millennia have made in the course and
appearance of the lower reaches of the Indus. In Alexander's time it
seems likely that the great Rann of Kutch was a gulf of the sea, into
which one of the two arms of the Indus emptied itself. It was at Pattala
that the river branched into these two arms, whose mouths, at the sea,
were more than 200 miles apart. Here Alexander began the building
of large dockyards and harbours, together with the fortification of the
citadel. Pattala was to be the starting-point for the fleet's voyage in
the Ocean; if it were discovered that communications with the central
satrapies were possible, it was to be the main naval station of India.
While the docks were being constructed and the fleet equipped,
Alexander himself, with a few ships, made a voyage of exploration
down the western arm of the Indus. After losing some vessels in a
storm and having others badly damaged after being left high and dry
by the ebbing of the tide—an unaccustomed phenomenon to men
from the Mediterranean—the flotilla came at length to the great
southern Ocean. After making the appropriate sacrifices, Alexander
sailed to an island out at sea, "to see, as he himself said, if any country
stood nearby in the ocean; but in my opinion, mainly that he might
have voyaged in the great ocean beyond India".[17] After returning to
Pattala, the King then sailed down the eastern arm to the sea and found
that it was better for navigation. After exploring the coast-line for
three days, he again returned to Pattala to finalise the arrangements for
the voyage of the fleet and for his own departure from India. It was now
September, 325.

The size of the exploratory fleet that was to follow westwards the
coastline of the Arabian Sea has been estimated at between 100 and
150 ships, with a total complement of between three and five thousand
men. Artillery and missile-troops were put on board with the crews
because of the necessity of landing each night on a possibly hostile
coast; ancient warships did not usually sail at night. Alexander, with
the army, was to march ahead of the fleet along the coast. The army's
official task was to dig wells and drop food supplies for the fleet to
pick up; but the King was not a little influenced to make the march
through the coastal desert by the stories of the disasters encountered in
similar ventures by the legendary Semiramis and the Persian monarch,
Cyrus. Alexander was seized with a desire to show that he could always
succeed where others had failed. Nearchus was chosen as admiral of the
fleet; in his writing he describes with no restraint to his modesty the
circumstances of his selection by Alexander; he also takes the oppor-

tunity of directing some sarcastic criticism at the motives which impelled the King to commission the expedition. The sailors seem to have been rather unhappy at the prospect of this voyage into the unknown, but, Nearchus informs us, the news of his selection raised their spirits greatly.[18] The fleet was to wait till the end of October, when the north-east monsoon was due to begin. At the beginning of October, in accordance with the agreed plan, Alexander and the army set out westwards, turning their backs on "India", to begin the disastrous march through the Makran.

It is easy to overemphasize the importance of Alexander's "conquest of India". For our Greek sources, on whom we are mainly dependent, influenced by the exotic and almost unknown nature of the country, themselves give undue prominence to the campaigns in their works on Alexander; thus Arrian devotes two of his seven books to the Indian expedition. But although Alexander and the army saw some of their hardest fighting in the country, the invasion can hardly be called any-thing more than a glorified raid. It has already been pointed out that Alexander never touched upon "India" in the modern geographical sense; and it helps to put the campaigns in their true perspective when it is realized that the name of Alexander—the great conqueror—is not found once in Indian literature. Alexander himself, though he maintained the fiction of attaching Punjab and Sind to the empire by the appoint-ment of satraps and the founding of cities, nevertheless realized the impossibility of holding India with the forces at his disposal. The Macedonian troops left in garrisons along the Indus were virtually condemned to death when Alexander departed westwards. Even while the King was present in the country, Abisares had openly and success-fully flouted him; and as soon as he had departed, the satrap Philippus was assassinated and Alexander could do no more than give Taxiles the formal title of satrap.

By 317 all traces of direct Macedonian authority in India had van-ished. Within twenty years of Alexander's death, the Mauryan Chandragupta (called Sandracottus by the Greek writers), who had in his youth actually seen Alexander, aided by the Brahmin Vish-nagupta, had liberated and unified the Punjab, had exterminated any Macedonian garrisons remaining in the Indus basin, had overthrown the great Nanda empire of the Ganges valley (aided in this by a Punjab rajah called Parvataka, i.e. Porus) and had established in North India the Maurya dynasty, the first great empire of India. In 306 Seleucus of Syria—Alexander's former marshal—crossed the Indus with an army. He was defeated by Chandragupta and compelled to cede the eastern satrapies of Paropamisus, Aria, Arachosia and Gedrosia.

Perhaps the indirect effects of the invasion were of greater consequence than the direct, political factors. By it the isolation of East from West was broken down; and there is evidence during succeeding centuries of a continuing contact between Indian rulers and the Successor-Kings, a contact both diplomatic and economic. It also enabled the rise in the middle of the third century B.C. of the great Greco-Bactrian monarchy, which ruled over Afghanistan and West Pakistan for almost 150 years. Indian art and science (especially astronomy) were also influenced by the contact with the Greeks. But the Greek influence "never penetrated deeply. Indian policy and structure of society, resting on the caste basis, remained substantially unchanged, and even in military science Indians showed no disposition to learn the lessons taught by the sharp sword of Alexander".[19]

---

1   Arrian V 20.4
2   Arrian V 21.2
3   See Onesicritus, Jacoby F.H.G. 134 F.21
4   Arrian V 24.5
5   Arrian V 25.3 ff.
6   Arrian, *Indica* 9 (Loeb translation)
7   W. W. Tarn, *C.A.H.* VI 411; *Alexander the Great* I, p.100
8   Arrian VI 2.1
9   Curtius IX 3.20
10 Arrian VI 3
11 Tarn, *C.A.H.* VI 413; *Alexander the Great* I, p.103
12 Arrian VI 12.2
13 Diodorus XVII 99.5
14 Arrian VI 15.4
15 Arrian VI 15.2
16 Diodorus XVII 102; Curtius IX 8.11ff.
17 Arrian VI 19.5
18 Nearchus, at Arrian, *Indica* 20
19 V. A. Smith, *The Oxford History of India* p.90ff.

17

The Return to the West

After leaving the neighbourhood of modern Karachi Alexander
marched westwards as far as the River Arabius (Hab). Here Hephaestion was left with the bulk of the army, while Alexander himself, with
a special detachment, moved down the river to the coast to make a
surprise attack on the Oreitae, the people who lived across the Arabius
and bordered on Gedrosia. Their crime was their failure to make submission to the King, by whom any behaviour that fell short of submission was regarded as open enmity. The column crossed the Arabius
and travelling by night crossed an expanse of desert. At dawn the
King's cavalry suddenly appeared in the area inhabited by the tribe
and devastated it with sword and fire.

When Hephaestion had rejoined him, Alexander moved on to the
main Oreitan settlement, a large village called Rhambacia. Impressed
by the site of the place, he decided to resettle it as another Alexandria;
Hephaestion was left to supervise the work and to impress the Arachosians from across the border to join the foundation. Alexander, with
his more mobile troops pressed on to the border between the Oreitan
territory and Gedrosia where a mixed host of both peoples were holding 'the main pass through the hills to prevent his advance. These,
however, took flight as the King drew near and dispersed. The Oreitan
leaders came and surrendered themselves and their people. A Macedonian officer, Apollophanes, was created satrap of the area; Leonnatus
the Bodyguard and a strong force of soldiers were left temporarily
with him. Leonnatus' duties were: to see that the fleet had a safe passage
along that part of the coast; to help with the building of Rhambacia;
and to police the Oreitan territory and make sure that the natives were

obedient to their new satrap. With what success he executed his orders will be told later. Alexander, now that Hephaestion had rejoined him on the border, crossed the border into Gedrosia and entered upon the worst two months of his career.

Bounded on the north by Arachosia and Aria, on the south by the Arabian Sea and on the west by Carmania, the satrapy of Gedrosia embraced some of the hottest and most arid country in the Northern Hemisphere. The southern part of the satrapy comprised the area now known as the Makran. Beginning roughly a hundred miles west of Karachi and continuing as far as the border between Pakistan and Iran is a range of high hills that sweep right down to the coast—the Talar-i-Bund, or Makran Coast Range. These hills compel any large force proceeding along the coast to make a wide detour inland—a factor which Alexander did not foresee and hence did not take into his calculations when entering Gedrosia. It was this detour which was to throw out of gear his plans for hugging the coast-line to supply the fleet and was to be responsible for all the miseries the army suffered in its march. Though the region is for the most part desert or semi-desert, with very little water, heavy rain-storms can fall on the high ground to the north, often producing rapid flooding in the lower-lying areas, the hard-baked earth not being able to absorb the rain quickly enough. As the satrapy approaches the Carmanian border—roughly a line drawn north-east-wards from the Straits of Aormuz—the country becomes more gentle; and it was here that the satrapal seat, Paura, was situated.

The inhabitants of Gedrosia were few and very backward; along the coast were scattered a few primitive—almost savage—communities of people who lived in stifling shacks (made, according to Nearchus,[1] from the ribs of stranded whales). Their basic diet was fish, which they even fed to the few sheep they possessed; the Greeks called them the Ichthyophagi—the fish eaters—and looked upon them as sub-human.

Despite the restraint of Arrian's narrative,[2] the horrors of the sixty days' march through the desert are easily imagined. It must be remembered that the number of fighting men formed but a small part of the expedition; that, in fact, a vast host of non-combatants accompanied the King—women and children belonging to the soldiers, and traders following in the army's wake—and these would be more prone to distress from the heat and thirst.

At first the heat and shortage of water created the greatest suffering, so that the army took to travelling between water-holes by night and resting during the heat of the day. This in itself created difficulties.

Men and pack-animals alike quickly grew exhausted from marching through the high, shifting sand-dunes and, as food grew scarcer and starvation was added to their plight, many simply dropped in their tracks and were left there by their comrades, themselves too weak to offer help. Since the night-marches were made in the hope of reaching the next water-hole by daybreak, the men who were thus left behind, if they did not die on the spot, might be lucky enough to drag themselves in the tracks of the army to the water-hole; but if, as often happened, water had not been reached when the sun rose, and the army was forced to push onwards during the heat of the day, then the plight of the men left behind was hopeless.

The discovery, too, of a shallow stream or water-hole presented its own dangers. For the thirst-crazed rush of both men and beasts to the water resulted in many of the weaker ones being trampled to death and the water being churned up and made undrinkable by the stampede. Many men drank the water to excess and either went mad or died. Eventually Alexander took to pitching his camp at some distance from the water to try to stop such insane rushes.

With the irrationality peculiar to such intemperate climates, when the army did not suffer from lack of water, it suffered from excess. On one occasion the force made camp—this time, at night—near the dried-up head of a small creek. Heavy rain had fallen earlier in the hills to the north, though there had been no sign of it in the desert. The result was the phenomenon known as a "flash-flood", in which water from the high ground rushes down a water course, flooding areas which themselves had received little or no rain. Such a flood suddenly hit the camp that night while all were asleep, sweeping away in its torrent all the tents (including Alexander's) and their contents, and drowning large numbers of the women, children and surviving pack-animals.

Food had become scarce long before this, and with the onset of starvation discipline degenerated rapidly. The men began secretly to kill off the precious pack-mules for food, and on one occasion, when a small stock of supplies had been procured at great expense, to be conveyed under escort to the coast for the fleet, the hungry troops broke the royal seals on the convoy and ate all the provisions; their comrades with Nearchus must manage as best they could. On both these offences the King turned a blind eye; for he saw that "the remedy for their [the soldiers] present distress lay rather in his pretended ignorance than in any connivance of what went on".[3] Indeed, the King realized that any attempt at stern disciplinary measures at this time would have been more than foolish on his part.

Nor were the guides who accompanied the army of great use to the King. The ever shifting appearance of the sand-dunes caused them to lose their way, and, though the marches were made by night, they had never learned to use the stars as an aid to direction. Hence the army wandered aimlessly in the desert for a considerably longer time than it need have done, till eventually Alexander himself took a party of cavalry and set off during the day in a southerly direction. When the horses were already beginning to wilt from exhaustion, the party came upon the coast. Here water was discovered through digging in the gravel, and the weary forces dragged themselves down to the shore. After this the King kept his route of march following the coast, and after seven days the guides once more picked up the trail. Striking inland again, they came to Paura, the satrapal seat, sixty days after entering the desert.

The march had turned out to be a great disaster and worthy of comparison with the retreat of Napoleon from Moscow in 1812. Arrian states it as the consensus of opinion among the historians he had read that all the troubles and toils which the army had endured throughout the whole of the rest of Asia were not to be compared with those it endured in the desert.[4] Of the great host who began the march, less than a quarter reached Paura (though, naturally, the greatest mortality rate was among the non-combatants); and the sight of the survivors, a weak, half-starved rabble, must have filled many Iranian hearts with a secret exultation. The blame for the disaster must be laid on the King's shoulders: it was his egotistical craving to achieve the spectacular and unprecedented that had motivated the march through the desert; and his inquiries concerning the difficulties to be encountered had obviously been of the most sketchy imaginable. The official version of Nearchus can do nothing but find Alexander guilty of gross incompetence—he took that route, says the admiral, because he did not have any knowledge of its difficulties.[5]

But, just as Kings can never lie,[6] so they can never make errors of judgement—especially if they are despots whose power is founded on the support of the soldiers. A scapegoat had to be found for the disaster, and at Paura the satrap of the Oreitae and Gedrosia, Apollophanes, was formally deposed from office. The charge was that he had failed to carry out his instructions to provision the army. His place was taken by a Macedonian nonentity, Sibyrtius, to whose satrapy Arachosia was

now added. Sibyrtius had been recently appointed satrap of Carmania
—which still had an Iranian governor—but now this distinction was
conferred on a certain Tlepolemus.

But for once the King had pounced too quickly on an intended
victim. For news was brought of a full-scale battle fought between
the troops left behind with Leonnatus and the Oreitae, in which
Leonnatus suffered heavy losses while the enemy escaped lightly; among
the Macedonian dead was Apollophanes. The defeat was, of course,
smothered up by the King: it was officially put out that Leonnatus had
won a great victory, killing 6,000 of the enemy and only losing fifteen
men himself. Leonnatus was later decorated at Susa for his Oreitan
"victory". No doubt Alexander, like Hitler in 1945, could make himself believe the lies he was disseminating. The search for a scapegoat had
to continue.

There now began a positive Reign of Terror among the high
officials of the empire. For when he reached Paura the King found that,
in addition to the disaffection in the army, the empire was in a dangerous
and chaotic condition. Many of the satraps, who had hoped when the
King disappeared into India that he would never return and who were
given confidence in their hopes by his long absence, had set themselves
up as virtually independent rulers. They had raised for themselves
strong private armies of mercenaries; in many cases had turned a blind
eye to or actually participated in acts of gross maladministration and,
with few exceptions, had lived like Kings in exquisite luxury. To all
these governors the reappearance of the King from the desert late in
325 was anything but welcome. An explosive situation was in the
making, with the possibility of a powerful combination of satraps rising
in revolt if a suitable leader could be found.

Such a man did exist, in the person of Harpalus, the royal Chancellor
of the Exchequer and boyhood companion of Alexander. Since the
King's departure Harpalus had moved his headquarters from Ecbatana
to the more congenial city of Babylon. Here he had freely helped
himself to the contents of the treasury entrusted to his keeping, and his
luxurious living was an open scandal: choice fish for his table were
brought to him regularly all the way from the Red Sea, and the two
Athenian women who were consecutively his mistresses—Pythonice
and Glycera—were set up as queens and the provincials were expected
to honour them as such. Harpalus had been forgiven once before by
Alexander but this time he could expect no mercy. For in addition to
abusing his position, Harpalus was guilty of a much more serious crime:

politically he had been allied to the disgraced and dead Coenus and, like that redoubtable champion of the rights of the private soldier, seems to have been implicated in the murder of Parmenion by Cleander (the brother of Coenus) and the other three generals. The generals commanded a powerful force of soldiers at Ecbatana; Harpalus controlled all the resources of the empire. Here was the makings of a dangerous group.

This time the King timed the situation nicely. Before leaving Paura (late November–early December, 325), orders were sent by express messengers to the various satraps to come to the King; to lull their suspicions, they were instructed to bring with them clothing and provisions for the army. Cleander and his fellow-commanders were also summoned to the royal presence, with orders to bring the bulk of their troops—ostensibly to fill up the gaps in Alexander's army.

As the army entered Carmania, affairs began to move more quickly. Astaspes, the Iranian satrap of the area, was removed from office on the grounds that he had been plotting rebellion; he was arrested and later executed. Craterus who now rejoined the King after his long detour, brought in with him another rebellious Iranian noble. Stasanor of Aria also arrived, and at the same time the satrap of Drangiana and the son of the governor of Parthyaea and Hyrcania, representing his father.

But the most important arrivals, as far as Alexander was concerned, were Cleander and the other three generals, accompanied by their army. Whether or not these officers had felt misgivings at the King's summons, they had not felt themselves strong enough to disobey it. They were followed by a large number of provincials who came— perhaps suborned by Alexander's agents—to lay charges against the generals of looting, temple robbery and other such abuses.

Alexander was now in a strong position. The generals were in his power; they were not popular with their troops because of the murder of Parmenion; and Harpalus was isolated. They were arrested on charges of maladministration and executed—an act that would at one stroke rid the King of four dangerous enemies and win some favour at least with the soldiers, who revered the memory of Parmenion. Like the Roman emperor, Tiberius, Alexander was skilful both in selecting his agents of destruction and disposing of them when it was convenient.[7]

Arrian faithfully repeats the official explanation for these executions —to deter other governors from wicked acts; "for it was not possible under Alexander's rule for subjects to be oppressed by their governors".[8]

The scandalous conduct of Cleomenes, who had usurped satrapal powers in Egypt, gives the lie to this statement. The reason for the executions was political and the first well-directed blow against a potentially dangerous group. Now that Harpalus was neutralized, the King felt himself strong enough to act against his satraps collectively, and he now issued a general decree to all provincial governors that they were to disband their armies of mercenaries immediately.

As the army moved through Carmania towards the main town of Salmous (unidentified) the King allowed a general relaxing of military discipline among the troops, and there were frequent scenes of drunkenness, not least from the royal quarters. Later legend inflated this indiscipline and depicted Alexander as leading his army through Carmania in a huge Bacchic revel, with Alexander and his intimate courtiers reclining in chariots and feasting, the army following behind, drinking and making merry, and the whole procession accompanied by the sounds of music.

At Salmous the festive mood in the army was maintained while trembling satraps awaited in suspense at court. After sacrifices had been offered for the "conquest" of India and the "safe passage" of the army through the desert, the men were treated to a series of games and artistic contests. The prize for singing and dancing was carried off by the eunuch Bagoas, who, though no longer a boy, was still held in favour by the King and capable, as will be seen, of exercising on him a sinister influence.

It was during these games that Nearchus suddenly appeared, safe from his sea-voyage. Accompanied by only a few of his officers, Nearchus had fallen in with a party of soldiers detailed to keep a watch for the fleet. The sailors had suffered dreadfully in their voyage from exposure, sunburn and shortage of food and water; their hair was long, unkempt and matted with salt, their skins were wizened from the sun and their clothes were in rags. The soldiers at first did not recognize the scarecrows nor immediately did the King, as they were escorted into his presence in the crowded theatre. His first thought was that the whole of the fleet had perished and these were the only survivors. Then when Nearchus had informed him of the truth, the King was overcome with joy and declared that this news caused him greater happiness than his conquest of all Asia. Nearchus was fêted and, at his own request, sent back to the fleet to continue his voyage along the coast to the Persian Gulf and the mouth of the Tigris.

At Salmous a significant administrative appointment was announced.

Peucestas, the King's shieldbearer, was promoted to the Bodyguard and proclaimed satrap of Persis. In this, the heart of the Persian empire, the satrap appointed by Alexander had died and a nobleman, Orxines, had taken upon himself the function of governor. Orxines was alleged to have acted oppressively and to have indulged in tomb- and temple-robbery; hence Alexander intended to depose and bring him to justice. Curtius gives a different picture: Orxines, he says, had brought gifts to Alexander and all his friends, but had insulted Bagoas. In revenge Bagoas himself and some cronies began a "smear" campaign against Orxines, which resulted in the unjust arrest and execution of that man.[9] Whichever is the correct version, it is certain that Orxines was put to death and that Peucestas was appointed to his position. Nor need this cause surprise. For Alexander's Iranian governors were not proving as successful as the King had hoped, and in replacing them Alexander was avoiding appointing high-ranking Macedonians, choosing instead men who, because they were obscure, were utterly dependent on him. Peucestas, hitherto unknown apart from his gallantry among the Malli and his subscription to the Indus fleet, was a particularly appropriate choice. In his eagerness to win his master's favour, he rivalled even Alexander in the orientalism of his dress and manners, and had learned to speak Persian fluently. His appointment to Persis was a bold step.

Peucestas did not have long to wait to take up his appointment. In the New Year of 324, Alexander moved northwards to Pasargadae, where Orxines was arrested. At the same time, another satrap reached the court—Atropates of Media—bringing with him as prisoners Baryaxes, an Iranian noble and his supporters; Baryaxes was accused of rebellion and pretending to the throne. At the King's orders all were hanged. Also at Pasargadae the tomb of Cyrus the Great was found to have been looted of all its costly jewellery and adornments. The Magi, who received a special allowance for protecting the tomb, were suspected by Alexander of complicity in the looting. They were arrested and tortured to make them disclose the culprits, but nothing was revealed.

It was about this time that Harpalus took fright at his own isolation and at the steady approach of Alexander towards Babylon. Already the satrap of Babylonia, who seems to have been a friend of Harpalus, had been replaced; and in Hellespontine Phrygia, the key to Asia Minor, where the Chancellor's cousin had been satrap, a new governor now took office. Collecting a force of 6,000 mercenaries—perhaps men from the central satrapies thrown out of a job by Alexander's recent decree—and taking from the treasury 5,000 talents of silver, Harpalus left Babylon and fled westwards, intending to make for Athens. Here he held honorary citizenship, conferred because of the aid he had given to the city during a food-crisis. He seems to have been well informed of the current of public opinion at Athens, and to have hoped to incite her to revolt from Alexander.

From Pasargadae the King continued his triumphant and vengeful advance towards Susa. As he passed through Persis, he again showed publicly that his kingdom was that of Persia; for he revived an old custom that the Persian King should distribute money to the women of Persis when he entered this, his ancestral home and the cradle of the race. At Susa, which he entered at the end of February, 324, Alexander struck again: Abulites, the satrap, was deposed and, along with his son, arrested on charges of extortion and of failure to bring provisions to the army in Gedrosia. The son, Oxythres, is said to have been killed by a spear-thrust from Alexander's own hand.

Here at Susa, with his governors in Asia reduced to their former subjection, the brief Reign of Terror ended. It cost the lives or the positions of at least eight satraps and four senior army officers, besides numerous other high officials whose names are not recorded. Even Arrian displays surprise at the extent and severity of the Terror and feels obliged to offer some explanation—perhaps the one he found in Ptolemy: Alexander at this time grew readier to listen to accusations and to punish severely even petty criminals, because he thought that people with such a mentality could easily commit major crimes.[10]

Now too Alexander's hand was greatly strengthened with regard to any future dealings with his Macedonians. For there arrived at Susa the 30,000 Iranian youths—the Epigoni—whom the King had ordered three years before to be armed and trained in Macedonian fashion. Camping outside the city, they demonstrated their skill and discipline to their monarch in military exercises. The Macedonian troops, not unreasonably, were filled with resentment—as yet not openly displayed; for they realized that Alexander was thus trying to rid himself of his dependence on them. Indeed, Diodorus specifically states that Alexander had trained them to be an *antitagma*—a counter-formation —to the Macedonian phalanx.

Then, as a sign of the harmony and unity that was supposed to exist at court and among the governing class, the King celebrated at Susa a mass-marriage ceremony in which leading Macedonians—eighty in number—were all given a noble Iranian bride. Alexander himself took two wives at the ceremony, both daughters of former Persian Kings, so he now had three concurrent queens. Hephaestion was given another daughter of Darius, because the King wished Hephaestion's children to be his own relatives. All the marriages were celebrated in the Persian manner and to all the bridegrooms the King gave dowries. The marriages also formally established an order of precedence at court, depending on the rank of the bride. Hephaestion was thus openly shown to be the second man in the empire and it is perhaps now that he assumed the title and functions of Grand Vizier (called Chiliarch by the Greeks). The ceremony further stressed that Alexander's empire was Persian in its basis and that co-operation along these lines would gain its rewards. Nor were the soldiers left out of this nuptial orgy: all who had taken an Asiatic concubine were given the chance to have the union regularized and were given a handsome gift.

That the Macedonian nobles took their Persian brides under strong royal pressure (or from obsequious compliance with the King's obvious desires) is seen from the fact that, with one exception, all rid themselves of their wives after Alexander's death. Nor were the soldiers made any better disposed to their leader. He was now viewed with deep suspicion and distrust by them: when he offered to pay off any debts the soldiers had incurred, if the debtors would register themselves and their bond with the auditors, the men suspected the King of using trickery to discover who was in bad debt, so that he might punish such offenders; and all refused to register themselves. Alexander was forced to proclaim that no names would be taken and the production of a bond would be sufficient.

Alexander's two final political actions at Susa were also his most important. In March two decrees were issued to the cities and communities of Greece: one contained instructions for the return to their native-land of all political exiles; the other was an announcement that their Hegemon had now become a god—that Alexander of Macedon, King Alexander of Persia, was now the god Alexander. Both these astonishing and extraordinary edicts require some explanation and it will be as well to begin with the so-called Exiles' Decree.

The reign of Alexander had resulted in many thousands in Greece being exiled from their native cities. For Alexander's policy *vis-à-vis* the Greeks was, wherever possible, to introduce and support puppet-oligarchies. The oligarchs rounded on their democratic (and anti-Macedonian) opponents and banished them, confiscating their property. The exiles, homeless and penniless, resorted in many cases to the only way of life open to them—service with the Great King of Persia as mercenaries. When Darius was succeeded by Alexander, these mercenary-exiles either joined the new Great King or entered the pay of one of his satraps. Some did neither and these joined the many thousands of Greeks in service with Darius in the early years of the war who had refused to join Alexander and had been thus condemned to outlawry by the League of Corinth. None of the mercenaries or the exiles had any cause to love Alexander or the Macedonians, but there was no other paymaster to be found; and during the ten years of the Asiatic campaign there was a large—and ever-growing—population of Greek mercenaries in Asia.

The royal decree to satraps to disband their private armies meant that thousands of mercenaries—many of them political exiles created by Alexander's own policies—were thrown out of work; and great social distress resulted from this as Asia became filled with bands of marauding and highly trained soldiers. The governing classes began to fear for their property and the possibility of revolution. It was, in fact, a highly explosive situation that was developing. Alexander tried to ease the problem by enlisting more mercenaries in his own army, but, apart from their excessive numbers, many simply refused to serve with the man responsible for all their troubles. Some of these mercenaries-exiles made their own way back to Greece, to the rocky promontory of Taenarum in Laconia (now the centre of an international market for mercenaries), where they were kept in pay by some officials of Alexander, who had fled from the Terror, and perhaps by Athens, whose thoughts were now wholly concerned with war. In the spring of 324 a former mercenary captain, the Athenian Leosthenes, conveyed many mercenaries across from Asia Minor to Greece by operating a secret ferry-service; Leosthenes seems to have been holding an official position at Athens at the time and to have had at least the unofficial support of the government there for his actions.

Alexander at Susa in March of 324 decided on a simple, but drastic, solution to this tremendous problem he had caused. To the exiles in general and the Greek cities in particular he issued a decree that all political exiles should be restored to their native states—an act that was a flagrant breach of his position and powers as Hegemon of the League of Corinth. This course of action involved a considerable political risk, lest he antagonize the states affected by the decree and lose control of them in the flood of returning democrats; but the King considered the risk worth taking—indeed, he hoped to win the support of the exiles. For the text of the decrees, as given by Diodorus,[11] carefully and cleverly attempts to transfer the responsibility of the exiles' plight from the King's person: "we (the royal plural) are not the cause of your exile; but we shall be responsible for your return home". It is perhaps Antipater, the regent in Macedonia, who is hinted at as being responsible for all the exiles' troubles. A Greek from Stagira, Nicanor, was entrusted with the task of delivering the decree, in the King's name, to the Greek states and of announcing it to the assembled exiles at the Olympic festival. Nicanor, travelling in ambassadorial pomp, reached Greece during June; soon after, amid the seething resentment caused by the decree, Harpalus and his money reached Athens. Harpalus himself was put under arrest by the People and his money impounded. After he had been allowed to escape, he made his way to Crete, where he was murdered by one of his lieutenants. His money helped to maintain the ever-increasing army of mercenaries at Taenarum.[12]

The King's demand for deification, one of the most important actions in Alexander's career, is also one of the most mysterious and obscure; for none of the major sources make any direct reference to it and other sources only in passing. Despite modern attempts to find political motives behind his action it is probably that Alexander demanded to be worshipped as a god from a genuine belief that he was now beyond merely human honours. From the early years of his life Alexander had been very concerned with his divine and mythical ancestors, especially Heracles, whose achievements he continually strove to surpass. That he already looked upon himself as set apart from the ordinary race of men as early as Asia Minor is seen from the writings of Callisthenes; and in Egypt he had been deeply influenced and impressed by his newly discovered relationship to Ammon.

Alexander's personality had never been stable; he was always prone to violent rages and was completely absorbed in himself and his own greatness. Now, after ten years, in which he had conquered the known world; had marched, fought, schemed and plotted without a break; had seen his greatest ambition shattered by a revolt of his army; had nearly died of a wound; and had suffered a terrible disaster in the Gedrosian desert, his mind seems to have become a prey to megalomania and delusions of grandeur, the manifestations of which became ever more frequent in the last two years of his life. Nor should he be utterly despised for his opinions of himself; for he had, in fact, surpassed the achievements of all other men in his conquest of Asia—and those of his divine ancestors too.

The belief in his own divinity had probably been growing steadily in Alexander's mind for some years. The sophist Anaxarchus is alleged to have said, as early as Bactria, that Alexander deserved to be worshipped for his achievements; and flatterers at court certainly encouraged such talk. Now, after his safe return from the unknown, it seemed the appropriate moment for the King to reveal this new truth. That the demand was made only to the Greeks need not cause surprise. For of the main racial groups in the empire (apart from the Egyptians, to whom he was already divine because of his position as Pharaoh), only the Greeks were sophisticated and flexible enough in their religious beliefs to accept his deification without being excessively scandalized. The Macedonians would certainly never accept their King as a god, and to the Persians such an idea was outright blasphemy.

It may be that there is some psychological connection between Alexander's belief in his divinity and the issuing of the Exiles' Decree. The deities whose exploits had always been a major source of emulation to Alexander were Heracles and Dionysus. These two were specially famed for the benefits they conferred on mankind in the course of their earthly careers; and it was his benefactions that had raised Heracles to the ranks of the immortals. It is possible to view the Exiles' Decree, not only as a drastic political move, but also as a misguided attempt by the new god to benefit a large section of mankind by restoring them to their homes, with a superhuman sacrifice involved in that most of these exiles were the King's personal enemies and very likely to stir up discontent against their benefactor when they returned home.

Whatever the annunciation of his godhead meant to Alexander and whatever traditionally minded Macedonians like Antipater felt, it is obvious from the casual way in which it is treated among the ancient writers that the Greeks, on the whole, did not find it an epoch-making event. For most of the states were more concerned with their own practical and political problems than with Alexander's aspirations to divinity. Thus at Athens, which, though little affected by the workings of the Exiles' Decree, was threatened with the loss of the island of Samos as the result of a recent decision of Alexander, both pro- and anti-Macedonian parties patriotically sank their differences and passed a decree that Alexander should become a god, hoping thus to divert the King's attention from the question of Samos. Demades, the Macedonian partisan, proposed the bill and his arch-enemy Demosthenes seconded it with the cynical comment "If Alexander wants to be a god, let him be one". A similar comment is attributed to one of the two Spartan Kings on the same occasion.

But not all the Greek states viewed Alexander's claims in this contemptuous light. Some established official cults of the God Alexander and as late as the fifth century A.D. the priesthood of Alexander at the city of Erythrae (significantly in Asia Minor, not on the mainland) was ranked as equal in prestige to that of Zeus in his capacity as the god of Friendship. At the time of its proclamation, however, the impact of Alexander's deification was deadened by the great turmoil created by his more earthly political acts.

NOTES

1 Arrian, *Indica* 29.16
2 Arrian VI 22–26
3 Arrian VI 25.2 (Loeb translation)
4 Arrian VI 24.1
5 At Arrian VI 24.1
6 Arrian I 1
7 Cf. Tacitus, *Annals* IV 71
8 Arrian VI 27.5
9 Curtius X 1.22ff.
10 Arrian VII 4.3
11 Diodorus XVIII 8.2ff.
12 For a full discussion of The Harpalus affair at Athens, see Badian, *Journal of Hellenic Studies* LXXXI, 1961, 16ff.

18

The End

The King left Susa early in the spring of 324. Using the fleet of Near-chus, who had accomplished the second part of his voyage from Carmania and reached Susa in time to receive a Persian bride and a decoration, he sailed down the River Eulaeus to the Persian Gulf. After coasting along to the mouth of the Tigris, which he had last seen seven years before, Alexander voyaged upstream as far as the town of Opis (about 200 miles directly north of Babylon), removing *en route* the artificial dams which the Persians had made to prevent any hostile fleet from sailing up the river.

Here at Opis there occurred yet another mutiny of the army—the worst and most bitter of all—whose origins require some explanation. Since the return from India an important change had been made in the organization of the Companion Cavalry. The eight Hipparchies which had operated in India had been so badly reduced by losses received both in battle and, especially, in the Gedrosian desert, that on his return to the west Alexander combined the remnants into four Hipparchies. Soon after, when strong Iranian reinforcements had been received, another Hipparchy was formed, making a total of five; its basis seems to have been the old *agema* of the Companions. Reinforcements—perhaps as many as 15,000 altogether—seem also to have been received from Macedonia; these perhaps represent drafts which had reached the central satrapies over the last few years, while Alexander was in India, and some which had come since his return. It was perhaps at Susa that the King took the momentous step of enrolling in the Companion Cavalry, as an integral part, the Iranians who hitherto had served *alongside* the squadrons of the Companions. In four of the Hipparchies the Iranians retained their native weapons; but in the fifth Hipparchy—the expanded *agema*—very select Iranians were enrolled as Companions and given Macedonian weapons. This *élite* cavalry unit was naturally under the command of Hephaestion.

Inevitably the enrolment of the Iranians caused bitter resentment among the Macedonians, who regarded it as an open move by the King to rid himself of his need of his fellow-countrymen; and with this resentment other complaints came to the surface, all of them stemming from the King's own Persian practices, his encouragements of such things in others, and his contempt of his ancestral way of life. The ordinary soldiers had long endured in silence this alienation of their King; now their anger burst out in great violence.

The immediate occasion for their mutiny took place at Opis, when Alexander announced his intentions of sending back to Macedonia those of the soldiers who were no longer fit for service. Though he promised to make them objects of envy to those at home, the soldiers in general, egged on by some rebellious elements, viewed the King's proposal as an underhand method of ridding himself of them all. When he tried to address them, he was shouted down and called upon to release *all* the soldiers from service; he could go, they said, and fight his wars with his "father's" help—a jeering reference to Ammon.

Alexander's response to this mutinous behaviour and these insults was immediate and violent. "When," says Arrian, "he had heard these things, since he was then rather violent tempered and no longer kindly disposed towards the Macedonians as a result of his Asiatic court, he leaped down from the tribunal along with the officers around him and ordered the arrest of the main troublemakers, himself pointing out with his hand to the Hypaspists whom they should arrest; and these came to thirteen in number".[1] The arrested men were led off for immediate execution.

Then, before the astonished troops had time to react, the King climbed back on to the tribunal and lashed them with a blistering speech, reminding the soldiers of their miserable plight before they were taken in hand by Philip and then Alexander himself, by whom they had been heaped with riches and made masters of the world. Reproaching the men for their ingratitude and their treachery in deserting the King, he concluded with a long and bombastic list of his conquests and the contempuous dismissal: "Tell them [back at home] that you have deserted your King and departed, leaving him in the protection of the defeated Asiatics. When you report this, it will, no doubt, be glorious among men and regarded as pious by heaven. Begone!"[2]

Jumping down from the tribunal, Alexander stormed into the royal quarters. For two whole days he shut himself away, refusing to speak to anyone but the most intimate of his Persian courtiers, who were called, according to the Persian custom, the King's "Kinsmen". Then on the third day he summoned to his quarters the chief dignitaries of the Persians and began to divide among them the various commands of the army. From the Epigoni—his trump-card in his dealings with the Macedonians—he began to organize infantry and cavalry units for these officers, on the Macedonian model and called by the Macedonian names: an Iranian *agema*, Iranian Companion Cavalry, Iranian Hypaspists and Iranian Foot Companions.

The Macedonians, meanwhile, had maintained a sullen silence in their camp. The King's anger and violence had overawed them, but they were not going to be broken this time by his silent rage. However, their pride and their resolution began to crack and finally broke down when they heard of the new Persian units which were taking their place; their King really did hold them in contempt and was finished with them. A sudden change of heart affected the soldiers, and flocking to the royal quarters, they stood outside and begged forgiveness.

Whether intentional or not, the King's handling of the mutiny had been a masterpiece of psychological manipulation—first the shock and violence of his reaction, then the uncertainty of his intentions, and finally the shaming of the soldiers by his organization of a new fighting-force from the despised Orientals. After keeping the men waiting in suspense for some time outside his quarters, the King came out and, with tears in his eyes, made the grand gesture of forgiveness. In an emotional scene an officer of the Companion Cavalry shouted out that the soldiers had been grieved that only the Persians were called Alexander's "Kinsmen" and allowed to receive the kiss from him. Alexander replied that henceforth he called them all his Kinsmen and any one who wished might kiss him.

The Macedonians, forgetful of their grievances after this apparent reconciliation with the King, marched back to their camp, singing and shouting. Soon after Alexander held a great banquet for the soldiers, which is said to have been attended by 9,000 people. Macedonians were given the places of honour, ahead of Iranians, and during the course of the banquet the King made his famous prayer "for all other good things, and for concord and partnership of the empire for Macedonians and Persians".[3] Much has been read into this prayer by admirers of Alexander, both ancient and modern. Plutarch talks of the King "mingling together as in a loving-cup, men's lives, characters and habits of life". Tarn speaks of "his (Alexander's) belief that he had a divine mission to be the harmonizer and reconciler of the world, to bring it to pass that all men, being brothers, should live together in Homonoia (concord), in unity of heart and mind . . . he gave it expression for the first time at Opis, tentatively".[4] In fact, the banquet at Opis and the prayer were nothing of the sort and in no way a statement of Alexander's intentions or aspirations. It cost him little, now that he had won his point, to flatter his men with a sumptuous dinner and even less to express a wish that henceforth they would accept the situation with a better grace.

The men now willingly accepted their discharge from the King. Almost 10,000 men are said to have been demobilized; this means that Alexander dismissed not merely the men who were no longer fit for service, but, in fact, all the Macedonians who had survived the campaigns up to this point. Every soldier was given his full pay and a large bounty on top of it. But they were forbidden—or dissuaded—from taking with them the children born of unions with Asiatic women (now, since Susa, the legal wives of many soldiers). The reason given was to avoid friction back in Macedonia, where, again, many soldiers had wives and families. But the King's promise to train all the male children in Macedonian military methods, followed by the vague statement that they would be returned to their fathers when grown up, indicates that his intention was to rear for himself an army of "children of the camp"—young men with no family ties whose only allegiance was to the King and the military surroundings in which they had been brought up. The soldiers seem to have been quite unperturbed at leaving behind their Asiatic wives and children—an indication of how much the mass weddings at Susa had meant to them.

As commander of the veterans on their march back home was assigned Craterus, with the sound, but uninspired, Polyperchon as his deputy. The command was intended purely as a temporary measure for Craterus; for on his arrival in Macedonia he was to take charge of Macedonia, Thrace and Thessaly (all the European empire) and look after "the freedom of the Greeks". Craterus, in fact, was superseding Antipater, to whom, at the same time, instructions were sent to relinquish his command and come to court, bringing fresh drafts of troops.

Despite Arrian's statement to the contrary,[5] relations between the King and his European Viceroy had long been strained. First there was the arrest and later the execution of Antipater's son-in-law, Alexander the Lyncestrian; then there came the murders of Parmenion and Philotas, old comrades-in-arms of the Regent, who is reported to have said, when the news of the deaths reached him, "If Parmenion was guilty, then who is to be trusted? and if he was not, then what is to be done?"—a remark which would make its way back to Alexander's ears. Again, Antipater was a close friend of Aristotle and had been of Callisthenes; and it has already been suggested that the King's letter threatening punishment to Aristotle after the arrest of Callisthenes also contains a veiled threat against Antipater too. The Viceroy was also known to be strongly opposed to Alexander's policies concerning the Orientals and to regard his claims to divinity as nothing short of blasphemy. He was, moreover, a man who wielded tremendous power through his control of the military resources of the European empire, a man of great prestige and influence among the Macedonians—nobles and ordinary soldiers alike—thanks to his way of life and military skill; —and a man who had been the subject of a continuous barrage of complaints and slander by Olympias. The King's jealousy and fear of Antipater go back at least to 331, as can be seen from his sneer at Antipater's great victory over the Spartans at Megalopolis. (see note p. 143). Moreover, the Viceroy was rumoured to have entered into secret negotiations, perhaps at the time of the big purge in Asia, with the Aetolians, the powerful Greek people who had no cause to love Alexander. The King's feelings towards Antipater can be well seen in his remark that outwardly Antipater was all white, but inwardly he was all purple—that is, his ambitions were nothing less than the throne.

The Viceroy, then, was in Alexander's eyes the most powerful, most feared and potentially the most dangerous man in the empire, now that the Asiatic purge was over; and he had to be replaced. Once he could be removed from his Macedonian stronghold and isolated at court, Antipater's career would be over. A charge would not be hard to find against him—perhaps maladministration in his capacity as deputy-Hegemon of the League of Corinth. For Antipater was not popular with the Greeks, and though it was in executing Alexander's policies that he had incurred this unpopularity, this was no safeguard. For, as has been seen with the Exiles' Decree, the King was adept at shifting responsibility from his own shoulders. Once the charge had been "proven", Antipater would go the way of Parmenion, Philotas, Cleitus and

Cleander. The choice of Craterus as his successor was a happy one; for Craterus, while an excellent soldier, was a natural second-in-command, who was not likely to let his ambitions raise him above his station; moreover, the move solved neatly the very real problem of keeping Craterus and Hephaestion from each other's throats.

The King's plans, however, did not mature as was anticipated. Antipater was made of sterner stuff than Harpalus, Cleander and the other satraps and officers in Asia. Instead of meekly submitting to Alexander, or taking to flight, Antipater, strong in his possession of the Macedonian homeland, refused to come to court. To prevent a showdown, which neither the King nor the Viceroy wanted, Antipater despatched his son, Cassander, to Asia, with instructions to negotiate with Alexander about his father's position. Craterus appears to have received information about the situation; nearly a year later, when the King died, he and his veterans, obviously watching events, had progressed no further than Cilicia.

Meanwhile, Alexander, to avoid the summer heat of the Mesopotamian plain, moved northwards to Ecbatana, the usual summer residence of the Persian monarch. Here pleasure was the order of the day, with athletic and literary contests and heavy drinking parties. It was due to immoderate drinking that Hephaestion was suddenly taken ill and died. In him the King lost his closest friend and confidant and his grief went beyond all measure and restraint, indicating how unbalanced his mind was at that time. He is alleged to have hanged Hephaestion's doctor; to have had the temple of Asclepius (the god of healing) at Ecbatana burned down; and himself to have eaten nothing for three days. Certainly the funeral pyre which was built by himself for the Vizier at Babylon, whither Perdiccas was ordered to convey the body, was the product of a mind possessed by megalomania. Five storeys high and with hollowed out Sirens on top, large enough to conceal persons singing a lament for the dead, it cost more than 10,000 talents. To Cleomenes, in Egypt, who had usurped the functions of satrap and had gravely abused his powers, the King wrote a letter ordering him to build hero's shrines of Hephaestion at Alexandria, which were to be outstanding in their size and costliness. The letter concluded: "If I find the Egyptian temples and the shrines of Hephaestion in good order, I shall acquit you of any transgression you have committed in the past; and in the future, no matter how great your crime, you will receive no unpleasant treatment at my hands".[6] Mourning was ordered all over the eastern part of the empire; and finally, as the King's letter shows, on the authority of Ammon of Siwah, Hephaestion was raised to the ranks of the "heroes", or demigods, with shrines for his worship and his name to be used in the most solemn of oaths and contracts.

The arrogant Hephaestion had been almost universally detested by the Macedonian officers and courtiers, with most of whom he was at enmity. But now, fearing the King's rage, all vied with each other in the expression of their grief and mourning. The royal secretary, Eumenes of Cardia, had a bitter feud with Hephaestion. Only recently it had erupted in open abuse and hatred, after Hephaestion, when the army was travelling to Ecbatana, had forcibly evicted some slaves of Eumenes, who had taken possession of a lodging-house for their master, and had installed therein his own favourite flute player. The two men almost came to blows and Alexander himself had attempted a reconciliation. The death of Hephaestion could have caused Eumenes little sorrow. Yet now, to avert the King's suspicion that he might be exulting over his dead enemy, Eumenes initiated the idea that the Companions of the King should dedicate themselves and their arms to the departed Hephaestion. Nor was a commander ever formally appointed, during Alexander's lifetime, to Hephaestion's Hipparchy; it was still known as "Hephaestion's" and the portrait-busts of the Vizier were still carved on the unit's standards.

As Achilles, in the Iliad, had commemorated the death of his companion Patroclus by means of lavish funeral games, so too Alexander celebrated the death of his Patroclus. The games were said to have been far more splendid than any before, the King providing 3,000 professional competitors; "and these," adds Arrian ominously, "are stated to have been competed not long after at Alexander's funeral".[7]

To console himself for the loss of Hephaestion, Alexander, late in 324, undertook the last campaign of his career. The Cossaei were a mountain-tribe, inhabiting the area south-west of Ecbatana. To reach this city from Babylon or Susa it was necessary to pass through their territory and the tribesmen had long been accustomed to levying a toll. on the Great King passing through to his summer residence; the rest of the time their main occupation was brigandage. The Persian government had never been able to clear the tribesmen out and considered it cheaper and easier to pay the annual passage-money. Now Alexander, who had learned much about guerilla- and mountain-warfare in Bactria and Sogdiana, undertook their subjugation; and in a campaign of forty days, assisted by Ptolemy, he virtually wiped out the tribe.

The following spring Alexander and his court passed through the Cossaean territory, making their way towards Babylon. *En route*, they encountered congratulatory embassies from as far away as Carthage and Etruria (in Italy); some writers even say that an embassy came from the Roman Republic and that Alexander foretold that people's future greatness. Arrian, a Greek by birth and a Roman by adoption, is torn between two loyalties on this point, but reluctantly decides that the Roman embassy is not true, and most historians today agree with him.

The entry into Babylon was inauspicious. As the King approached the city, he was met by some of the Chaldaeans who informed him that an oracle given by Bel warned him not to enter the city; or if he must, he should avoid entering the city from the eastern side. Alexander at first tried to shrug the warning off with a sneer. He suspected that the Chaldaeans were trying to prevent his entry because they had not performed the task with which they had been entrusted seven years earlier—of restoring the temple of Bel—in order that they might themselves enjoy the revenues of the god, there being no religious use to which they could be put. Despite his apparent scepticism, Alexander was sufficiently impressed by the Chaldaeans as to attempt to enter the city from the western side. But the proximity of the Euphrates to the city made this impossible and he was eventually forced to go against the oracle and enter by the eastern side.

In Babylon the King threw himself wholeheartedly into a recently formed plan, which entailed nothing less than the conquest and colonization of the Arabian peninsula. Another expedition had already been initiated—the exploration of the Caspian Sea. This according to Arrian, was the result of a *pothos*—the irrational desire to do something unprecedented—and men had been sent to Hyrcania to build ships. The object of the expedition was to discover if the Caspian was really a vast gulf of the Ocean and if so, to see if it joined up with the Black Sea on the west and the Ocean that encircled India on the east; it was also probably to be the prelude to an attack on the nomadic Scythians of the north.

The Arabian expedition was to be on a vaster scale altogether, in keeping with its basic aim of conquest. Alexander was stimulated by the reputedly immense wealth of Arabia in spices and precious stones— hence the colonization following conquest, to exploit these fabled riches. The official reason for the expedition was that the Arabian tribes had not made any overtures or offers of submission to the new Great

King and had made no complimentary gestures at all to him; but perhaps Arrian's sarcastic remark is nearer the truth, that Alexander was never satisfied unless he was always winning something new.[8] There may also be more than a grain of truth in the story that the King heard that the Arabs worshipped only two gods, equated with the Hellenic Uranus and Dionysus, and felt that he himself should be added, as a third god, since he had achieved more than Dionysus. At any rate it does not reflect well on Alexander's concern for his empire that, with all the abuses which so obviously still existed in the Asiatic satrapies, with Greece seething with discontent, and with Antipater in Macedonia on the point of open rebellion, the matter of prime importance to him was the undertaking of new and difficult conquests. As one writer has said, "there is no sign that he had any taste for the humdrum routine of administration".[9]

The nucleus of the great armada was to be the fleet which had sailed with Nearchus, but many other ships were being built in Babylonia and a further fifty had recently arrived from Phoenicia. They had been dismantled there, carried across to Thapsacus, reassembled and sailed down the Euphrates to Babylon. Recruiting agents had also been sent to Phoenicia, with 500 talents to purchase skilled sailors. At Babylon, Alexander had begun a grandiose scheme of building a harbour and docks for the fleet; they were to be large enough to accommodate a thousand warships. Preliminary—and not very thorough—reconnaissance of both the eastern and western coast of the Arabian peninsula had been made. One ship had coasted as far as Bahrein and its captain reported that Arabia must be nearly as big as India; this news was most gratifying to the King's thirst for conquest.

While the preparations were going on, the restless monarch left Babylon to make a voyage down the Euphrates to inspect the marshes and lakes south of the city and especially the Pallacopas "canal", a large cut which drained off the flood waters of the river. While returning to the city, he encountered an unpleasant omen: the Kings of ancient Assyria were all buried in the marshes; whilst he was sailing through these, the King's hat, with the royal diadem, was blown off his head. The hat fell in the water and sank, but the diadem became caught on one of the tombs of the Kings. When a sailor went to fetch the diadem, he put it on his own head to stop it getting wet. The royal diadem landing on a tomb, and another man putting it on his head—the signs were clear enough. It is said that Alexander gave the sailor a talent for his pains—and then decapitated him to avert the portent. Other similar warnings of impending disaster began to occur with greater frequency—or are said to have occurred to increase the sense of drama at the King's death.[10]

Back at Babylon the King found the faithful Peucestas, who had arrived from Persis with an army of 20,000 trained Persians. Peucestas was publicly commended for his loyalty and efficiency and the Persians were enrolled in a new phalanx, in which there was a ratio of twelve Persians to four Macedonians. Assuming that all the Persians were enrolled, the full strength of the new phalanx would be nearly 27,000 men, incorporating half of Alexander's available Macedonian troops. Both races were to retain their natural weapons—the Macedonians, the long sarissa, the Persians, the bow and the throwing javelin. This new phalanx—or rather its conception—has been praised by historians on the grounds that it would introduce a new flexibility and offensive variety into the royal army; but it is hard to see what use it would have been in battle, in view of the absolute superb training and discipline that would be needed to make such a mixed force manageable.

About the same time as Peucestas, there arrived at court embassies from the Greek city-states (perhaps from each member of the League of Corinth). That they came to offer the King their congratulations on his new-found divinity seems to be implied in Arrian's sarcastic remark that they had arrived "like religious envoys to honour a god".[11] They probably also came to refer to the King some of the many difficulties—restoration of property, dissolved marriages and such—that had arisen from the workings of the Exiles' Decree, and also to lay complaints before the King's sympathetic ears against Antipater. This seems to follow from the arrival of Cassander at court at the same time; he had been sent by his father to negotiate with the King.

The reception Cassander received at court showed clearly what sort of fate his father could expect, if he were to entrust himself to the tender mercies of the King. He immediately fell foul of Alexander over a matter of court-ceremonial. For the first time he saw the Persian courtiers prostrating themselves before Alexander, he burst out laughing. The King is said to have flown into a violent rage at this and having seized Cassander by the hair, to have banged his head against the wall. Moreover, throughout the brief time left to him, Alexander went out of his way to be as unpleasant to Cassander as he could be. When Cassander, soon after his arrival, attempted to refute charges which were being laid against his father by the Greeks, Alexander interrupted him, saying, "Would these men have made such a long journey, if they were making false charges?". Cassander replied, "The fact that they have come such a great distance from the proofs of their charges shows that these charges are false". To this Alexander sneered, "These are the famous quibblings of the Aristotelian school, arguing for both sides of a point" (a reference to eristics, see Chapter I). "But you and your father will be sorry if it appears that you have harmed these men even slightly."[12] It is not hard to understand the hatred which Cassander felt for Alexander for the rest of his life.

It was now the beginning of June and preparations for the Arabian expedition were almost complete. But *dis aliter visum*; on the evening of June 3rd the King attended a dinner-party, which lasted late into the night. As he was leaving to retire to bed one of his more intimate courtiers, Medius, a Thessalian from Larissa, persuaded him to come and join a party he was giving. The party lasted until well on into the following day and after leaving it Alexander began to feel ill. Despite this, he again went to Medius' the following evening and again drank till late at night. A few days later the King was very weak and feverish and had to be carried on a litter to perform his usual religious obligations. Another two days and he was almost speechless. The soldiers, who had heard rumours of his illness, believed that he was actually dead and that the officers were trying to conceal this fact. Marching to the palace, they demanded to be let in and were eventually admitted. They filed past the King's couch and he, unable to address them, could only motion with his hand and raise his head slightly. The following day, June 13th, King Alexander died. He is said to have removed his signet-ring shortly before breathing his last and to have handed it to Perdiccas, the senior officer present, as a sign that Perdiccas was to assume control of the administration. When asked by his closest Companions to whom he bequeathed his Kingdom, he whispered "To the strongest"; others state that he also added to these words, "I can see there being a mighty funeral contest over me", hinting at the struggles which would take place to see who was "the strongest".

It is commonly thought that the cause of the King's death was a fever, aggravated by heavy drinking and a weakened constitution. The course of the illness as described above is drawn from Arrian and Plutarch, both of whom claim to be transcribing a document which they call the "Royal Journal".[13] However, the ancient writers knew of another alleged cause of Alexander's death, and since the authenticity and even the existence of the "Royal Journal" is both dubious and disputed, it may not be profitless to examine it in some detail.

It is said that the King died as the result of poison, though this was hushed up for a long time after his death. The agents of the poisoning were Aristotle, the former tutor of the King, Antipater and Cassander. Aristotle prepared it; Antipater entrusted it to his son, when he despatched him to court. At first sight it appears a most unlikely triumvirate to devise and accomplish such a deed, especially in the person of Aristotle, revered by the medieval scholars as one of the select few pagans who would escape hell-fire. But on closer examination, a good case can be made out for the likelihood, at least, of this version.

Aristotle and Antipater, as has been seen, were close friends and both stood in personal danger from the King. But apart from personal fears, they were united by what might be called ideological motives of action against Alexander. For both strongly disapproved of—even abhorred— the King's orientalism in all its manifestations. Aristotle, as has been seen in Chapter 1, despised all Orientals and their way of life, especially their subservience to tyranny in the person of the Great King. His advice to the young Alexander on how to deal with Orientals will be remembered; yet the same Alexander was not only treating the despised race with respect and honour, but actually associating himself and his ideas with it, making Greeks and Macedonians dance attendance on him in the process. Again, the murder of Callisthenes had been the act of a typical despot, and was viewed as such by Aristotle and his followers. Alexander was a tyrant and as the philosopher himself says, "no free man will voluntarily endure such a system".[14] Antipater, too, apart from his disapproval of Alexander's Persian habits, had been shocked by a succession of murders of his close relatives and old comrades-in-arms, beginning with his son-in-law, Alexander of Lyncestis, then Philotas and Parmenion, then Cleitus. The death of Callisthenes must have caused a similar repugnance in him to that caused in his friend Aristotle. Now, with the Reign of Terror on the King's return from India, he could see himself as the next intended victim; and the treatment accorded to Cassander at court must have confirmed in his son such a belief.

Then in 324 Alexander had shown a further, alarming development in his character, when by his demand for deification he added blasphemy and megalomania to his despotism. A letter written by Aristotle to Antipater at this time gives some indication of how the philosopher felt with regard to the deification: "Alexander," he says, "may be proud of being ruler over many peoples; but those who hold true views of the gods have no less reason to be proud."[15] Here surely is an indirect reference to the one man who above all did not hold "true views of the gods" because he wanted to make himself a god. Antipater, too, regarded the deification with horror and refused to countenance it after the King's death.

On both personal and ideological grounds, then, Aristotle and Antipater had strong motives for wanting the King's death; and Aristotle had the necessary skill to bring this death about. Himself the son of a doctor, he was also the most famous botanist of his age and certainly well acquainted with the common root poisons, such as hellebore (known as protoveratrine) and strychnine. Theophrastus, Aristotle's colleague at the Lyceum, describes in his *History of Plants* the usages of strychnine in medicine, saying that in small doses the drug is beneficial (as a stimulant), but fatal in large doses.[16] The last illness of the King contains some features similar to slow poisoning by strychnine, including lassitude and an increased body temperature, as is shown by his continual desire for bathing. Strychnine, a poison easily extracted from a root of common occurrence, can also be kept in an effective condition over a long period of time. Hence its conveyance from Greece to Babylon presents no problems.

Finally, the three men had an excellent opportunity for administering the poison. For the King's chief wine-steward (*archioenochous*) was a certain Iolaus, who was none other than a son of Antipater (perhaps the eldest); and he, if anybody, had the means of mixing such a poison in the King's drink. It may be objected that surely such an opportunity is too good to be true and that Alexander would never have entrusted such a position as chief wine-steward to a close relative of Antipater. But such a flamboyant gesture, intended to show how little he had to fear from Antipater, would be quite in keeping with Alexander's character. His father, it will be remembered, had been assassinated because of a similar gesture, intended to demonstrate that Philip also felt himself sufficiently protected from harm by the universal goodwill towards him. It is interesting to note that at the party given by Medius the King was drinking pure, undiluted wine (the ancients always mixed their wine, which was much stronger than modern wine, with water; to drink unmixed wine was considered a sign of a really strong drinker). Theophrastus, in the passage quoted above, says that the best way to administer strychnine as a medicine—to overcome the bitter taste—is to mix it with pure wine.

Thus, though it can never be proven conclusively, there exists a strong possibility that the King did not die of natural causes. Perhaps a reconstruction on the following lines is within the bounds of credibility: as Alexander returned to the west, Antipater and Aristotle began to take thought together on their future course of action; then, when the news of the Terror, the demand for deification and Antipater's supersession came through, Cassander was despatched to court with the poison prepared by Aristotle, with instructions to sound out the King's reaction to a possible settlement which would leave Antipater in undisturbed control of Macedonia. If conditions at court were as bad as reports made out and if the King proved intractable over Antipater, then he was to be assassinated. Whether any others of the senior Macedonian officers at court were implicated cannot be said. If poison was the cause of the King's death, it is hard to imagine that some of them did not entertain suspicions of the fact. But the officers themselves were probably content, if presented with a *fait accompli*, to connive at its suppression and were more concerned with dividing up among themselves the spoils of the dead monarch's empire; and this, as the King had predicted, turned out to be "a mighty funeral contest".

NOTES

1 Arrian VII 8.3
2 Arrian VII 10.7
3 Plutarch, *Moralia* 329 C
4 W. W. Tarn, *Alexander the Great*, II, p.447–8
5 Arrian VII 12.5ff.
6 Arrian VII 23.8
7 Arrian VII 14.10
8 Arrian VII 19.6
9 P. A. Brunt, *Greece and Rome* XII no. 2 1965 p.213
10 Cf. Plutarch, *Alexander* LXXIII and Diodorus XIII 116 for such portents
11 Arrian VII 23.3
12 Plutarch, *Alexander* 74
13 Arrian VII 25; Plutarch, *Alexander* 76ff.
14 Aristotle, *Politics* 1295a 21
15 Suidas, s.v. *Antipatros*
16 Theophrastus, *Hist. Plant* VII 15.4; IX 11.5ff.

EPILOGUE

The Man and his Achievement

To sum up the character and achievements of Alexander of Macedon
in a few pages is a difficult task, but one which must be attempted.
We may examine the King's career from the aspects of his personality;
his abilities as a statesman and administrator; his influence in the development of the world; and his capacities as a soldier.

Within Alexander's personality were several features that would
fit into the Aristotelian picture of the "great-souled" man. Thus he was
extremely generous with his money, lavishing it in all directions without
regard to the quantity that was spent. For his intimate and trusted
friends—an ever decreasing number—he always displayed a deep
affection and concern for their well-being. Towards women—at least
of high rank—he was usually considerate and almost chivalrous; the
example which most readily springs to mind is that of the captive
womenfolk of Darius, but there are several other well attested in-
stances.[1] Towards his mother he always showed himself a most
affectionate son, and his attitude towards sexual matters may well be
the result of her influence over him from an early age. For though he
took over the institution of the harem along with the position of Great
King of Persia, there is little to indicate that Alexander found relations
with the opposite sex a source of pleasure, while his affection for the
eunuch Bagoas seems to be beyond question. That he was a man of
great personal charm and magnetism, when he wanted to be so, can
hardly be doubted; and such was the sheer force and drive of his will
that there are almost Nietzchian qualities about his personality.

But it is perhaps fair to say that in Alexander the most outstanding
features of his character are, to the modern reader, also the most
repellent. He was a deep and intemperate drinker, with a violent and

almost maniacal temper which he found difficult to control at any time, but which, under the influence of wine, could lead to the most dreadful tragedies. The supreme instance of this is the killing of Cleitus at Bactra. He could be treacherous, cruel and ruthless when faced with any potential danger, as the affair of Parmenion and Philotas clearly shows; and his reign both opened and closed with a welter of political murders. His treatment of Callisthenes and—if it is true—the Persian governor of Gaza shows that there was within him a strong streak of vindictiveness. His actions at Thebes, Tyre and Gaza were savage and cruel beyond what was necessary, and no amount of apology can explain his treacherous slaughter of the Indian mercenaries at Massaga.

There are, in fact, too many indelible stains on Alexander's record for him to be judged both a great and a good man. One must, however, bear in mind before condemning Alexander's brutality in too strong terms that he was a Macedonian King and not an English gentleman of the nineteenth century. Macedonia and its people, despite the attempts of several of its rulers, was still a comparatively primitive – even backward – community both socially and politically. To use a modern analogy, conditions in Macedonia would be far closer to those in one of the small Balkan states before the Great War than those even in sixteenth century England. In Macedonian politics there was no such concept as "Her Majesty's Loyal Opposition": a Macedonian King, though the nobility liked him to act as no more than *primus inter pares*, was an absolute monarch—in fact, he *was* the Macedonian state—and opposition to his politics or person could only take one form—conspiracy and revolt. Few Kings in that country before the time of Alexander had died a natural death and Alexander must always have had before him the example of his own father's end. Opposition had to be crushed before it could crush the King; hence to survive the King must be at least one degree more treacherous, and more ruthless than his enemies, both real and potential. If Parmenion, Philotas, Cleitus and such men were dissatisfied with the way Alexander was conducting his rule, then there was a strong possibility that sooner or later they would be found leading a revolt against the King's authority. Thus, when tensions began to increase between the King and his officers over the question of his growing orientalism, together with the nervous strain of several year's continuous warfare, it is hardly surprising that Alexander became increasingly irritable and his temper even less controllable, or that he resorted more and more to the consolation of drink; and hard and intemperate drinking had always been a characteristic quality of the Macedonian governing class, even under Philip.

Equally unattractive perhaps is the King's complete absorption in and concern with his own glory and renown. This is manifested in his identification of himself with Achilles and with his strivings to surpass the mythical feats of the gods and heroes; and it was eventually to lead to his demand for deification. Here again a defence, or at least explanation, of this trait can be offered. For the signs are all that Alexander was a deeply religious man, who worshipped the gods of his ancestors with sedulous attention to ritual detail; oracles and omens really had some meaning for him, and Aristander the seer was a more influential person with the King than Callisthenes the philosopher. From early in his life he had been taught to regard himself as set apart from other men, as being involved in a special relationship to the gods and having a duty to live up to the achievements of his divine ancestors. His religious convictions were sincere, but unsophisticated: the idea that he and his mission were divinely inspired and divinely protected were spread by Callisthenes for propaganda purposes, but Alexander himself probably believed in the truth of this propaganda; and whatever was said or done at Siwah, Alexander certainly regarded himself as being in a special relationship with that god. Add to all this the fact that in a career of uninterrupted success Alexander had conquered the whole of the Persian empire and in India had surpassed the feats even of Heracles and Dionysus, and it is not surprising that under the persuasive and persistent influence of flattering poets and courtiers such a young man could come to look upon himself as being more than human—a veritable god incarnate.

It was from his conquests that Alexander obtained the glory he was striving after and there can be no doubt that he was a great conqueror. indeed, he quickly became the type of the great conqueror and as such exerted considerable influence on that most militaristic of peoples, the Romans: the great Republican general Pompey looked upon himself as a second Alexander; Julius Caesar, it is said, when governor of Spain wept before a statue of Alexander at Cadiz because he had not accomplished at that age one fraction of what the Macedonian had achieved; Augustus venerated the tomb of the King at Alexandria; and Trajan, in his despatches to the senate after his victorious campaigns in Parthia, boasted that he had surpassed the achievements of Alexander. But Alexander's glory was purchased at the cost of hundreds of thousands of dead and maimed. The chivalrous treatment of Darius' family was a poor compensation for the hardships inflicted on both Persia and Macedonia and for the way in which the inoffensive Darius was hounded to an inglorious and wretched death.

Granted that Alexander was a great conqueror, are there any indications that his acts and intentions ever went beyond pure conquest? The answer, unhappily, must be that the indications are few. Despite the glowing praises of panegyrists both ancient and modern, there is hardly any evidence to show that Alexander was interested in the art of governing or in the welfare of his subjects; and the grandiose operations that were about to begin at the end of his reign, when the whole structure of the empire urgently required a thorough overhaul, strongly argue against his having any deep interest in administration. The satrapal system of government had been shown by Achaemenid experiences to be highly inefficient; yet Alexander took it straight over (though with the modification in some satrapies of separate finance-officers and military commanders; and these innovations were made rather for the King's own security than for the welfare of his subjects). Again, after Darius' death Alexander stepped into the autocratic position of the Great King and throughout his reign made no attempt to change the basis of his rule so as to give the peoples of his empire an interest in their government or even a sense of loyalty towards the government. What he *might* have done, had he lived, belongs to the realm of pure speculation; his recorded actions do not show him rising above the traditional standards of behaviour of an oriental despot. The masses of Asia remained apathetic; the Iranian nobility, with few exceptions, refused to accept Alexander; and the Greeks hated him.

The Greeks had good cause for their dislike. Whatever intentions Philip may have had for the Greeks and the League of Corinth, Alexander's attitude was simple: the Greeks were a part of his domain and where they could be held down by means of garrisons and the imposition of pro-Macedonian governments, these were used. Antipater was the instrument in the execution of Alexander's policies; but the Greeks realized who their author was and it was Alexander they hated. Thus even Thessaly, for a long time the stronghold of Macedonian influence in Greece, rose in revolt at the King's death. Again, when the Greek world was distressed by a great food scarcity during the years 330–326, there is little to show Alexander or his administrators helping to ease the shortage. Harpalus, on his own initiative, sent corn to Athens; but the sharp practices of Cleomenes in Egypt, the greatest grain-producing area in the Mediterranean, were actually encouraged by Alexander—and the Greeks knew this. Above all, the problem of Greek exiles and mercenaries at the end of his reign the King solved by the crude method of ordering all the cities to receive back all their exiles, without taking any thought for the hardships such a measure would involve. A long inscription from Tegea in Arcadia records the difficulties created by the Exiles' Decree in such matters as restoration of property, citizen rights, the status of wives who had remarried during their husband's absence. The Tegeans even bind themselves by law not to harbour resentment against the restored exiles or to do them harm.[2]

On the important question of economics Alexander has met with much praise for his financial measure in reforming the coinage and bringing into line with each other the decimal currency of Persia with the duodecimal system of Macedonia.[3] This was done by adopting the Attic currency standard and making the gold stater of Persia equal to twenty silver Attic drachmae; thus, it is claimed, the King refrained from competing with the coinage of Athens and practically made that city a partner in trade. This may be true; but otherwise there is no evidence for Alexander ever having formed any far-reaching economic policy. In the field of trade it can be argued that the foundation and rapid growth of Alexandria in Egypt, far from helping to make Athens a trade-partner, was actually injurious to the commerce, not only of Athens, but of Rhodes and the trading-cities of Phoenicia. The huge flood of Persian gold—at least 150,000 talents—released by Alexander's conquests and lavish spending produced the inevitable reaction and inflation on a large scale quickly became prevalent. The prices of food, clothing and housing rose steeply, without any corresponding rise in the basic wages; thus the poorer classes, into whose hands the Persian gold did not make its way, were hard hit. After Alexander's death the gap between rich and poor increased and with it the fear of social revolution.

But perhaps nowhere has Alexander received so much praise as in the ideas and intentions for his huge empire that are attributed to him. Foremost among these ideas are the Fusion of Races and the concept of the Brotherhood of Man. As evidence of the former are adduced the King's wearing of Persian clothes and adoption of Persian habits and his city-foundations; of the latter, the famous prayer made at Opis for "unity of purpose and partnership of the realm for Macedonians and Persians". (cf. above, Chapter 18).

As regards Alexander's orientalism, it has been demonstrated thoughout this book that the King did not adopt Persian clothes and customs as a means of conciliating his new subjects, but because he acquired a strong taste for oriental luxury and splendour and fell in love with the absolute power that was in the hands of the Great King. The more he fell under the influence of the Persian way of life, the more he grew to despise the more frugal—and more primitive—customs of his own land and to resent the concept of the King as no more than *primus inter pares* among his noble retainers.

Alexander has been called by Tarn "the greatest city-builder of all time";[4] and the same writer states that "the new towns were designed to promote the fusion of Europe and Asia on a basis of Greek culture".[5] But to call Alexander the greatest city-builder of all time is only true in terms of the number of cities he founded. But of the twenty-five or so foundations which can be substantiated very few survived the King's death by a long period; and in most cases "city" is a grandiose title for what these places really were—military fortresses, manned by time-expired Macedonians and Greeks, with the purpose of policing the far outposts of the empire. Any cultural effects these "cities" might have had were purely incidental. A few of the foundations, such as Alexandria Eschate on the Jaxartes, perhaps also had economic motives attached to their foundation, though the economic aspect was rather that of the traditional agrarian economy (i.e. the surrounding soil was very productive) rather than that of trade and commerce.

One obvious exception to such city-foundations was Alexandria Rhacotis in Egypt which flourished greatly and rapidly became the most splendid and populous city in the Mediterranean. In the third century it was both the centre of Mediterranean commerce and the home of Greek science and literature; but much of the credit for this is due to the early Ptolemies who lavished money and energy in building and encouraging Greeks to come to Egypt to settle.

Intermarriage between the Macedonian and Asian peoples Alexander certainly did encourage, as is shown by the evidence of the Susa weddings and the gifts to soldiers who took an Asian wife; and Diodorus attributes to the King the intention of transferring large masses of people from Asia to Europe and vice versa.[6] But it seems that the purpose of the Susa weddings was to demonstrate to the Macedonians that henceforth they were to be but part of the one wide empire of the Great King and on the same level in his eyes as the Iranian governing class; and a major purpose of the encouragement of the soldiers to marry was to produce children who would grow up and become loyal soldiers, having lived their whole lives in the camp. The population transfers, if the idea can be accepted as true, was a practice that had been pursued by the Persians and was to be adopted by the Romans, whereby for the sake of peace and security potentially dangerous peoples were uprooted from their native soil and sent far away to dwell among people foreign to them.

Nor must a great deal be read into the famous—indeed, too famous—prayer at Opis after the soldiers had mutinied. If the prayer had any significance at all, it was as a statement that the ruling class of the empire was to be a mixture of Macedonians and Persians; but more likely it was merely a rhetorical gesture in the festivities that celebrated the ending of what had been for Alexander an extremely delicate and unpleasant situation. To read into the prayer, with Eratosthenes, that Alexander "tried to mix all races in one loving-cup",[7] or with Tarn that "he proclaimed for the first time . . . the Brotherhood of Man"[8] is to go beyond the evidence and to attribute to Alexander ideas that belong to later thinkers and philosophers.

Perhaps the greatest of Alexander's achievements stem unintentionally from his life and career. Thus, for example, his demand for deification paved the way for the institution among the Hellenistic Kings of the ruler-cult, as practised by the Seleucids and Ptolemies. The monarchs took one step further Alexander's belief that he was worthy of deification because of his great deeds and formulated the principle that the ruler was worthy of such an honour merely in virtue of his position as King: Kings, in fact, were regarded as "born of Zeus".[9] The Hellenistic ruler-cult was in turn taken over by the Roman emperors, who used it in their world-state as a unifying force, a means of focusing the loyalties of widely differing nations on the one central government.

But more important, the conquest of the Persian empire resulted in the opening up of western Asia to penetration by Greek civilization on a far wider scale than had ever been possible before. Under the rule of the Successor Kings cities based on Greek models sprang up all over western Asia and the native aristocracies rapidly became Hellenized to a greater or lesser extent, though the native peasantry was never affected by the alien culture. The modified Athenian tongue that was spoken by the inhabitants of these new centres of civilization—the *koinē*—was for hundreds of years the international language, not only of diplomacy but of all cultured people in the Mediterranean area. The new capitals of the Successor Kings—Alexandria and Antioch—became cosmopolitan centres of international learning, where national barriers were, to a large extent overcome; thus, for example, it was at Alexandria in Egypt that a group of Greek scholars translated into their native language the seventy books of the Jewish Old Testament, the Septuagint. It was the conquests of Alexander that made possible the so-called "Hellenistic" Age, the age of the dynastic Successors to the conqueror's empire; and this was the Greek civilization with which the Romans came into contact, absorbed and diffused even further through their world-empire. It is truly said that after Alexander the old order was gone for good, a new era had opened, and "nothing could again be as it had been".[10]

It is in the person of Alexander the conqueror that we may see the one quality of the King about which there can be no controversy—his military genius. He had his reverses—the annihilation of Pharnuches' force by Spitamenes and the disastrous march through the Gedrosian desert—but his career of success is so nearly perfect that, had he been a Roman general, he would surely have assumed the title of "Felix", "The Fortunate". There can hardly be anyone who would deny Alexander a place among the very greatest of military leaders.

His genius as a soldier was displayed in every aspect of warfare. His success in every siege-operation he undertook is sufficient commentary on his abilities in this direction. In the rapidity of his marches he is on a par with Napoleon and he often succeeded in taking his enemies by surprise and compelling them to modify their plans. His lines of communication were carefully guarded so that reinforcements never experienced difficulty in reaching the main army. Discipline among the soldiers was, for an ancient army, good; and the King knew how to relax discipline when the occasion demanded. Moreover the men were frequently encouraged by rewards of money or days of rest when athletic contests were held.

As a tactician simplicity was his motto. In the set battles the decisive moment was usually the nicely timed charge of the Companions, while the phalanx fought a holding battle. But he was ready to adapt and modify his tactics as the need arose: thus the Granicus was essentially a cavalry contest from the very outset; in the fight with Porus the infantry was used to administer the *coup de grâce* because the cavalry could not face the Indian elephants; and though essentially an attacking general, he was willing to fight a defensive battle at Gaugamela until the moment was ripe for turning defence into attack. But his tactical genius is perhaps seen at its best and most adaptable in the way in which he successfully countered and defeated the desert-tactics of the Scythian nomads at his first meeting with them.

From the beginning of his reign he demonstrated his ability to grasp the strategic needs of a situation. Thus the campaign in the Balkans aimed at winning the Danube as a strategic frontier for Macedonia. In Asia, once he had formulated the strategy of destroying the Persian navy by capturing all its land-bases, he adhered to it even after Issus, when he could have pursued Darius into the heart of the empire. After Gaugamela, also, he abandoned the pursuit of Darius in order to overrun the strategically important nerve-centre of the empire; and among the motives behind the advance eastwards after Darius' death was the need to protect the centre of the empire by establishing control of the wild areas to the north and the east. When he allowed Darius time to gather and train a large army after Issus, he showed himself a precursor of Napoleon in the "strategy of overthrow", that is to say, seeking out the largest possible concentration of the enemy and annihilating it.

As a person Alexander was "terrifying perhaps rather than attractive";[11] as a ruler and administrator he displayed some measure of competence, but never rose above the times in which he lived. It is as a soldier and conqueror that he lays the most deserving claim to fame; and in this field he was truly "Alexandros Aniketos"—"invincible Alexander".

NOTES

1   Cf. Plutarch, *Alexander 12* for Timocleia at Thebes
2   M. N. Tod *G.H.I.* II, p.202, with commentary; cf. also 201
3   Cf. *C.A.H.* VI 428; Tarn's *Alexander the Great* I 130
4   *C.A.H.* VI 429; *Alexander the Great* I 132
5   *C.A.H.* VI 430; *Alexander the Great* I 134
6   Diodorus XVIII 4.4
7   Quoted by Plutarch, *Moralia* 329C
8   *C.A.H.* VI 437; *Alexander the Great* I 147
9   Cf. Theocritus, *Idyll* XVII 73
10 *C.A.H.* VI 436; *Alexander the Great* I 145
11 C. B. Welles, *Greece and Rome*, vol. cit. p.228

APPENDIX I

The Dissolution of the Empire

Alexander's last words were soon proven correct. In Greece the news of his death was at first disbelieved: "if it were true", said a leading Athenian politician, "the whole world would stink of his corpse". But when the confirmation came through, the Greek states formed a coalition to shake off the now hated Macedonian domination. Athens was the moving spirit—as was to be expected —and her general, Leosthenes, held the chief command of the confederate forces, amongst whom were the many mercenaries ferried over from Asia to Greece by Leosthenes in the previous year. In Bactria 20,000 Greek settlers, most of them mercenaries, rose in revolt (see Chapter 13 for details). The two risings, at opposite ends of the world, may well have been part of a concerted plan. At first the confederate army in Greece was successful: Antipater and his Macedonians were blockaded in the Thessalian fortress of Lamia and victory was in sight. But then Leosthenes was killed, Antipater succeeded in joining forces with Craterus and his veterans, and the allied coalition began to crumble. At sea the Athenian navy was defeated in two battles by the Macedonian fleet and on land the last battle for Greek independence, fought at Crannon in Thessaly, ended in a victory for Antipater (322 B.C.). The day of the autonomous city-state was gone forever.

In Asia, even greater events were being set in motion. The marshals of the dead King gathered at Babylon, suspiciously watching each other and afraid of being passed over in the division of the spoils of empire. Roxane produced a baby son, whom the nobility and cavalry proclaimed as Alexander IV; the infantry, more traditionally minded and disgusted with the new oriental empire, produced a rival candidate in the person of Alexander's imbecile half-brother, Arrhidaeus. A compromise was reached, whereby both Arrhidaeus and Alexander IV should rule jointly, but under the control and guidance of a Regency: Craterus was made guardian of the idiot Philip and Perdiccas, assuming the office of Vizier, acted as guardian in Asia for the infant Alexander. Perdiccas, to whom the dying King had handed his signet-ring, was *de facto* the central authority in the Asiatic empire. In the re-allocation of commands and satrapies the other senior officers all secured for themselves positions of influence: Seleucus became Hipparch of the Companion Cavalry; Antipater, contrary to Alexander's intentions, was confirmed in his European command; while Antigonus retained a greatly extended Phrygia; Leonnatus and Lysimachus received Hellespontine Phrygia and Thrace respectively; but the main prize was gained by the cunning Ptolemy, who became satrap of the rich and easily defended province of Egypt.

Of the great marshals perhaps only Perdiccas, the representative and executor of the regal power, was concerned with maintaining the unity of the far-flung Asiatic empire. The objective of the others was to seize as large a slice of the empire as they could and establish themselves as independent rulers. The history of the next twenty-two years is the history of the struggle for power among the marshals, and the convulsions and dismemberment of the empire. It is a tedious story of warfare, treachery and ever-changing alliances, in the course of which most of the leading personalities of Alexander's reign came to a violent end. Of the marshals Leonnatus, Craterus, Perdiccas and Antigonus all perished on the field of battle, while the aged Antipater alone died a natural death. Alexander's terrible mother, Olympias, seized control of both Macedonia and Arrhidaeus for a brief while after Antipater's death. After murdering Arrhidaeus and instituting a Reign of Terror against the supporters of Antipater, she was herself put to death by Antipater's ruthless son, Cassander. Six years later, in 310 B.C., Roxane and her thirteen-years-old son were murdered and again the regicide was Cassander. With the extermination of the Kings, the Argead dynasty came to an end and there was no descendant of Alexander left to lay claim to the sole rule of his empire.

By 301 the four surviving marshals had succeeded in dividing up Alexander's empire amongst themselves; all by now had assumed the title of King. Cassander was recognized as ruler of the Macedonian homeland; Lysimachus' realm straddled Europe and Asia, consisting of Thrace and the northern half of Asia Minor; Seleucus bequeathed to his descendants, the Seleucids, a huge empire made up of southern Asia Minor, Syria and the central satrapies; and Ptolemy had extended his rule from Egypt over the Levant as far north as Tyre. Twenty-five years later and the pattern in Europe had changed again: Cassander, like his father, had died a natural death, but Lysimachus had lost his life and his kingdom in battle. Macedonia and Thrace were once again united, under Antigonus—a grandson of Antigonus, the former Phrygian satrap—who founded the dynasty of the Antigonids.

By 287 the "great funeral games" of Alexander were finally over. Three great dynastic houses—the Antigonids, Seleucids and Ptolemies—had proved themselves "the strongest" and had succeeded to the power and empire of the great conqueror. They are known to history as the kingdoms of the Diadochi, the Successors of Alexander; and the era of Greek history which they represent has become known to scholars as the Hellenistic Age to distinguish it from the era that preceded it—the era of the free and independent Greek city-state.

The life-spans of these dynasties were of varying duration: the Antigonid kingdom, being the first to encounter the growing might of Rome, was the first to succumb, the last Antigonid King, Perseus, being deposed by the Romans in 168 B.C., and his kingdom turned into four independent Republics. The Seleucid empire survived a century longer, with ever dwindling boundaries, until the Roman general Pompey turned the last remnant into the Roman province of Syria. Longest lived was the kingdom of Ptolemy, who had invested his rule with an aura of divine sanction by diverting the cortège bearing the body of the dead Alexander and entombing it in the capital, Alexandria. Ptolemaic rule in Egypt survived until 31 B.C. and the last of the descendants of Ptolemy, the queen Cleopatra, may be numbered among the greatest of his line. Famous for her liaisons first with Julius Caesar and then with Mark Antony, she used both these men to help her rebuild the power and influence of Egypt; and to the Romans she became as great an object of fear as Hannibal had been. After her suicide in 31 B.C. Egypt was annexed to the Roman empire.

APPENDIX II

Notes on the sources

To enter into the vexed and much disputed problem of the quality of the sources for Alexander's career is beyond the scope of this book, and the purpose of this appendix is essentially to provide the reader with some biographical details of the five major ancient writers whose works on Alexander have survived. The earliest of our extant sources, Diodorus, wrote almost 300 years after Alexander's death, while Justin, the latest, did not write until nearly 500 years after. Thus all five writers are essentially "secondary" sources. They did, however, have a wide range of contemporary, or near contemporary, writers on whom to draw for their accounts; unfortunately the works of all these primary sources have perished—perhaps because *"habent sua fata libelli"*—though in many cases fragments of their works have survived in the form of quotations or citations of particular passages by other ancient writers, often with comments on the quality of their works. These fragments have been collected together by F. Jacoby, (see bibliography) and translated into English by C. A. Robinson (*History of Alexander the Great*, vol. I, cited in bibliography). The best and most sober discussion—in English—of these fragmentary historians is that of L. Pearson in *The Lost Histories of Alexander the Great* (cited in bibliography). The fullest discussion of the source problem is that of W. W. Tarn in *Alexander the Great* vol II (cited in bibliography); unfortunately much of the value of his discussion is vitiated by what might be called "special pleading" and many of his most important conclusions have been successfully refuted since the publication of his book. Modern books and articles which deal specifically with the sources and the problems they present are marked in the bibliography with an asterisk.

Diodorus: a Greek from Agyrium in Sicily, wrote between 60 and 30 B.C. a Universal History in forty books from the earliest times down to the Gallic War of Julius Caesar. The whole of Book XVII is devoted to the history of Alexander's campaigns and affairs in Greece during Alexander's absence. There is a large gap in the text at the end of Chapter LXXXIII, with a jump from the capture and death of Bessus to the capture of Massaga. The table of contents at the beginning of the book supplies a summary of the contents of the missing section. The best English translation of Book XVII is that of C. Bradford Welles in the Loeb Classical Library series (Heinemann, 1963); this volume has an excellent introduction and discussion of the sources followed by Diodorus in Book XVII.

Curtius Rufus: a teacher of rhetoric, active at Rome in the first half of the first century A.D. It is my contention that he wrote his *Historiae Alexandri Magni* late in life under the emperor Nero (A.D. 54–68) and completed it soon after the accession of Vespasian (late 69 or early 70 A.D.). His history, the first full-scale work on Alexander in Latin, was composed in ten books of which books I and II are completely missing, while books V, VI and X have large lacunae in the text. The work is a rhetorical *tour de force*, but contains much useful information and makes good lively reading. The best modern English translation is again to be found in the Loeb Classical Library series, by J. C. Rolfe (1956); this volume also contains a useful introduction to the work.

Plutarch: a Greek from Chaeronea in Boetia, *fl. c.* A.D. 46 to after A.D. 120. Plutarch is best known for his *Parallel Lives* of famous Greeks and Romans, of which the *Alexander* and *Julius Caesar* form a pair. His account of the life of Alexander is not a work of history, as he himself stresses at the beginning. He is writing a *biography* with a moral purpose; and thus, while he tends to follow a chronological sequence, he frequently digresses to cite anecdotes which illustrate a particular aspect of the King's character and it is to these anecdotes that we are indebted to Plutarch for many personal details about Alexander. Plutarch was not a critical writer, but he was a voracious reader and the sources he cites in the *Alexander* show that he had read pretty well the whole of the available Alexander literature. Also extant from the pen of Plutarch are two essays, in the form of orations, "On the Fortune or Virtue of Alexander" (*Opera moralia*, 333D—345B), in which the writer sets out to prove that Alexander's success was due to his virtue and not to the favour of Fortune. The best English translations of the *Life of Alexander* are those of John Dryden (in the Everyman Library series, 1957) and B. Perrin (in the Loeb Classical Library series, 1949).

Arrian: (full name Flavius Arrianus), a Greek from the Roman province of Bithynia. His floruit is *c.* A.D. 96–*c.* A.D. 180. As a Roman citizen, Arrian entered upon a public career in the imperial service. Appointed governor of Cappadocia in 131, he defeated in this capacity an invasion in 134 of the barbarian Alani; he was thus a man with some claim to military skill. He was also a devoted and admiring pupil of the great stoic philosopher Epictetus, whose lectures he collected and preserved. His passionate interest in Alexander is shown in his historical writings: apart from his *Anabasis*, he wrote an *Indica*, or history of Alexander's Indian campaign based on the writings of Nearchus, and a history of the events following Alexander's death; of these two works, the former survives intact and is usually appended to the *Anabasis*, while the latter has perished except for fragments. His most famous work is the *Anabasis* or "March up country": this title he borrowed for his history of Alexander from the more famous work of Xenophon. The *Anabasis* has survived entire in seven books and is based primarily on the histories of Ptolemy, son of Lagus, and Aristobulus, son of Aristobulus, both of whom accompanied Alexander's expedition; though Arrian makes it clear that he had read a great deal of the other primary historians of Alexander. His account of the King's career is admittedly the best from the aspects of military campaigns and administrative measures, but is open to suspicion on more "controversial" matters. For Ptolemy, his main source, was undoubtedly an "official" writer whose tendency was to suppress or distort any incident unfavourable to Alexander. The best English translation of the *Anabasis* is that of A. de Selincourt, in the Penguin Classics series; the Loeb Classical Library translation of E. Iliff Robson is marred by many inaccuracies and is not to be trusted by a reader without a knowledge of Greek.

Justin: (M. Junianus Justinus), made in Latin, about the middle of the third century A.D., an epitome of the *Philippic History* in 44 books of Pompeius Trogus, who wrote under the emperor Augustus. Books XI and XII deal with the career of Alexander and there is little of value to be found in them that is not in the other sources. There is no English translation of Justin available.

SELECT BIBLIOGRAPHY

This bibliography is far from exhaustive and has deliberately been confined mainly to the more important publications in English, though a few of the major works in French and German are also cited.

Abbreviations

A.H.R. — American Historical Review

A.J.A. — American Journal of Archaeology

A.J.Ph. — American Journal of Philology

A.U.M.L.A. — Australian Universities Modern Languages Association

C.Ph. — Classical Philology

Class. Quarterly — Classical Quarterly

C.R. — Classical Review

E.H.R. — English Historical Review

J.C.S. — Journal of Classical Studies

J.H.S. — Journal of Hellenic Studies

P.C.Ph.S. — Proceedings of the Cambridge Philological Society

R.E.G. — Révue des Etudes Grecques

T.A.Ph.A. — Transactions of the American Philological Association

Books

Adcock, F. E. — *The Greek and Macedonian Art of War* (Berkeley, 1962)

Bellinger, A. — *Essays on the Coinage of Alexander the Great* (New York, 1963)

Berve, H. — *Das Alexanderreich auf prosopographischer Grundlage* (Munich, 1926)

Bieber, M. — *Alexander the Great in Greek and Roman Art* (Chicago, 1964)

Burn, A. R. — *Alexander the Great and the Hellenistic Empire* (London, 1947)

Casson, S. — *Macedonia, Thrace and Illyria* (Oxford, 1926)

Ehrenberg, V. — *Alexander and the Greeks* (Oxford, 1938)

Fuller, J. F. C. — *The Generalship of Alexander the Great* (London, 1958)

Griffith, G. T. — *Mercenaries of the Hellenistic World* (Cambridge, 1935)
    —*Alexander the Great, the Main Problems* (Cambridge, 1965)

Hogarth, D. G. — *Philip and Alexander of Macedon* (London, 1897)

Instinsky, H. U. — *Alexander der Grosse am Hellespont* (Godesburg, 1949)

Jacoby, F. — *Die Fragmente der griechischen Historiker*; Teil IIB, nos. 117–153 (Leiden, 1926)

Jouguet, P. — *Macedonian Imperialism* (London, 1928: English translation)

Kornemann, E. — *Die Alexandergeschichte des Königs Ptolemaeus I* (Berlin, 1935)★

Kromayer and Veith — *Heerwesen und Kriegführung der Griechen und Römer* (Munich, 1928)

Marsden, A. E. — *The Campaign of Gaugamela* (Liverpool, 1964)

Nadell, J. — *Alexander and the Romans* (Ann Arbor, 1959)

Olmstead, A. T. — *History of the Persian Empire* (Chicago, 1948)

Parke, H. W. — *Greek Mercenaries* (Oxford, 1933)

Pearson, L. — *The Lost Histories of Alexander the Great* (American Philological Association, 1960)★

Radet, G. — *Alexandre le Grand* (Paris, 1950: 6th edition)

Robinson, C. A. — *The Ephemerides of Alexander's Expedition* (Providence, 1932)
    — *The History of Alexander the Great* (Providence, vol. I, 1953; vol. II, 1963)

Schachermeyer, F. — *Alexander der Grosse* (Graz, 1949)

Stein, A. — *On Alexander's Track to the Indus* (London, 1928)

Tod, M. N. — *Greek Historical Inscriptions*, vol. II (Oxford, 1949)

Tarn, W. W. — *Hellenistic Naval and Military Developments* (Cambridge, 1930)
    —*Alexander the Great*, vols. I and II. (Cambridge, 1948): volume I is a reprint, with minor alterations, of Tarn's chapters in *C.A.H.* VI; volume II contains studies of the sources and other specialized problems.

Tarn, W. W. and Griffith, G. T. — *Hellenistic Civilization* (London, 1952: 3rd edition)

Wilcken, U. — *Alexander the Great* (London, 1928: English translation)

The Cambridge Ancient History, vol. VI (Cambridge, 1953: 3rd edition)

Greece and Rome, vol. XII, no. 2, October 1965, is an anniversary edition devoted to Alexander, containing articles (with bibliographies) by eminent scholars on the main aspects of Alexander's career, e.g. his early life; the Macedonian background; his generalship; his administration of the empire; his aims and achievement.

Articles

Adcock, F. E. — *Proc. Brit. Acad.* XXXIX, 1954, 163–80: "Greek and Macedonian Kingship".

Badian, E. — *Class. Quarterly*, n.s. VIII, no. 3 and 4, 144 ff.: "The Eunuch Bagoas".

— *History Today*, vol. X, 1960, pp. 779–87 "Ancient Alexandria".

— *Historia*, VII, 1958, 425–44: "Alexander the Great and the Unity of Mankind".

— *T.A.Ph.A*, XCI, 1960, 324–38: "The Death of Parmenio".

— *Historia*, IX, 1960, 245–6: "The First Flight of Harpalus".

— *J.H.S.* LXXXI, 1961. 16 ff.: "Harpalus".

— *A.U.L.M.A.* 17, 1962, 80 ff.: "Alexander the Great and the Loneliness of Power".

— *Phoenix*, XVII, 4, 1963, 244 ff.: "The Death of Philip II".

— *J.H.S.* LXXXV, 1965, 160: "Orientals in Alexander's Army".

Balsdon, J. P. V. D. — *Historia*, I, 1950, 363 ff.: "The 'Divinity' of Alexander".

Bickermann, E. — *R.E.G.* XLVII, 1934, 346 ff.: "Alexandre le Grande et les Villes d'Asie".

Brown, T. S. — *A.J.Ph.* LXX, 1949, 225 ff.: "Callisthenes and Alexander".

— *A.J.Ph.* LXXI, 1950, 134 ff.: "Cleitarchus".★

Brunt, P. A. — *Class. Quarterly*, XII, 1962, 144 ff.: "Persian Accounts of Alexander's Campaigns".★

— *J.H.S.* LXXXIII, 1963, 27 ff.: "Alexander's Macedonian Cavalry".

Burn, A. R. — *J.H.S.* LXXII, 1952, 81 ff.: "Notes on Alexander's Campaigns, 332–30 B.C.".

Frederichsmeyer, E. A. — *A.J.A.* LXIV, 1960, 184 ff.: "Alexander, Midas and the Oracle at Gordium".

Griffith, G. T. — *J.H.S.* LXXVII, 1947, 77 ff.: "Alexander's Generalship at Gaugamela".

— *J.H.S.* LXXXIII, 1963, 68 ff.: "A Note on the Hipparchies of Alexander".

— *P.C.Ph.S*, n.s.4, 184, 156–7, 3 ff.: "Makedonika: Notes on the Macedonians of Philip and Alexander".

— *P.C.Ph.S*, n.s.10, 190, 1964, 23 ff.: "Alexander the Great, an Experiment in Government".

Hamilton, J. R. — *J.H.S.* LXXVI, 1956, 26 ff.: "The Cavalry Battle on the Hydaspes".

— *Class. Quarterly*, n.s. V, 1955, 218 ff.: "Three Notes on Arrian".

— *Historia*, X, 1961, 448 ff.: Cleitarchus and Aristobulus".★

Instinsky, H. U. — *Historia*, X, 1961, 284 ff.: "Alexander, Pindar and Euripides".

Merlan, P. — *Historia*, III, 1954–5, 60 ff.: "Isocrates, Aristotle and Alexander the Great".

Milns, R. D. — *Latomus*, XXV, 3, 1966, 490 ff.: "Curtius Rufus and the 'Historiae Alexandri' ".★

— *Greek, Roman and Byzantine Studies*, vol. 7, no. 2, 1966, 159 ff.: "Alexander's Seventh Phalanx Battalion".

— *J.H.S.* LXXXVI, 1966, 167–8: "Diodorus XVII 10.4 and Alexander's Macedonian Cavalry".

— *Historia*, XV, 1966, 256 ff.: "Alexander's Pursuit of Darius through Iran".

Omuta, A. — *J.C.S.* X, 1962, 88 ff.: "The Deification of Alexander".

Pearson, L. — *Class. Quarterly.* n.s. I, 1951, 80 ff.: "Notes on Two Passages in Strabo".

— *A.J.Ph.* LXXIII, 1952, 72 ff.: "Aristobulus the Phocian".★

— *Historia*, III, 1954–5, 429 ff.: "The Diary and Letters of Alexander the Great".★

Powell, J. E. — *J.H.S.* LIX, 1939, 229 ff.: "The Sources of Plutarch's 'Life of Alexander' ".★

Robinson, C. A. — *Hesperia*, supp. 8, 299 ff.: "Alexander the Great and the Oecumenē".

Robinson, C. A. — *A.J.Ph.* LXIV, 1943, 286 ff.: "Alexander's Deification".

— *A.J.A.* LIX, 1945, 422 ff.: "Alexander the Great and Parmenion".

— *A.J.Ph.* LVI, 1952, 169 ff.: "Alexander's Brutality".

— *A.H.R.* LXII, 1956–7, 326 ff.: "The Extraordinary Ideas of Alexander the Great".

Samuel, A. E. — *Historia*, XIV, 1965, 1 ff.: "Alexander's 'Royal Journals' ".★

Stark, F. — *Geog. Journ.* CXXII, 1956, 294 ff.: "Alexander's Minor Campaigns in Turkey".

— *J.H.S.* LXXVIII, 1958, 102 ff.: "Alexander's March from Miletus to Phrygia".

Strasburger, H. — *Hermes*, LXXXII, 1954, 251–254: "Zur Route Alexanders durch Gedrosien".

Sumner, G. V. — *A.U.M.L.A.* 15, 1961, 30 ff.: "Curtius Rufus and the 'Historiae Alexandri' "★

Tarbell, F. — *C.Ph.* I, 1906, 285 ff.: "The Form of the Chlamys".

Walbank, F. — *Phoenix*, XVI, 1962, 178 ff.: "Surety in Alexander's Letter to the Chians".

Welles, C. B. — *Historia*, XI, 1962, 271 ff.: "The Discovery of Sarapis and the Foundation of Alexandria".

Wüst, F. R. — *Historia*, II, 1953–4, 418 ff.: "Die Meuterei von Opis".

— *Historia*, II, 1953–4, 177 ff.: "Die Rede Alexanders des Grossen in Opis".★

Reviews of some works cited in Bibliography

Badian, E. — *J.H.S.* LXXXIV, 1964, 206: "Tarn's *Alexander*".

Brown, T. S. — *A.J.Ph.* LXXII, 1951, 75 ff.: "Schachermeyer's *Alexander*".

Burn, A. R. — *J.H.S.* LXVII, 1947 (published 1949), 141: "Tarn's *Alexander*".

— *Class. Quarterly,* n.s.I 1951, 100 ff.: "Schachermeyer's *Alexander*".

— *E.H.R.* LXXV, 1960, 143.: "Fuller's *Generalship*".

Cawkwell, G. L. — *C.R.* X, 1960, 57 ff.: "Fuller's *Generalship*".

— *C.R.* XV.2, 1965, 203.: "Marsden's *Gaugamela*".

Griffith, G. T. — *J.H.S.* LIX, 1939, 156.: "Ehrenberg's *Alexander and the Greeks*".

Jones, A. H. M. — *Class. Quarterly.* LXIII, 1949, 122 ff.: "Tarn's *Alexander*".

Robinson, C. A. — *A.J.Ph.* LXI, 1940, 498: "Ehrenberg's *Alexander and the Greeks*".

— *A.J.Ph.* LXX, 1949, 192 ff.: "Tarn's *Alexander*".

Walbank, F. — *Gnomon,* 1950, 188: "Schachermeyer's *Alexander*".

— *J.H.S.* LX, 1950, 79 ff.: H. U. Instinsky, *Alexander der Grosse am Hellespont.*

Welles, C. B. — *A.J.A.* LV, 1951, 433 ff.: "Schachermeyer's *Alexander der Grosse*".

Index

A

Abisares, Indian prince: 207, 208, 209, 218, 219, 223, 229

Abreas, Macedonian officer: 225, 226

Abulites, Persian satrap: 131, 132, 239

Achilles, Homeric hero: 18, 19, 24, 44, 56, 97, 251, 261

Ada, Carian satrap: 62, 64

Acuphis, Indian noble: 207

Agamemnon, Homeric hero: 44, 53

Agis, King of Sparta: 81, 82, 83

Alcimachus, Macedonian officer: 59

Alexander (1) III of Macedon, "The Great", 356–323 B.C.: mother's influence on, 19–20; and Aristotle, 20–25, 256–8; and the murder of Philip II, 30–1; and the League of Corinth, 35; Balkan campaign of, 36–9; and the passage of Mt. Climax, 67; and the Gordian Knot, 70–1; negotiations with Darius, 87–8, 95–6, 116; crowned Pharaoh of Egypt, 101; founds Alexandria 102–4; visits Siwah oasis, 104–7; and the destruction of Persepolis, 137–9; and the family of Parmenion, 27, 34, 73–4, 117, 143–4, 158–165; becomes Great King of Asia, 152; his orientalism, 156–7, 194–5,

238–40, 264; and the massacre of the Branchidae, 170; marries Roxane, 183; and Cleitus, 189–194; and Callisthenes, 195–200; and Antipater, 25, 31, 66, 199, 249–50, 256–8; and the invasion of India, 202; and the Hyphasis mutiny, 221–3; seriously wounded in India, 225–6; disastrous Gedrosian march, 232–4; and Harpalus and the Reign of Terror, 235–9; and the Susa Weddings, 239–40; and the Exiles' Decree, 240–2; demands deification, 240, 242–4; and the Opis mutiny, 245–8; and Hephaestion's death, 250–1; projected Arabian campaign, 252–3; his death, 255–8; his attitude to sex, 259; his drinking habits, 259–60; his brutality, 260; his religious beliefs, 261; his statesmanship and ideas, 262–5; effects of his career, 265–6; his military genius, 266–7

Alexander (2) IV, son of Alexander and Roxane: 268

Alexander (3), of Epirus, Brother of Olympias: 28, 29, 30, 111

Alexander (4), son of Aeropus, "The Lyncestian": 26, 33, 40, 58, 66, 163, 249, 256